Hard to Love

Hard to Love

Essays

and Confessions

Briallen Hopper

BLOOMSBURY PUBLISHING

NEW YORK • LONDON • OXFORD • NEW DELHI • SYDNEY

BLOOMSBURY PUBLISHING
Bloomsbury Publishing Inc.
1385 Broadway, New York, NY 10018, USA

BLOOMSBURY, BLOOMSBURY PUBLISHING, and the Diana logo are trademarks of
Bloomsbury Publishing Plc

First published in the United States 2019

ISBN: HB: 978-1-63286-880-0; eBook: 978-1-63286-879-4

LIBRARY OF CONGRESS CATALOGING-IN-PUBLICATION DATA

Names: Hopper, Briallen Elisabeth, 1978- author.
Title: Hard to love : essays and confessions / Briallen Hopper.
Description: New York, NY : Bloomsbury Publishing Inc., 2019.
Identifiers: LCCN 2018016387 | ISBN 9781632868800 (hardcover) |
ISBN 9781632868794 (ebook)
Subjects: LCSH: Hopper, Briallen Elisabeth, 1978- | Love. | Friendship. |
Interpersonal relations. | Essays.
Classification: LCC HQ801 .H737 2019 | DDC 302.3—dc23
LC record available at https://lccn.loc.gov/2018016387

2 4 6 8 10 9 7 5 3 1

Typeset by Westchester Publishing Services
Printed and bound in the U.S.A. by Berryville Graphics Inc., Berryville, Virginia

To find out more about our authors and books visit www.bloomsbury.com
and sign up for our newsletters.

Bloomsbury books may be purchased for business or promotional use. For information on
bulk purchases please contact Macmillan Corporate and Premium Sales Department at
specialmarkets@macmillan.com.

to my friends and families

CONTENTS

The times I didn't write, maybe I was in love. Or beloved.
Somebody was making me the object of love. It's not bad.
It's short, but not bad.

—TONI MORRISON

Overbrim and overflow,
If your own heart you would know;
For the spirit born to bless
Lives but in its own excess.

—LAURENCE BINYON

LEAN ON

A Declaration of Dependence

I LIKE TO lean. Too much of the time I have to hold myself up, so if an opportunity to swoon presents itself, I take it. When I'm getting a haircut and the lady asks me to lean back into the basin for a shampoo, I let myself melt. My muscles go slack, my eyes fall shut, and there is nothing holding me except gravity and the chair and the water and her hands on my head. I feel my tears of bliss slide into the suds.

In photos I am often leaning. When I'm not resting my head on someone's shoulder, I am hugging a column in a haunted castle in Great Barrington, or bracing myself against a big block of basalt on a pedestal in a Barcelona park. At home alone I improvise with bookshelves and doorjambs, but sometimes I need to lean on something alive. Seeking support on a stormy night, I run out into the rain and lean against the dogwood tree in front of my house until the wet bark soaks through my coat. The world is my trellis.

Ten years ago I bought a Gordon Parks print of Paul Newman and Joanne Woodward leaning against each other by lamplight on a big brass bed. They are sitting side by side, eyes closed, serene. He is leaning more heavily, his body slanted into hers, his head on her shoulder. She is resting more gently, her cheek against the top of his head. Her face is half-illuminated, half-eclipsed. They seem solemn and private and young. He is quiet in her shadow.

I hung the photograph over my bed. Next to it I tacked another 1950s Paul and Joanne picture I tore out of a book. They are leaning on a bed again, and he is still slumped against her shoulder, but this time the lean seems more in league with an audience. They are both meeting the photographer's gaze and smiling small smiles. Her eyebrows are slightly raised; she might be sly or smug. She is holding a cup of tea in one hand, and his head, proprietarily, with the other. He is supine and sated and holding a glass of wine.

Paul and Joanne liked to lean for the camera. For their 1968 *LIFE* cover promoting *Rachel, Rachel* (she starred, he directed), they are layered on wall-to-wall carpet; she is reclining in the foreground, and he is her blue-eyed backrest. In yet another famous photo from an earlier era (Joanne is still in gingham, not yet in Pucci), they are leaning back to back with their shoulders against each other, their mutual pressure holding each other up, with an isosceles triangle of space between them, and a sturdy baseline of brick patio beneath them.

I like to fall asleep under images of leaning every night, and wake up beneath them every day.

I like to believe that leaning is love.

∿

I was raised to believe in the romance of leaning. My parents turned the tale of how they met into a bedtime story, and they told it to us until we had it memorized. My dad's version was simple and sunny: My mom showed up at the commune where he was living, a vision of loveliness in green corduroy pants, and it was love at first sight. My mom's version was heavier. She was a moody adolescent, with formless feelings that often overwhelmed her and a future that loomed without a shape. She was nineteen when she met my dad, and he seemed youthfully exuberant and dependably good: someone she could structure her life around. They married within a few months.

What happened ever after was not part of the story they told me and my siblings, but we could see it playing out before us as the years went by. My mom could depend on my dad to work hard, hammering nails and hauling two-by-fours in all kinds of weather, slowly and quickly wrecking his body to try to pay the bills. My dad could depend on my mom to stay in the marriage and to keep six kids fed, clothed, washed, wrangled, read to, and rested, even when he broke his back on the job site falling from a high, rain-slicked beam onto the concrete foundation and was immobilized for six months; even when he was unemployed for a year and a half and people from church who knew we were broke were delivering food to our door; even when he became almost catatonic with depression for years, no longer recognizable as the man she had married.

I was formed by this story, both as an aspiration and as a cautionary tale, and in my own youthful romances I leaned heavily. I was moody like my mom, plagued by sudden spells of panic, and depressed like my dad, susceptible to an undertow of doom, so I spent most of my twenties in long-term relationships with men who seemed so even-keeled that they couldn't be capsized—so sunny and strong that they couldn't possibly lapse into sadness for long. My college boyfriend was a safe person to lean on. He had a saintly serenity that came from his mystical and untroubled religious faith; the years he'd spent as the precociously responsible son of an intermittently single mother; the hours he spent fishing, mountain biking, and stargazing in the countryside; and his nightly dose of marijuana. He was warm to the core, and utterly unfazed by my dependence on him. It might even have reassured him.

My grad school boyfriend was a much more dangerous person for a leaner to date. He was attracted to vulnerable women, but he disapproved of dependency. When I was in a writing vortex he would bring me sandwiches and coffee and give me expert editorial advice, and when I was shaking with fear and dark thoughts I couldn't name, he would hold me until his warmth and weight and smell and steady breathing soothed me. But he also told me, not as a threat but as a simple statement of fact (but of course it felt like a threat, and it was a threat), that he needed to know that any woman he was with would be fine and functional either with or without him. He did not sign up for panic attacks and yawning existential dread. If I wanted to be with him for the long haul, I would have to get it together.

And so I mostly did. For years I lived with the knowledge that if I ceased to be a successful, self-motivated, ambitious, size-six Ivy League blonde, I would lose love. And I knew I couldn't live without love, so I stayed as successful and self-motivated and ambitious and size-six and Ivy League and blonde as I could. I formed friendships to tide me over between our times together. I learned to self-soothe. I tried to quell myself.

The paradox was that my newfound self-reliance was a symptom of my utter reliance on him. I depended on his demand that I not depend. I leaned on not leaning on him.

The irony was he left me anyway.

≈

I blamed our breakup on Ralph Waldo Emerson. Almost the whole time we were dating, my grad school boyfriend was writing his dissertation on Emerson, who is best known as the author of "Self-Reliance"—the ultimate anti-leaning manifesto. (After we broke up I wrote my dissertation on feelings.) "Self-Reliance" is a soaring sermonic essay that has so permeated American popular consciousness that it reads at times like clusters of vaguely libertarian coffee-mug quotes:

Trust thyself: every heart vibrates to that iron string.

Whoso would be a man must be a nonconformist.

Insist on yourself; never imitate.

My friend Mary tells me that she often sees Emerson name-checked on men's dating profiles along with Bukowski and David Foster Wallace as part of a macho literary trifecta.

The self-reliant man, as Emerson describes him, seems like he would make for a comically terrible boyfriend, simultaneously entitled, dismissive, and hard to get. He has "the nonchalance of boys who are sure of a dinner, and would disdain as much as a lord to do or say aught to conciliate one":

independent, irresponsible, looking out from his corner on
such people and facts as pass by, he tries and sentences them
on their merits, in the swift, summary way of boys, as
good, bad, interesting, silly, eloquent, troublesome. He
cumbers himself never about consequences, about interests: he gives an independent, genuine verdict. You must
court him: he does not court you.

We know this man. He is Rhett Butler, Mr. Big, Wyatt Earp,
Donald Trump. (Or rather: He is the person Donald Trump
is trying to seem to be.) He's a high plains drifter; a gambler
and a ghoster. He's a lone cowboy judging the world from
under the brim of his hat. My own grad student version
was deceptively mild-mannered and soft-spoken and wore
button-downs and khakis, and I courted him like crazy.

I courted him both despite and because of the fact that I've
always fiercely disapproved of Emerson's version of self-
reliance, in practice and on principle. Emerson believes in
self-made men, but I experience myself as someone formed
and sustained by others' love and patience, by student loans
and stipends, by the kindness of strangers. Emerson thinks of
people as independent individuals, like an orderly orchard
of freestanding trees, but I see them as an overgrown tangle of
undergrowth, mulch, mushrooms, and moss, or as an indivisible ocean of brinedrops. I believe we are all obviously a
part of one another, elements of one ecosystem, members of
one body, all of us at the mercy of capitalism, weather, genes,
and fate. Independence, to me, is nothing but a dangerous
delusion. So I pushed back. And the more my craving to lean
was thwarted, the more I defended my desire to depend,

maybe even my right to depend. (Hence the shout-out in my ex's book acknowledgments: "Thanks to Briallen Hopper for her skepticism about Emersonian self-fashioning.")

What I didn't fully understand at the time is that maybe my swooning and skepticism were as necessary to my ex as his sunny sturdiness was to me. Because classic American self-reliance is often expressed as a defensive response to a gendered set of threats. As Emerson puts it: "Society everywhere is in conspiracy against the manhood of every one of its members." And it's impossible to ignore that these threats are often figured as feminine. The essay's epigraph is a poem calling for a baby boy to be cast out into the wild so he can be nursed by a wolf instead of a woman, and grow up to be tough instead of weak. The disapproval of an educated consensus is described as a kind of "feminine rage" to be scorned; an outmoded theory is a "harlot" to be fled from. "Self-Reliance" is a man's world, but it requires many metaphorical women in the wings acting like milky, emotional, seductive sirens. And that was a role that my twenty-something self felt born to play, no matter how shameful it might be.

Because for Emerson, the primary emotional threat posed by dependence is shame. There's shame in agreeing with what someone else says instead of being the person to say it first (i.e., being "forced to take with shame our own opinion from another"). There's shame in being an object of empathy. (Emerson believes the person we feel sorry for should be "ashamed of our compassion.") And there's shame in capitulating to requests for help ("Though I confess with shame I sometimes succumb and give the dollar, it is a wicked dollar which by and by I shall have the manhood to withhold").

As it happens, none of the supposedly shameful things Emerson mentions has ever made me feel ashamed. Unlike Emerson, I love it when someone says what I've been thinking; it makes me feel less alone. I crave commiseration—I often sigh melodramatically, hoping my roommates will hear and ask what's wrong so I can complain at ludicrous length. I am endlessly susceptible to GoFundMes and nonprofit fundraising appeals, and I try to remember to carry cash for panhandlers. (We are all members of one body; we are all at the mercy of fate.)

Still, as the adoring girlfriend of an aspiring Emersonian, I found myself tangled up in shame. My shame came not from the consciousness of my utter dependence but from my perverse attraction to a man who represented every clichéd, obvious, all-American thing I didn't want to want: unshakable entitlement, supreme self-satisfaction, and the seemingly effortless ability to wake up cheerful every day and be confident and productive and tall and Southern Californian and win prizes and eat vegetables and go to the gym like clockwork. It was as though through loving him I was outsourcing my craving for independent individualism and discernible muscle definition. I wanted white male privilege by association. I was frankly in love with it. It wasn't pretty. And my resulting shame spirals were simultaneously unsustainable and hot.

Because shame is hot. It's a flush, a burning, a fire glowing behind your ears and between your legs and underneath your toes. I was ashamed that I needed him emotionally and existentially in ways he didn't seem to need me. I was ashamed of my desire to hitch my wagon to his star so he could tug us both to overeducated upper-middle-class security and possibly the New York Times Weddings section. And I was ashamed of my willingness to settle for a love life in which my desire to twine like a vine was constantly thwarted by a man who was always carefully disentangling himself from my tendrils and tentacles.

(At one point, years before we broke up, he Microsoft Painted an ostensibly affectionate cartoon of me as a blonde octopus in bright red lipstick, eager to surround him with all my arms, as he wielded a mortar trowel and built a brick wall to keep me away. The picture was doom in pixels—there was no recovering from it—but it was also the way we stayed together so long: turning our difficult love into a cutting joke. Meanwhile, frustrated by his unassailable self-sufficiency, which felt like a challenge I couldn't refuse, I called him undentable; the Teflon Boyfriend; the Unmoved Mover. He would chuckle ruefully, and then open his arms and give me another crack at him.)

Toward the end of "Self-Reliance," Emerson writes admiringly about how the typical Maori man (or "naked New Zealander") is, unlike effete white Americans, immune to wounds: "If the traveller tell us truly, strike the savage with a broad axe, and in a day or two the flesh shall unite and heal as if you struck the blow into soft pitch, and the same blow shall send the white to his grave."

This is obviously a convenient belief for a settler colonial to have, since it makes any amount of white violence against brown people seem as harmless as slicing tar. It's also a vision of self-reliant masculinity that is inhuman, even monstrous.

Emerson idealizes beings who are so independent that they can survive all-out assault without any need for succor, sympathy, or balm.

In his book, amidst hundreds of pages of praise, my ex briefly describes the most extreme form of Emersonian self-reliance as "an almost grotesque invulnerability." When I read that fleeting phrase years later I saw a trace of my own skeptical perspective; a slight scar I had left on his invulnerable pitch-perfect mind.

Emerson wants men to know that "they are not leaning willows, but can and must detach themselves." I was a leaning willow, and when my man could and did detach himself from me, I learned that leaning willows, unlike mighty oaks, are built to withstand quakes and storms. They can bend almost to the ground without breaking.

~

At first I didn't know I wasn't broken. When I found myself abruptly single after six serially monogamous years, I thought I was thrown back on myself, a vine without a trellis. I made a long and ridiculous list of 102 things I thought I'd lost forever, including meaning, hope, sanity, security, snowball fights, the Sunday *New York Times*, consolation, ecstasy, peace, pleasure, ritual and tradition, teasing, making dinner, quotidian contentment, taking care of someone, being taken care of, leaning on someone, and the Pacific Ocean. (My ex and I had driven up and down the Pacific Coast Highway together, and when I divided up our memories in my mind, he got everything.) I honestly believed that as far as I was concerned, all joy in life was gone, and the ocean bed was dry.

I had come to a pivot point: a moment when I could have turned in desperation to the next plausible straight man to lean on, or, failing that, tried to reinvent myself as a self-reliant, independent Emersonian cowgirl. In the end I did neither: I was too wary to fall back into love and too much of a leaner not to lean. But I wasn't yet sure what a third option would be, and in the meantime I kept sinking deeper into shame.

~

Once, as an antidote to a shame spiral of her own, Joan Didion wrote herself a modern woman's version of "Self-Reliance" called "On Self-Respect." It's an essay so consummately cool that, even though I'm hopelessly wedded to dependence, I'm still sometimes tempted to dip it in ice water and drape it across my brow whenever the shame fever starts to rise. It represents a path not taken; a way I occasionally imagine my life could have gone had I been constructed with fewer tendrils and a bit more fiber.

Like me, Didion was once a young woman reeling from rejection, but she'd been rejected by Phi Beta Kappa, not by a man in khakis. In the wake of this rebuff, which shattered her belief that her various merits "automatically guaranteed me not only Phi Beta Kappa keys but happiness, honour, and the love of a good man," she rebuilt her system of values. Instead of depending on honor societies and external accolades for her worth, she decided to depend on herself. "Although to be driven back upon oneself is an uneasy affair at best," she writes, "rather like trying to cross a border with borrowed credentials, it seems to me now the one condition necessary to the beginnings of real self-respect."

It's hard for me to imagine a less self-sufficient scenario than an attempted illicit border crossing—one is dependent first of all on someone to borrow credentials from, and then on the unpredictable power of border officials. But for Didion, there is something liberating about the idea of moving through the world without worrying about stamps of approval. "People with self-respect exhibit a certain toughness, a kind of moral nerve; they display what was once called *character*," she declares. Character, for Didion, is "the willingness to accept responsibility for one's own life." The essay is written in the clear, uncompromising voice of a woman who leans against yellow Stingrays and Malibu balconies and nothing else.

When she wrote the essay in 1961, Didion, a fifth-generation Californian raised in a military family, was still a libertarian Republican, a Goldwater Girl in the making. Perhaps it is not such a surprise that as examples of self-respect, she invokes, unironically, the Victorian Major General Charles Gordon, who "put on a clean white suit and held Khartoum against the Mahdi"; the British soldiers who learned to fight on the playing fields of Eton; the British imperialists who insisted on dressing for dinner in the middle of the jungle; her own Californian settler ancestor Narcissa Cornwall, who reacted "coolly" when her house was swarmed with "strange Indians"; and, of course, Rhett Butler. Didion is also a fan of "the careless, incurably dishonest Jordan Baker in *The Great Gatsby*," who "took her own measure, made her own peace, avoided threats to that peace."

People who don't make the cut as models for Didionesque self-respect include some fairly formidable heroines: Cathy in *Wuthering Heights* (too dramatic) and Helen Keller (too dependent on Annie Sullivan, the blind teacher who taught her how to speak sign language and read and write Braille). Indians, meanwhile, are neither self-respecting nor the reverse, but simply an opportunity for white people to prove their own coolness: "People who respect themselves are willing to accept the risk that the Indians will be hostile."

Though Didion is careful not to conflate self-respect with undentable masculinity (she openly admires "that genius for accommodation more often seen in women than in men"), it's not difficult to see how her scorn for dependent disability à la Keller or public passion à la Cathy echoes Emerson's distaste for weakness and woundedness, just as it's impossible to ignore how much the glamour of Didion's tough and cool attitude depends on the dubious mythologies of Manifest Destiny, *Gone with the Wind*, and fabulous Roaring Twenties parties thrown by the 1 percent. To revere these mythologies as Didion does requires you to see self-respect in cowboys and not Indians; in Rhett and not Mammy; in Jordan Baker and not the residents of the valley of ashes.

Didion's existentialist insistence on the authenticity of aloneness has been harder for me to dismiss. It's tempting to attempt to redeem rejection by reimagining it, as she does, as a kind of purification process, a necessary stripping away of the obscuring tangle of social mendacity. Didion believes that the person you are when you're alone is the person you really are. "Self-deception remains the most difficult deception," she writes. "The charms that work on others count for nothing in that devastatingly well-lit back alley where one keeps assignations with oneself." Others may fall prey to our obfuscation or be taken in by our charm, but a self-respecting self sees itself at its worst (Didion meets herself in an alley; I imagine my own hypothetical self-confrontation happening in an empty locker room, each self naked, goose-bumped, and floodlit by fluorescents), and coolly accepts itself for what it is.

Without such unflinching self-respect, Didion believes, one can't help but become a captive audience for what must be the worst film in the world:

> an interminable home movie that documents one's fail-ings, both real and imagined, with fresh footage spliced in for every screening. *There's the glass you broke in anger, there's the hurt on X's face; watch now, this next scene, the night Y came back from Houston, see how you muff this one.*

From this sour cinematic experience it is but a short step to insomnia and despair. "To live without self-respect," she explains,

> is to lie awake some night, beyond the reach of warm milk, phenobarbital, and the sleeping hand on the coverlet, counting up the sins of commission and omis-sion, the trusts betrayed, the promises subtly broken, the gifts irrevocably wasted through sloth or cowardice or carelessness.

Sleeping alone is the existentialist endgame, the would-be self-reliant self-respecter's ultimate test. "However long we postpone it," she warns,

> we eventually lie down alone in that notoriously uncomfortable bed, the one we make ourselves. Whether or not we sleep in it depends, of course, on whether or not we respect ourselves.

Didion isn't wrong about the self-lacerating documentary screening in HD and surround sound at inconvenient hours. I have seen that movie before (my own personal version is titled *Shame Spiral: The Reckoning*), and insomnia is occasionally how it ends. But only sometimes. Most of the time, for me, it ends with sleep.

In fact, over the years my own experience of a solitary bed has been far from Didionesque. It's actually become quite comfortable, whether despite or because of the fact that I've done my best to avoid confronting myself naked and alone under grim bluish lights. If I were to catch a glimpse of myself, I don't expect I'd respect what I saw. I admit that my ability to sleep without self-respect is probably a symptom of the self-obfuscation that lulls me into complacency and lets me off the hook. But I'm not truly troubled by this possibility because, unlike Didion, I don't believe that my solitary self is my truest self. I'm not even sure that my solitary self exists at all.

My skepticism about the authenticity of solitude is partly rooted in experience. I don't see why the person I am when

I'm rising to the occasion for students in the classroom is less truly myself than the person I am when I come home and kick off my shoes and collapse on the couch. There are verses of hymns I know by heart that I can only remember in church, but they'll still be a part of me till I die. I never feel more myself than when I'm writing, and I always write for readers. My sisters know I'm bossy and my friends know I'm kind, and when I'm alone I'm neither, but really I'm both. My identity is not an independent state.

I can't imagine a solitary self even in theory. What would it even mean, after all, to be truly alone with yourself, an independent and dispassionate critic of your own individual character? You would need to be able to trace the contours of your personality as if they had never meant anything to anyone; to scour your brain of love's neural traces; to forget where your hands have been. You would need a body and soul free of microscopic chimeras, unmarked by social judgments past and present. You would need to redact yourself from every file and delete yourself from every inbox. You would need an unlisted number and a rotary phone with a severed cord. You would need to have forgotten all the books you'd read, or never read them in the first place. You would need to be the last living speaker of a dying language. You would need to have been abandoned as an infant by a wolf who refused to raise you.

I could never clear away the cloud of social meaning that surrounds and supports me, and I don't see why I should want to try.

In the wake of my breakup, after my initial collapse, I didn't think I would ever lean again. But when I instinctively turned to my friends, not daring to hope for anything more than some social sorrow-drowning, I was met with surprisingly sturdy affection, and I unexpectedly learned to lean more confidently and steadily than I ever had before. Rather than resting all my weight on one unreliable man, I began to spread myself out. I learned to practice mutual, broadly distributed leaning: to depend on care that was neither compulsory nor conditional, and on lavish, unrationed, unanticipated kindness.

The forms of love that had once been ancillary and supplemental became, collectively, everything. In the winter I threw and dodged snowballs again. In the summer I raced my friend down a beach under the bright suspended-steel span of the Golden Gate Bridge and got my ocean back. And I began the long process of learning how to lean without the simultaneously reassuring and panicking pressure of a marriage plot, or any other plot. The urgent question of my twenties was always, "Is this relationship going somewhere?" Was the steel strong enough? Was the engineering sound? Was the love sturdy enough to bear a lifetime's worth of weight? It never was. But leaning on friends is never going anywhere, it is not proof of anything, and there are no mandatory standards for it to meet or fail to meet. You just find yourself together, side by side, and then one day you are depending on each other, bearing one another's burdens, basking in each other's warmth, for decades or only for a moment.

"To free us from the expectations of others, to give us back to ourselves—there lies the great, the singular power of self-respect," Didion writes. "Without it, one eventually discovers the final turn of the screw: one runs away to find oneself, and finds no one at home." But what if locating yourself by yourself is like trying to use a compass without the North Pole, and what if the expectations of others are constellations to navigate by? What if self-possession is the tautology you are trying to escape?

Didion was thrown back on herself, but I was thrown back on my friends.

Although to be driven back on your friends is an uneasy affair at best, rather like falling from a fire escape into the net below, for me it was the one condition necessary to the beginning of sustainable dependence, and accepting my need to lean without shame. Because despite what America and Emerson would have us believe, "self-reliance" is often less a virtue than a myth. And it has been clear to me, from the first day I was supposedly on my own, that independence is impossible for me, even if I wanted it. As Elizabeth Warren reminds us, we do not build the roads we drive on or rely on our own personal fire trucks to put out our house fires, and this principle holds true for our emotional infrastructure as well.

To do without the illusion of independence is to be given a new vision of our painful past through the filter of friendship. It is a reprieve from the relentless self-scrutiny of the independent lens; it is a newly restored home movie that documents the miraculous moments our own severity or selective memory might have forced us to forget. *Look, there's the time you rose to the occasion, and there's the time you were surprised by kindness; watch now, this next scene, the night I needed you, see how you were there to meet me.* Even our faults and flaws can become bearable when mediated through the eyes of others, since our closest friends can show us the awful sides of ourselves that we would never have seen, but in ways that sharpen us instead of wearing us away.

To give up on self-reliance and self-respect is to trade the harshness of insomnia for the bliss of drowsiness. It is to lie half-asleep at night with your phone resting against your ear, listening to your friend regale you with stories of jokes shared, promises kept, gifts given.

To give us back to one another—there lies the great, the singular power of learning to lean on others. Without it, one eventually discovers the final turn of the screw: One runs away to find love, and finds only oneself.

~

I've spent more than a decade now leaning broadly and shamelessly, and I no longer worry that I'll break or fall. When I start to panic or lose myself I just make a call, or place my palm against a plinth until I'm steady. My fierce dependence has never failed me yet. It's become second nature.

It's natural to me now, but that doesn't mean it's easy. And it's hard partly because dependence is so despised in our culture, from psychology to politics. To radically revise Emerson: "Society everywhere is in conspiracy against the leaning of every one of its members." "Codependence" is a beautiful word that could mean mutual support but instead means mutual harm. We all depend on various chemicals to survive, but "chemical dependency" is a euphemism for drug addiction. "Depend" is an adult diaper brand that provides an essential product but also reinforces the connections between dependence, weakness, and public shame. The conservative coinage "culture of dependency" evokes not a community of care but racist stereotypes of deadbeat dads and welfare queens. I live in a country where the idea that children would get a free school lunch is untenable to many; when kids can't pay, cafeteria workers are instructed to dump their lunch in the trash rather than feed them, and politicians have proposed the plan of making poor children do janitorial work to earn their food. In America, even kindergarteners are taught to be ashamed of depending on others for their sandwiches and milk.

Of course, kids are usually allowed to do a fair amount of leaning at home. But for adults, romantic partnership can sometimes seem like the only socially sanctioned reprieve from the demand to self-rely, aside perhaps from the military or team sports. Emotional and material dependence within couples is both accepted and expected, and even though in practice romantic love is not necessarily a license to lean, it is commonly understood that marriage, in the words of the *Book of Common Prayer*, "was ordained for the mutual society, help, and comfort, that the one ought to have of the other."

No wonder I've spent so much of my life leaning on the man I was sleeping with, or sleeping with the man I was leaning on. No wonder so many people I know try to save all their leaning for their romantic partner.

The flipside of the love-and-marriage exception is that other kinds of relationships of dependence are subject to constant criticism and condescension. A few years ago, when I was rearranging my life to care for a friend with cancer, an acquaintance of ours took me to task, telling me that certain kinds of care should be provided only by romantic partners, not by friends. He may have been trying to protect me, but in doing so he was enforcing a norm, and I didn't see why my friend should be deprived of care and I should be protected from the hard parts of love just because both of us happened to be single. Meanwhile another friend who wants to be a mother has told me that she's not sure she can have kids without a partner, because when she was growing up she absorbed the prevailing attitude that unwed parents had made irresponsible choices and were not entitled to approval and support. Even though she no longer believes this, she can't quite shake the shame, and as a brown woman with an immigrant family background, she knows she would be judged especially harshly if she ever needed help—and of course she would need help; all parents need help.

The obstacles to shameless leaning are all around us, and they are also inside us. Insofar as leaning in America has often been characterized as feminine or foreign, and independence has been declared to be a prerequisite for citizenship and dignity, these obstacles might even constitute us. Dependence does not have the same social meaning for everyone, and its weight is not equally borne. Even when it is necessary, it can be an unaffordable privilege or an unsustainable loss of power. Leaning, or being leaned on, can make one feel luscious, melting, known, held, solid, suspended, steely, light. It can also make one feel used, worn out, weak, diminished, infantilized, guarded, sick, spent. Leaning can be love. It is also an improvisation and a risk.

Long ago, in a season of romantic despair, I wrote a melodramatic email to two old friends asking for empathy.

One thanked me for reaching out and sent love, the other rebuked me for my emotional excess and cut off contact; both were sure they'd acted appropriately, and perhaps they both were right. In one of my friendships, an immense financial gift that I thought might wreck us with the weight of obligation instead wove us together like a heartfelt vow, while in another friendship, a period of temporary financial dependence coincided with unprecedentedly bitter fights and recriminations. There have been times in caregiving situations when I've felt the kind of profound physical connection with a friend that one might have with a longtime lover: the ability to read someone's face and body and to know the subtle signs, imperceptible to others, that they are tired, overwhelmed, in pain, at peace. And there have been times when the intimacy of giving and receiving care was so intense, the fear of loss and self-loss so great, that it required carefully sustained mutual resentment and exasperation.

Some of the difficulty of dependence is inevitable, and it may be indistinguishable from the difficulty of intimacy itself. But some of it is exacerbated by the awkwardness of leaning in unscripted and uncoupled configurations. And a lot of the time *all* leaning seems unnecessarily hard: as if we are far too prone to punish ourselves and others for needing something we can't exist without.

It doesn't help that the American canon celebrating self-reliance is vast, encompassing the Declaration of Independence, Emerson, Didion, perennial bestseller Ayn Rand, most noirs, most Westerns, and a large percentage of congressional legislation. Popular celebrations of adult dependence, if you leave out romantic dependence, are harder to find, and they often portray it as a pre- or post-couplehood phase (e.g., *Friends* or *The Golden Girls*). For a full-fledged paean to leaning there is mainly just Bill Withers, whose anthem "Lean on Me" was inspired by the West Virginia coal-mining town that raised him.

I'll never stop singing along with Bill Withers. I believe we all need somebody to lean on. But sometimes it seems like there are two American creeds, self-reliance and marriage, and neither of them is mine.

∼

A few years ago, when I was trying to figure out (still, again) how to lean, my friend Adrienne introduced me to Gwendolyn Brooks's 1953 novel, *Maud Martha*, and it was exactly what I needed. It's a series of brief, poetic, impressionistic chapters that document the eponymous heroine's life from childhood through her mid-thirties—an ordinary midcentury black Chicagoan existence that at one point Maud Martha sums up as "Decent childhood, happy Christmases; some shreds of romance, a marriage, pregnancy and the giving birth, her growing child, her experiments with sewing, her books, her conversations with her friends and enemies."

But though Maud Martha's existence is ordinary, her experience of it is not. In each chapter she wryly and reverently attends to the details of the world around her, pondering small gestures and phrases, savoring dandelions in the yard and cocoa in the kitchen, sharing a porch swing with a man who makes her whole body sing, magnanimously freeing a mouse from a trap, refusing to endure microaggressions from a white woman at work, reading newspaper headlines about lynching and war, and soaring high on a surge of postpartum elation. Through it all, she is privately and urgently working out her desires, their meanings, and by extension the meaning of life. In a two-page chapter called "posts" (my paperback falls open to it, the spine broken between the pages), Maud Martha turns her skeptical attention to leaning and love.

The most life-giving thing about Maud Martha's response to the cult of self-reliance is that she refuses even to acknowledge its existence. Instead, from the very first sentences, she treats the need for dependence as a self-evident truth, universal and incontrovertible:

> People have to choose something decently constant to depend on, thought Maud Martha. People must have something to lean on.

For Maud Martha, an independent identity is never an option.

She then relentlessly proceeds to dispose of the love-and-marriage myth as well, seeing love not as a static solution to the problem of dependence, but rather as a chronic condition of flux and latent loss:

> But the love of a single person was not enough. Not only was personal love itself, however good, a thing that varied from week to week, from second to second, but the parties to it were likely, for example, to die, any minute, or otherwise be parted, or destroyed. At any time.

Friendship and other forms of love are not reliable either:

> Not alone was the romantic love of a man and a woman
> fallible, but the breadier love between parents and chil-
> dren; brothers; animals; friend and friend. Those too
> could not be heavily depended on.

It's a bracing refusal of all the conventional consolations—a
guarded assessment of the strength of all affections.

What then is left to help bear the weight? At first Maud
Martha turns cosmic, contemplating nature and its impersonal "system of change"—the orbits and seasons that offer
"some order of constancy." But this is an austere kind of
leaning, presumably not intimate enough. What she settles on
instead is a carefully constructed kind of domestic structure:

> The marriage shell, not the romance, or love, it might
> contain.

The marriage shell as Maud Martha describes it is a list of
habits that make up a habitation—

> A marriage made up of Sunday papers and shoeless feet,
> baking powder biscuits, baby baths, and matinees and
> laundrymen, and potato plants in the kitchen window.

It's a list that evokes the bodily intimacy of shared space,
shared nourishment, shared movement through history, shared
responsibility, shared screentime, and the care of living and

growing things. On any given day the love itself may be lost or inaccessible, but the biscuits will still rise in the oven, and the potato plant will bring forth another leaf, in the faith that love will return, or in love's memory.

I tend to let myself lean more heavily on personal love than Maud Martha does, but I know my loves might all be fragile and fallible too. And so, in the absence of a marriage shell, I've spent years attempting to construct a friendship shell that will hold me and my friends up, and hold us together. I bake gingerbread for my friends in the winter and shortcake in the summer. I light candles and pray for them morning and night. I invite them over to celebrate many holidays that are on the calendar and a few that aren't. And across years and oceans, my distant friends and I co-create structures of togetherness through group texts and phone dates and regular reunions. We are trying to safeguard our love against the ravages of space and time.

But we are all bodies as well as voices and minds, and there is no satisfying substitute for shared daily life. That is something I can't always count on from year to year, as friends and roommates come and go. As a result I'm irrationally attached to the symbolism of a shared lease, or even a shared Shop-Rite membership, and I carry keys to my friends' houses like talismans even though I rarely need to use them. I'm also especially reliant on small daily leans. For two years my former roommate would ask me what the day's weather was going to be, and I would google it for him while he put the kettle on for my tea. We could easily have done these things for ourselves, but swapping two-second tasks sometimes meant the difference between a day with mutual care in it and a day without.

Of course, making and maintaining this structure requires a kind of mutuality that's not always available. In the very next chapter, after she describes the marriage shell, Maud Martha, simmering with resentment, defends her sometimes solitary struggle to build the kind of shell she wants:

> What she had wanted was a solid. She had wanted shimmering form; warm, but hard as stone and as difficult to break. She had wanted to found—tradition. She had wanted to shape, for their use . . . a set of falterless customs.

For Maud Martha, these customs include a peaceful family Christmas around the tree like the ones she grew up with, but instead her husband invites his rowdy friends over for takeout and Blatz beer. It's a crack in the shell that symbolizes the loss of the kind of intimate family life she'd always wanted. In a moment of frustration, as she peels her husband's tipsy friend's arm from around her waist, Maud Martha stubbornly depends not on her husband's love, not even on the marriage shell itself, but rather on the intensity of her desire for its shimmering form; on the fervency of her belief that what she had wanted to make of her life was meaningful, was worth wanting.

If Maud Martha's struggle is finding a way to lean within a marriage, mine is finding a way to lean without one. Neither is easy, but nothing matters more. Because I believe, with Maud Martha, that learning how to lean might be the primary ethical problem, the all-encompassing question and quest. As she says:

> Was, perhaps, the whole life of man a dedication to this search for something to lean upon, and was, to a great degree, his "happiness" or "unhappiness" written up for him by the demands or limitations of what he chose for that work?
>
> For work it was. Leaning was a work.

∾

We all need something decently constant to lean on.

Even Didion, who radically reversed her take on the value of pioneer self-reliance in *Where I Was From*, arguing that Westerners' rhetoric of independence masked and enabled "this extreme reliance of California on federal money, so seemingly at odds with the emphasis on unfettered individualism that constitutes the local core belief." Didion, who turned to marriage as an alternative to psychiatry when she had a breakdown in her late twenties, as she tells us in "Goodbye to All That"; and whose utter reliance on her husband—she described them as "terrifically, terribly dependent on one another"—caused her to lose her sanity for a year after he died. Her memoirs of grief are elegies to leaning.

Even Emerson, who depended every day on his wife and their servants, though he didn't like to admit it (in distinct contrast to Maud Martha, he writes disgustedly in his essay on "Love" about the way marriage customs can cause the language of love to degenerate into something with "a savor of hams and powdering-tubs"). Emerson, who *did* admit to a kind of dependence on friendships ("when they are real, they are not glass threads or frostwork, but the solidest thing we know"), and who, beyond that, imagines self-reliance itself as kind of extreme and total leaning—an infantile dependence on a cosmic force that is the origin of all things. "We lie in the lap of immense intelligence," he writes with unstrung pleasure, as if he is a Transcendentalist Paul Newman leaning on some all-intelligent, all-powerful Over-Soul version of Joanne Woodward.

Even Paul and Joanne, whose decades-long lean was doubtless not always as serene as it looked. Ten years ago, when my friend Greg and I were sitting on my bed under the Gordon Parks picture, he told me it reminded him of "Man and Wife" by Robert Lowell, a poem about a long-married couple wrung out from a fight. Ever since then, the poem has intermittently filtered my idyllic vision of the image with a red haze of tranquilizers and mid-conflict exhaustion.

And even me—a self-avowed leaner who is sometimes disinclined to lean. Because while it's true that I love nothing more than leaning back and melting into bliss at the beauty shop, sometimes I fear that if I start to melt I'll never stop, so I cut my own hair with pinking shears over the sink. After spending so many years with the circles labeled LEANING and ROMANTIC LOVE stacked directly on top of each other in my personal Venn diagram, I find I am now unable to get them to overlap at all. These days I'm not sure what falling in love would mean if it weren't a free fall, so I save all my leaning for my friends.

I build a friendship shell, and it cracks apart, so I build another, or maybe I find another, like a hermit crab. I walk through the world with my eye always out for sturdy leaning walls with a mix of sun and shade. I try to mend the broken trellises, or to tie them temporarily together, or at least to cover their cracks with leaves. I try to lean neither too little nor too much; I try to bear others up even as I burden them; I try to let them lean on me as lightly or heavily as they like. I try to shape shimmering forms, warm and solid. I try to keep shame at bay. Sometimes I fail. But I never rest in my quest for rest.

Because leaning is a work.

HOW TO BE SINGLE

1. First, get rid of your lover, partner, fiancé, or spouse. A define-the-relationship talk is the classic way to do this, but glacially cold and slow emotional withdrawal is also effective, as are Post-its. Emojis are efficient and expressive (peace out, broken heart, Edvard Munch scream!). Process servers are legally binding. Ghosting is for lazy people. Poison should be attempted only if you are in an Agatha Christie story and are dying to meet Miss Marple.

2. Alternatively, you can make your significant other get rid of you. Try mysterious dick pics, unrealistic ultimatums, and a series of phantom pregnancies.

3. Now you are single. Congratulations! The trick is to stay that way. You can start by throwing out your razor and canceling all your salon appointments.

4. Be aware that the instant you become single, everyone in the world will join in a relentless conspiracy to get you paired off. The most obvious way to thwart them is to build an

indoor fort out of old newspapers and fill it with feral raccoons and refuse to leave your apartment. Do not rule this out just because it's a cliché. It works.

5. If you can't afford to quit your job and go full newspapers-and-raccoons just yet, you could try reconnecting with your ex. Don't actually date them, but text them, theorize them, narrate them, hook up with them, sleep with their picture under your pillow, and write them ten-page tear-stained love letters that you send through the U.S. Mail, walking slowly and deliberately all the way to the post office while the hand that is clutching the letter throbs as if it were full of embers. Do this for as many months or years as it takes for you to get bored of it.

6. Your friends are going to want you to date online. It is hard to avoid online dating entirely, but there are many strategies you can use to maximize dating websites' preexisting propensity to perpetuate singleness in order to maintain their customer base.

The simplest way is to start with the path of least resistance and cheerily play along. Tell your friends, with a little wobble of emotion in your voice, that you're finally ready to put yourself out there! Ask them to help you make a cool OKCupid profile. Solicit their advice about which pictures to include (smiling face from a clear-skin phase, full-body pic from a restricted-eating phase, National Park selfie with a photogenic mountain!). Put a lot of thought into your answers. Be the right amount of light and the right amount of open, with an unthreatening garnish of wit and an appealing soupçon of snark. Choose favorite novels that are approachable without being clichéd. Choose favorite TV shows that are critically acclaimed and full of sex scenes. Inform the people of the internet that you're interested in short- or long-term dating, you're cool with both cats and dogs, and you want kids someday! Act like you mean it! Then set your profile to invisible and try to pretend the whole thing never happened.

7. At some point one of your married friends will say, "Hey, whatever happened to the online dating thing? Don't you think you should give that another try?" She may even insist that you reactivate your account, and subsequently sit down next to you on the couch with your laptop on her lap and sift through your entire inbox looking for plausible messages, because surely they can't ALL be bad.

There are a few ways you can play this. One way is to make sure your friend reads the absolute worst messages right away and hope that she'll be so amused by the astonishing grammatical manglings and surreal spellings that she'll fall into helpless giggle fits and forget why she is looking at your messages in the first place.

Better yet, she'll be so appalled by the messages' corrosive subtext of misogyny and self-loathing that she'll suddenly slam your laptop shut as if it is a radioactive Pandora's box and she is trying to protect you from the horrors of the world.

8. Another way to deflect the threat of online dating is to go ahead and reply to a message from a plausible person and agree to meet them for a date. This is a bit more labor intensive, as you will in fact have to put on some nice clothes and go out

into the world (only the most incorrigible single people actually stand dates up). You should be pleasant and warm during the date—you don't want to give your friends ammunition to blame you for your own singleness. You can even go ahead and have fun! Why not? The stakes are infinitely low. Kiss the person or hook up with them. Or don't. It's immaterial.

After the date one of the following things might happen:

The person might send you a text saying it was nice meeting you but they didn't really feel like you had chemistry.

Or they might go home and instantly block you.

Or they might subtly, gradually disappear.

In any of these cases, you're golden!

Alternatively, the person might text you and make some kind of clever, bantery allusion to some aspect of your conversation, or a flirty reference to your physical intimacies, in which case you should send them a Havisham GIF, either Helena Bonham Carter from Mike Newell's 2012 version of *Great Expectations* or Gillian Anderson from the 2011 BBC version or Martita Hunt from the 1946 David Lean version. (Anne Bancroft from the 1998 version is too hot.) If your date tries to keep bantering or flirting, just keep sending Havishams until they stop.

Or your date might text you and say, "Hey! I had a really nice time the other night. I'd really like to see you again." To which you should reply, with a kind of flat, obtuse, withholding finality: "Huh. I guess that is nice of you to say." Then delete their number from your phone, and tell your friends that they didn't seem that interested.

9. Tinder is great because it doesn't matter which way you swipe as long as you never meet anyone in person.

Bumble is too much work.

10. Once you've mastered the internet, staying single in real life is relatively straightforward. The main thing to remember is always to gaze raptly into the middle distance, whether you're walking down a crowded street or schmoozing at a party full of attractive people. Do not allow your vision to focus on exciting new faces or bodies! Pay attention only to people you could never imagine dating (people of an incompatible gender or sexuality or political persuasion; people who are wearing wedding rings and actually holding their partner's hands). Let the people you might be attracted to fade into the landscape until eventually you don't see them anymore.

11. The middle-distance gaze works beautifully for sidewalks, cocktail parties, and public transportation, but it's a lot harder to deploy at work or during dinner parties or in other small-scale social gatherings. Sometimes an eligible person comes into focus despite your best attempts to the contrary. Sometimes you gaze at them and they remind you of nerve endings you'd forgotten you had. Sometimes you feel their attention as if it's painting you with brushstrokes of fire. Sometimes you lie in bed and think of them and melt slowly into your mattress as if the memory foam holds the memory of all the pleasure you've ever known. Sometimes when you're alone you remember something they said and laugh aloud with involuntary joy.

When this happens, it's best to friend-zone them aggressively right away. Talk to them about your exes, your crushing student debt, your toenail fungus. Tell them that you're planning to become a single parent any minute now through surrogacy or donor sperm. Dye your hair a steely gray and pretend that you're old enough to be their parent (or, if you actually are that old, lean into it!), and supply them with a steady stream of patronizing unsolicited advice prefaced by "When I was your age" until they begin to squirm. You could even try to force them to listen as you tell them all about how to be single.

ON SPINSTERS

It's the queers who made me. Who didn't get married . . .
—*HILTON ALS,* WHITE GIRLS

I WOULD CERTAINLY SEEM to be an ideal reader for a book called *Spinster.* After all, I'm someone who sometimes identifies as a spinster, who reveres "spinster" as a cultural category, and who was clunkily complimented by a fellow grad student when I was twenty-nine for "the bold way you are resignifying the term." I predictably preordered Kate Bolick's ode to singleness as soon as I heard about it: I was eager to read something about being a woman that wasn't about getting married, leaning in, or having it all.

Bolick's book was inspired by something she calls her "spinster wish," which is "shorthand for the extravagant pleasures of simply being by myself." A fragment she quotes from her diary describes "a long, perfect spinster wish of a Sunday, read all day, took two naps." But despite all the lounging, to Bolick the embodiment of a spinster wish is not a couch potato but an Art Deco sprite:

In my mind's eye, the spinster wish was the shape of that small, steel sylph gracing the nose of a Rolls-Royce, arms outstretched, sleeves billowing, about to leap from her earthbound perch and soar.

Spinsterhood, for Bolick, is not simply being an unmarried woman. Nor is it cat-collecting, celibacy, or the social indignity of life as a human Old Maid card. Instead it is something luxurious, coveted, and glamorous, associated with long days of reading, plenty of room to sprawl in bed, ecstatic self-communion, and, as befits the former executive editor of the decorating magazine *Domino*, a well-appointed apartment of one's own.

Bolick's sensuous vision of solitary self-care and self-indulgence recalls the glorious *Live Alone and Like It*, a classic 1936 self-help guide by Marjorie Hillis that's listed in Bolick's bibliography but never directly cited in her text. But *Live Alone* is much clearer about its topic than *Spinster*, and much grittier. Its subject is less sylph-inspired wishes and more, well, living alone. And its brisk, humorous tone is miles away from Bolick's wistful reveries. Like a true first-wave feminist, Hillis rejects words that define women by their relationship to marriage:

If you are in the habit of thinking of yourself as a widow or a spinster, this, too, is something to get over as speedily as possible. Both words are rapidly becoming extinct—or, at least, being relegated to another period, like bustle and reticule. A woman is now a woman, just as a man is a man, and expected to stand on her own feet, as he (supposedly) stands on his.

But eighty years later Bolick still thinks of herself as a spinster, even though for her the word is so metaphorical as to be almost meaningless. For Bolick, spinsterhood is quite compatible with dating (she is seemingly never not dating), cohabiting, and even marriage. Ultimately Bolick defines spinsterhood as an identity available to any woman, married or single, who sometimes feels suffocated by conventional cohabitation and who has decided to prioritize me-time: "For the happily coupled . . . spinster can be code for remembering to take time out for yourself."

As I read *Spinster* I found myself resisting it on almost every page. This is partly because I don't really share Bolick's solitary spinster wish: Most of the time I would rather sprawl and read with someone I love nearby, and luckily I get to do this a lot of the time. But more significantly, Bolick lost me at the beginning of the first chapter with this astonishing set of statements:

Whom to marry, and when will it happen—these two questions define every woman's existence, regardless of where she was raised or what religion she does or doesn't practice. She may grow up to love women instead of men, or to decide she simply doesn't believe in marriage. No matter. These dual contingencies govern her until they're answered, even if the answers are nobody and never.

I don't do well with anachronistic absolutes. "Too much," I wrote in the margin. (As Laura Kipnis observes in her excellent review on *Slate*, "All this seems far too sweeping.") I'm in my thirties and haven't married yet, but marriage is not in my own top five questions and hasn't been for some time. I'm much more interested in whether I'll write books or have kids, and much more defined and governed by race, class, gender, and the changing climate. I might feel differently if I were a socialite or a sorority sister or a member of a fundamentalist religious community, but the world Bolick describes is not the one I live in.

She goes on to ask,

You are born, you grow up, you become a wife.
But what if it wasn't this way? . . .
What would that look and feel like?

with dramatic line drops between each question, as if she is blowing our minds; as if these exact questions haven't already been asked and answered by generations of women for decades or centuries. I couldn't help but wonder: Why does Bolick's account of women's existence seem so much more archaic than a book published in 1936?

Spinster begins with overstated claims about the all-importance of marriage, but it quickly turns around and acts as if marital status is irrelevant—an equally inaccurate assumption. Over its three hundred pages Bolick answers her questions about what "spinster" lives might look like with micro-biographies of five women from the early-to-mid-twentieth century—the two you've probably heard of are

Edith Wharton and Edna St. Vincent Millay—who all were born, grew up, and became wives. Some of them also got divorced or separated or had open marriages and/or second marriages, but none of them were spinsters according to any standard definition of the term. Nor is marriage all that Bolick's "spinsters" have in common: All of them were writers who lived in the American Northeast; all of them were white; almost all of them were redheads. Bolick calls them her "awakeners"—the ones who helped her cultivate her ethereal "spinster wish." These five women may not have known much about what it's like to not become a wife (or about what that would look and feel like!), but their stories allow Bolick to rhapsodize about many of the things she loves the most: magazine writing, interior decorating, New York City. I'm fond of all those things too, but I would have enjoyed *Spinster* a lot more if it had been titled *Red-Headed Writers* or *Dating and Divorce*.

But my fundamental resistance to *Spinster* isn't just about the bait and switch of its title and content. It comes down to the way Bolick's small and not especially spinster-based archive radically limits the potential of her book, both culturally and politically.

Because the spinster, in history and literature, is not typically cool and stylish like Bolick's glamorous "awakeners." She is often weird, difficult, dissonant, queer—like an unnerving dream, or a pungent dose of smelling salts. And her social and emotional life is not primarily oriented around the familiar forms of straight romance—dating men, hooking up with men, living with men, getting engaged to men, marrying men, divorcing men, etc.; in other words virtually all the important adult relationships given significant space in Bolick's book. Instead, the spinster may find herself immersed in an ocean-deep existential solitude that remains impervious to Tinder or brunch. Or she may forge powerful forms of female love, friendship, commitment, and community, like the Boston marriage, the matriarchal family, or the settlement house. These varied modes of life are what make spinsters different from single ladies, debutantes, divorcées, and wives. Why would a book called *Spinster* gloss over them?

Chronically unmarried women have long endured the injustice of being set aside, ignored, dismissed, made invisible. This experience of social erasure is at the heart of the drama of many spinster stories. And the irony of *Spinster* is that despite its title it is often curiously committed to ignoring actual spinsters. I was floored when Bolick mentioned the boy-crazy, glamorous, and/or eligible Henry James heroines Isabel Archer (married) and Daisy Miller (a teenager) as "New Woman" precursors for what she's calling a spinster, but name-checked *The Bostonians* only as a way to signify the "WASP decorum" of the *Atlantic* office where she worked. Has Bolick even read *The Bostonians*? Henry James is practically the poet laureate of Spinsterland, and Olive Chancellor of *The Bostonians* is one of the greatest spinsters of all time. As James explains:

> There are women who are unmarried by accident, and others who are unmarried by option; but Olive Chancellor was unmarried by every implication of her being. She was

a spinster as Shelley was a lyric poet, or as the month of August is sultry.

Olive is the Platonic ideal of James's magnificent spinsters, out-spinstering even the spurned and spurning Catherine Sloper of *Washington Square* and the triumphant pyromaniac Miss Tina of *The Aspern Papers*. Passionate, twisted, harsh, awkward, indecorous, bold, bitter, and self-immolating, she probably wouldn't fit in well at the *Atlantic* offices, or anywhere else for that matter. And a book called *Spinster* that excludes Olive and the rest of the literary spinster pantheon while honoring Isabel Archer does violence to my soul as a spinster, a spinster fan, and a scholar of nineteenth-century literature.

You would scarcely guess it from *Spinster*, but the figure of the never-married woman of a certain age evokes a vast constellation of abrasive, eccentric, no-nonsense, sour, strong-minded, or socially invisible women who were born to inspire drag queens, tomboys, lesbians, late bloomers, loners, joiners, haters, do-gooders, nuns, divas, misfits, misanthropes, saints, wallflowers, or various combinations of the above. This starry host includes towering archetypes of female genius such as Jane Austen, Emily Dickinson, and Flannery O'Connor; haggard paragons of power such as Elizabeth I; and the apotheosis of the fictional spinster, the formidable Miss Havisham of Dickens's *Great Expectations*, with her ragged wedding dress, spidery cake, and quenchless thirst for revenge.

It also includes voluble and vulnerable women like Miss Bates in *Emma*, brave late bloomers like Joanne Woodward's eponymous schoolteacher in *Rachel, Rachel*, sadder and wiser fallen women like Marian the Librarian in *The Music Man*, conflagrations of thwarted lust like Rosalind Russell's schoolteacher in *Picnic*, the feral and fabulous Little Edie of *Grey Gardens*, the radiant spinster-in-training played by Julia Roberts in *My Best Friend's Wedding* (whose happy ending is dancing with the marvelous Rupert Everett), Agatha Christie's Miss Marple (who uses her social invisibility to solve murders!), Frances McDormand's despairing and heroic nursery governess in *Miss Pettigrew Lives for a Day*, the centuries-old Aunt Ester who presides over all August Wilson's plays as the ancestor of her people, the varied church ladies and pink-collar workers and fag hags of Barbara Pym, and the consummate artist Pym herself.

And it encompasses busy "career women" of various stripes: educational innovators like Maria Louise Baldwin, educational cautionary tales like Miss Jean Brodie, social visionaries like Jane Addams and Louisa May Alcott (who each get a brief shout-out in *Spinster*, but whose decidedly queer and/or woman-oriented emotional lives are ignored), odd-couple friends like Mary and Rhoda on *The Mary Tyler Moore Show*, and tenacious, long-lived professional sister pairs like Susan and Anna Warner, Sadie and Bessie Delany, and Alice and Harper Lee.

These many magnificent spinsters and their unnamed sisters expand the range of femininity far beyond the familiar territory of the cute, cool, or easily commodified, and ignoring or shunning almost all of this classic spinster pantheon—as Bolick does—has political consequences. Above all, it domesticates the threat that the spinster poses to normative systems of love, sex, and power. There is a reason the word "spinster" has long been a queer-tinged insult with a straight-slicing edge—a reason why Katharine Hepburn, one of cinema's great spinsters (*Summertime! Desk Set! The African Queen!*), was devastated in *The Philadelphia Story* when her ex-husband called her a "married maiden" and her estranged father called her a "perennial spinster." Historically, spinsterhood has meant a kind of radical unavailability to straight men, implying either rejection of them or rejection by them or both.

This sought or unsought rejection has the potential to be experienced by women as a source of strength. It can mean making the choice not just to set your own terms on the marriage or meat market, but to opt out of the market altogether. To quote the introduction of the great 1970s second-wave anthology *Solo: Women on Women Alone*, another book that was published before I was born but feels infinitely more modern than *Spinster*:

> Under the theme of independence, there are stories about women who are coping with, even enjoying the state of singleness. In this group of stories, the women are not only effectively managing solitary existences they may not have sought, but they are actively creating self-contained existences that leave them relatively free of what those forces that govern growing up had defined to them as a "natural need"—dependence on men. We see them in the process of "kicking the habit."

The editors of *Solo* celebrate independence from men using the language of creativity, freedom, and recovery. And this language is important because all too often female independence without the approval stamp of male desire is seen as a source of shame, and blamed on the spinster's supposed spiritual or sexual frigidity, and/or her ugly or invisible body. Spinsterhood is commonly interpreted as a symptom of a guarded soul and hardened heart.

In this way the challenge that spinsterhood poses to patriarchy is contained and punished by the imposition of a sexual stigma. And too often the prescribed patriarchal cure for spinsterhood is reorienting spinsters' lives around straight men. Hepburn's remedy in *The Philadelphia Story* involves remarrying her ex-husband, a man who once toppled her to the ground by shoving her in the face. Meanwhile, a self-loathing self-identified spinster writing under a pseudonym on *Salon* describes her decision to hire a male sex surrogate to "fix" her spinsterhood: a kind of reparative therapy. She falls in unrequited love with the man she hires to have sex with her, an attachment that causes new shame and pain, but apparently anything is better than the shame of being a spinster.

Too often our culture tells us that a spinster needs a man like a fish needs water. This is part of why I'm so disappointed in Bolick's self-narration, which barely passes the Bechdel test. Bolick writes page after page about her ex-boyfriends, delving deep into their personalities and relationship dynamics, but she spends only a few paragraphs writing about female friends she's known for decades, who remain relative ciphers. With the exception of Bolick herself, the only women who really matter in *Spinster* are dead. Bolick thus takes the teeth out of the trope by making spinsters into a kind of dream girlfriend for Nathaniel P.–type Brooklyn boys: exactly as man-oriented as every other girl, except maybe less interested in commitment.

Throughout *Spinster*, Bolick defends spinsters in unthreatening, individualistic terms. She accepts the heteronormative assumption that conventional romantic and familial relationships constitute "strong ties" while other forms of relationships are "weak ties," and she equates being a spinster with prioritizing oneself, as opposed to committing oneself to different but equally demanding forms of love and connection. According to Bolick, spinsterhood is aloneness, and being single "means having nobody to help you make difficult decisions, or comfort you at the end of a bad week." Even when she writes about Charlotte Perkins Gilman's *Herland*, a 1915 utopian novel about a communal, matriarchal society of Amazons raising their female children together as one family, her takeaway is incorrigibly individualistic: Bolick zeroes in on the way the women must sacrifice a measure of "personal joy" for the greater good of their society. For Bolick, the primary lesson of *Herland* is not the exhilarating potential for new women-oriented or collective forms of social and emotional life, but rather an individual lament that whether you're in *Herland* or the United States, you can't always get all of what you want.

I love *Herland*, but my own favorite spinster manifesto (which doesn't appear in *Spinster*) was written almost half a century earlier, in 1869. It's a chapter in Louisa May Alcott's misleadingly titled *An Old-Fashioned Girl*, a novel about being a youngish woman in Boston (which Bolick herself once was, but there the resemblance ends). Polly is an unmarried music teacher struggling with loneliness and depression; her friend

Fan is an unmarried lady of leisure also struggling with loneliness and depression. When Polly suddenly becomes happier,
Fan assumes her good mood must be because she's falling in
love with a man, but Polly corrects her: "No; friendship and
good works." Polly takes Fan to see her new spinster friends,
whom she describes as "lively, odd, and pleasant," and the
young women share an improvised indoor picnic ("it's so
much jollier to eat in sisterhood") and a riotous feminist
discussion at the home of Becky and Bess, both artists, who
are partners in a Boston marriage. As Polly explains, Becky
and Bess

> live together, and take care of one another in true Damon
> and Pythias style. This studio is their home . . . they work,
> eat, sleep, and live here, going halves in everything. They
> are all alone in the world, but as happy and independent
> as birds; real friends, whom nothing will part.

Becky is sculpting a giant statue of the woman of the future,
"bigger, lovelier, and more imposing than any we see
nowadays," who is "strong-minded, strong-hearted, strong-
souled, and strong-bodied." The women all admire the
statue-in-progress and make suggestions. Becky refuses to
put a child in the woman's arms or a man's hand in her hand,
but she places a ballot box, pen, and broom at her feet. When
Kate, an author, announces that one of their mutual female
friends is getting a trip to Europe, all expenses paid (cour-
tesy of another female friend), everyone celebrates: "It was
good to see how heartily these girls sympathized in their
comrade's good fortune. Polly danced all over the room, Bess

and Becky hugged one another, and Kate laughed with her eyes full, while even Fanny felt a glow."

Fanny is astounded at how rich women's lives can be without men at the center:

> She listened, finding it as interesting as any romance to hear these young women discuss their plans, ambitions, successes, and defeats. It was a new world to her . . . Below the light-heartedness each cherished a purpose, which seemed to ennoble her womanhood, to give her a certain power, a sustaining satisfaction, a daily stimulus, that led her on to daily effort, and in time to some success in circumstance or character, which was worth all the patience, hope, and labor of her life.

Spinsterland in nineteenth-century Boston is not yet a *Herland*-style utopia. Women still can't vote, and they work too hard for their money: Fanny observes that "Kate looked sick, tired, and too early old." But they have "the religion of their sisterhood" to sustain them, and nothing could be stronger than that faith.

It's impossible not to compare Alcott's grand, broad-shouldered statue symbolizing women's strength, labor, and potential political power to Bolick's small silver hood ornament on an unaffordable car. I won't dwell on what the comparison says about Bolick's spinster wish. Instead I'll just say that Alcott writes about spinsters as women of substance, comrades, friends, activists, and insatiable eaters of sardines whose conversations and shared hopes cause one another's hearts to glow. And if you want to read a book about spinsters that will inspire you to pursue a purpose in life beyond your own personal wish fulfillment, you should read *Herland* or *An Old-Fashioned Girl*.

∼

When I was first learning how to be a spinster, my mentors were three straight African American women, ten or twenty years ahead of me, who had spent long years of their youth in a small, mostly white town in suburban New Jersey. All of them had lives full of friendship, faith, family, community, political purposefulness, significant caregiving responsibilities, dazzling professional success, and, occasionally or eventually, real romance. But they also had lives marked by the demographic reality of blackness in America. None of them had the standard story of most of their white peers: pair off in your twenties or thirties; marry; have kids. From these women I learned to measure singleness not in months but in years, or even decades. As one of them quipped when I asked about her love life when she was my age, "I know why the caged bird sings."

These women taught me to question my own entitled white-girl assumptions about relationships and marital status: that marriage (or spinsterhood) is a simple matter of figuring out what you want and waiting for it to happen, or making it happen. They taught me not to self-dramatize or presume, and not to project my own experiences onto others. I remember one of them telling me, clear-eyed and matter-of-fact, "If I'd met someone when I was younger and we'd had kids together, that would have been my life, and I would have had those experiences. But I didn't, so this is my life instead, and now looking back it's hard to imagine it any other way." For them, marital status was less about chasing wishes or fulfilling a destiny and more about making something meaningful with the life you have.

My mentors taught me that friendships are family and friendships are love. One of them told me that even though she'd spent many years in romantic relationships, it was her friendships with women that first taught her about intimacy and caregiving. They taught me to think systemically, and to question the structural injustice that honors the commitments of couples and married people but fails to recognize the validity of other forms of family and the immense caregiving work done by daughters, sisters, aunts, and friends. Once I was assigned last place in a grad-student housing draw because I was single and the housing authorities were giving priority to couples because they might need more space. I was bummed out, but my mentor was incensed. "They don't know your life! Just because you don't have a boyfriend or girlfriend doesn't mean you're always home alone. Anyway you're all paying the same. You should be treated the same." In a way these women taught me a new kind of entitlement: one that insists on the value of my life and relationships, and resists all the ways, large and small, that lives are diminished by the dominance of the couple form.

There are urgent reasons why spinsters need to look beyond the self and resist the system. As Alcott's insistence on the ballot box suggests, insofar as the conversation about unmarried women remains a conversation about choice and individual temperament and not about politics, it is missing something important. Even though the contingencies of when and whom I marry don't define my existence, marriage is still an important legal and social category with implications for many practical and symbolic aspects of adult life. Because in our culture, marriage is a choice, but it also isn't. It's a rom-com ending and a party with a cake, but it's also a systemic mechanism that separates the enfranchised from the disenfranchised, the included from the excluded.

And unfortunately, the momentous *Obergefell v. Hodges* Supreme Court decision remedies some of these injustices while shoring up others. In too many important ways, marriage and the couple form are still the legal and social prerequisites for the sharing of resources and lives, the care of the sick, the parenting of children. This arbitrary conflation of marriage with the commitments and responsibilities of adult life sometimes turns unmarried people into second-class citizens, while devaluing many necessary forms of love.

I'm glad gay marriage is now legal. But as a spinster who craves connection and community above all and who has found it outside of the standard couple form, I've come to realize that I owe an immeasurable debt to the intersecting groups of people who have historically been barred from the privileges of marriage by law and demography and have learned to create intimate lives apart from it. In other words, I'm indebted to queer people and to African Americans, and to all who have seen their loves and families treated as nonexistent or pathological, and who have had marriage used as a weapon against them or as a compulsory straight and narrow path to equality. These people are more than "awakeners": They have done the hard work of loving and world-making in defiance of the powers that be, and all unmarried people continue to benefit from their centuries of emotional and material labor.

For years, queer people have made lives and loves without access to most legal protections or religious rituals. Now, in the age of legal gay marriage, many queer people are being forced to adopt the traditional form of marriage (regardless of whether it fits the shape of their lives) in order to access health benefits or shared custody, a prospect that is often less than liberating. Meanwhile, from the cruelty of slavery to the callous "marriage cure" of the George W. Bush administration, from the Moynihan Report to the million and a half "missing" black men, marriage has been made simultaneously compulsory and unattainable for millions of African Americans whose family formations and most cherished relationships are honored neither by American society nor the state. And there are so many others whom marriage fails to recognize or protect: all whose families are torn apart by citizenship status and national borders; all whose loves and commitments exceed the boundaries of the nuclear family norm.

The author of *Spinster* champions an individualistic kind of feminism, but she is apparently uninterested in reflecting on the politics of marriage as a system and the way its oppressiveness might prompt privileged people like herself to seek alliances with people she pushes to the margins: poor people, queer people, people of color. This marginalization is not an accident. Single black women feature as a kind of cautionary tale in the *Atlantic* article on which Bolick's book is based, but in *Spinster* she repeatedly makes the conscious decision to exclude them altogether. At one point she starts to compare one of her "awakeners" to Billie Holiday, only to stop abruptly after a few sentences, informing her reader that it would be "specious" for her to attempt to include black women in her book, because they should have a (separate but equal?) spinster book of their own. Meanwhile, Bolick's willfully oblivious defense of the absolute whiteness of her "awakeners" has infuriated every woman of color I know who has read it:

> Not until I was driving through my blindingly white hometown did I realize that the only characteristics all five women had in common were a highly ambivalent relationship to the institution of marriage, the opportunity to articulate this ambivalence, and whiteness—each of which, arguably, was inextricable from the rest. During the period I was drawn to—primarily, the turn of the last century—vanishingly few women of color were given the privilege to write and publish and, therefore, speak across the decades.

If Bolick is interested in writing only about pale redheads, she should own this preference and not use words like "vanishing" to try to make it go away. Because the late nineteenth- and early twentieth-century period she writes about was in fact full of writing women of color with ambivalent relationships to the institution of marriage: Nella Larsen and Zora Neale Hurston are not exactly obscure writers, and they wouldn't even have required Bolick to look beyond New York City. When Bolick says whiteness was an "inextricable" characteristic of women who wrote ambivalently about marriage, she is perpetuating racism, not describing it.

The truth is that Bolick didn't need to do a deep archive dive to find out how women create full lives without being wives. She could have chosen to pay attention to the lives of women of varied classes and colors living in her own city right now. But Bolick's spinster wish is not political. It is pretty and private and pristine and pale. And this is a problem. As Jessa Crispin has tweeted, "if the pretty people now get the word 'spinster' I am comfortable switching over to 'hag.'"

"Hag" is a splendid word, but I don't think we need to surrender "spinster." We still need spinster. We need Connie Sun's wry *How to Find Love: Lessons from an Old Maid* at *McSweeney's*, and Ashley Boney's bold "I'm a Single Black Girl and I Refuse to be Scared by the Statistics Saying I Will Never Get Married" in *xoJane*. We need the humane voice of Sara Eckel, who writes so wisely about midlife loneliness and love's randomness, and the affectionate and much-missed spinster love of *The Toast*, and the passion of Emily Rapp Black's tear-stained love letter to the spinsters who taught her about "Transformation and Transcendence: The Power of Female Friendship." We need satire and protest and unapologetic in-your-face stigma and courage and unhinged adoration and matter-of-fact, no-nonsense happiness. We need fierce female loves.

I cling to the word "spinster" in the second decade of the twenty-first century because it serves as a challenge to the way our society still conflates coupledom with love, maturity, and citizenship, while seeing unmarried people as—to quote Justice Kennedy—"condemned to live in loneliness." And, to borrow a phrase from second-wave historian Carroll Smith-Rosenberg, I cling to the word because it links me with my spinster sisters throughout history in a shared "female world of love and ritual." I cling to it and hold it close because, to riff on a refrain from Hilton Als, it's the spinsters who made me.

~

It's the spinsters who made me. Who made farm-share feasts with me for our family dinners and watched *Golden Girls* with me every night. Who sent me silver-framed photographs of us at a Houston diner, and glitter-framed photographs of us at Graceland, and magnet-backed photographs to put on my fridge of us sharing a bed at a Palm Springs hotel. Who talked with me for hours on the phone as we lay a thousand miles apart in bed in the dark until one of us finally fell asleep. Who asked me to help them choose their mother's gravestone. Who told me about their abortions. Who bought me a dress for my yet-to-be-adopted daughter. Who made me the aunt of their one-eyed Chihuahua. Who sat next to me in church. Who swayed on the piano bench as they accompanied the gospel choir with a ring on every finger, playing from "sheet music" that was simply a piece of paper saying "Abundantly Blessed in F." Who burned sage in my apartment and said blessings and jingled bells and burned small sticks of aromatic Panamanian wood to drive out the bad energy after my roommate's psychotic break. Who came into money unexpectedly and paid off my $65,000 student loans and changed my life forever. Who left me long, delirious voicemails on the happiest day of their life with their voice stretched almost to breaking with joy. Who sent me lilies on my birthday

("It's Heavenly to Be With You" in the language of flowers) and filled my Easter basket and stuffed my Christmas stocking and made me black-eyed peas on New Year's for good luck. Who invited me over for cava in the garden or vinho verde on the deck. Who invited me to stay with them during a hurricane when my house was shaking. Who were my family and made me their family as they lived with metastatic cancer. Who called me "Lovely" and "Lady" and "Sweetie-pie" and "Dear." Whom I called "Lovely" and "Lady" and "Sweetie-pie" and "Dear." Who are my readers and editors and muses and collaborators and confidants. Who are my loves. Who know that, although in the eyes of the world and the law we are alone, we are not alone.

~

So often with spinster stories it is the endings that betray us—with their tall, handsome boyfriends who appear in the nick of time (as happens in *Spinster*), their well-tamed shrews and prettified tomboys, their inevitable weddings. Of course I finished the first draft of this essay while attending a glorious wedding in the Catskills on the very same weekend that Ireland voted to legalize gay marriage, and of course I finished the final draft on the weekend that SCOTUS followed suit. Of course I wept with joy when my glowing friend read her wedding vows in the dappled May sunshine and leaned against her new husband with utter trust, and I wept with gratitude when I read the tweets of all the Irish people who traveled #hometovote, and I rainbowed my Facebook profile picture along with everybody else. I could feel the tide-like tow of the marriage plot and the ancient satisfactions of the Hollywood happy ending, and I was susceptible to conflicting surges of spinsterish and unspinsterish feeling. All of this is perfectly predictable and understandable—after all, I've written other essays about my love for straight men and wedding vows—but ambivalence is not where this essay is destined to end, because unrelenting spinster endings are too hard-won.

I'll leave you instead with benedictions from three of my favorite spinster texts, each with a different spin on the spinster and her final fate. I don't know what the future holds for me and the rest of my spinster sisterhood, but I know I would rejoice to have any of these as my epitaph.

Louisa May Alcott, *An Old-Fashioned Girl* (1869):
Lest any of my young readers who have honored Maud with their interest should suffer the pangs of unsatisfied curiosity as to her future, I will add for their benefit that she did not marry Will, but remained a busy, lively spinster all her days.

Bette Davis as Charlotte Vale in *Now, Voyager* (1942):
Don't let's ask for the moon. We have the stars.

Emily Nussbaum, "Difficult Women," on a counterfactual version of *Sex and the City* in which Carrie does not marry (2013):
What if it were the story of a woman who lost herself in her thirties, who was changed by a poisonous, powerful love affair, and who emerged, finally, surrounded by her friends?

PANDORA IN BLUE JEANS

THE PHOTOGRAPH CAPTIONED "Pandora in Blue Jeans" is one of the most widely circulated portraits of a woman in history. Like most people, I first saw it on the back of a pulpy paperback book. A black-and-white 1950s author photo that seems like a snapshot, it is a side view of a solidly built young woman in a pre-hipster buffalo plaid shirt and men's jeans, sitting at a table with a typewriter on it in what looks like a kitchen. She's not wearing makeup and her hair is pulled back in a lumpy ponytail, and she's leaning forward with her hands folded anxiously or pensively in front of her face, so we can't really see what she looks like. There's a half-smoked cigarette in the ashtray next to her typewriter, and a messy stack of papers behind it. She is staring at what she's writing, and she seems not to know or care that the photographer is there.

Some author photos develop a life of their own, and they often seem to be the ones that bend a gender or pose a challenge. Perhaps the first of these was the engraved daguerreotype of Walt Whitman from the 1855 *Leaves of Grass*. The book didn't disclose Whitman's name on the title page, but it included his full-page frontispiece portrait as a personal welcome, his shirt unbuttoned and his undershirt showing, a hand on his hip, a hand in his pocket, his gaze direct, his head cocked. "I look so damned flamboyant," he later said about this image, "as if I was hurling bolts at somebody—full of mad oaths—saying defiantly, to hell with you!" Flamboyant, yes, without a doubt, but the direction of the defiance is harder to read. Is he really saying to hell with us, or is he defying us to look away? Does he want his lightning bolt to fatally pierce us, or does he just want to electrify us?

For his authorial debut almost a hundred years later, on the dust jacket of the 1947 first edition of *Other Voices, Other Rooms*, Truman Capote went Whitman one better by draping himself on his back on a couch, one hand on his stomach and one on his crotch, and looking up at the viewer with a knowing gaze. Hilton Als reads this author photograph as both a metamorphosis and an expression of desire. The image turned Capote into "an American woman of style," Als writes in *White Girls*, and "the woman he became in this photograph— itself better written than *Other Voices, Other Rooms*—wanted to be fucked by you and by any idea of femininity that had fucked you up."

The woman at the kitchen table in "Pandora in Blue Jeans" has undoubtedly been fucked up by femininity, as all women have, but she does not appear to want to be fucked by it or by us. Indeed, she doesn't seem to want anything from us at all. If Capote's photo is famously seductive and come-hither, "Pandora in Blue Jeans" is famously unsexy and go-away. Circulating on the back of one of the most sexual and successful books of the decade, Grace Metalious's scandalous 1956 mega-bestseller *Peyton Place*, "Pandora in Blue Jeans" represents a white girl's rejection of white-girl conventions, an unprecedented opting out of mainstream commercial feminine iconography that still managed to be wildly popular (if rarely imitated) and made an unlikely icon of a woman whose life seems to consist of unglamorous obliviousness, unremarkable domesticity, and totally depraved thoughts.

It's an icon that doesn't quite fit with Als's compelling account of gender and author photos at midcentury, which focuses on a higher class of author. In contextualizing Capote's pose, Als tells the story of ambitious literary women performing a certain kind of anxious drag in order to be taken seriously: "In 1947, women did not publish books. So determined to be authors were they—Jean Stafford, Carson McCullers, Marguerite Young, say—that they buttoned themselves up on dust jackets in some Hemingway-influenced image of a male American author." This gendered story of authorly aspiration might explain Capote's self-presentation—Als suggests that as a man he ironically had more room to be womanly—but it hardly explains that of Grace Metalious. She was aspiring to a very different kind of authorship than Stafford's, McCullers's, or Young's—less glossy *New Yorker*, more high-acid pulp paperback—and her homely mise-en-scène of cheerful curtains and pleasant potted plants is worlds away from Hemingway.

Still, the woman in "Pandora in Blue Jeans" is bending a gender and posing a challenge. But what is her angle, and what is her challenge?

"In her blue jeans, sneakers, and flannel shirt," Ardis Cameron claims in *Unbuttoning America: A Biography of "Peyton Place,"* "Metalious offered women a sartorial counterpart to the antiestablishment Beats." Cameron is right that Metalious's clothes overlapped with the Beats' (and, like theirs, prefigured grunge), but this account of what the image offers doesn't seem exactly right either. Like Jack Kerouac, Metalious was a Franco-American from a New England mill town whose literary persona depended on an outsider status. But her style seems less a women's answer to the countercultural clothes of the self-consciously subversive male Beats, who bought their working-class castoffs in thrift stores on road trips, and more a reflection of what ordinary housewives actually wore—at least the ones who weren't wearing pearls while vacuuming, as in Madison Avenue fantasies. In the 1950s, blue jeans could reference Kerouac, James Dean, or Marilyn Monroe, but in this photograph they are something utterly uncinematic: the unfraught, unstudied, everyday drag of borrowing your husband's worn-in work clothes without bothering to ask, thus giving a literal meaning to the phrase "effortless style."

Though Cameron is alert to the image's countercultural undertones, she sees the primary appeal of the picture as the friction between Metalious's status as a humdrum wife and mother and her fiction's salacious focus on the abuse, abortion, incest, and murder thriving within quaint New England villages. Clearly that is a part of it. But I think what "Pandora in Blue Jeans" offers women is something even more subversive than overt rebellion or explicit sex, or the frisson of a PTA mom who writes in the language of "a bellicose longshoreman," to quote from a contemporary review. Instead, "Pandora in Blue Jeans" illustrates the shocking combination of utter apathy and utter focus. This woman is DGAF about us and the kitchen, her husband and children are nowhere in sight, but she is riveted, thunderbolted to the chair, by the vision of her own words on the page. She is not herself an object of desire, but she has one, and she gazes at it steadily, seduced by the sight of her book in progress.

The picture is perverse in its refusal to perform for the viewer's expectations, not just because "Pandora in Blue Jeans" is an ordinary housewife who wrote dirty books, but because she is an unkempt woman who doesn't seem to care what we think of her, and who cares intensely about something else. What could be more disturbing, after all, than the possibility that unremarkable, unenviable, uninviting women might have searing stories burning inside them? Maybe only the possibility that a woman might not need to try to please us; that she might not ever choose to look up from her page.

Almost immediately, pulp fiction fan-fic began to be written in response to this unsettling new author persona and the threat it posed. One notable novel inspired by Metalious's life and image was *The Girl on the Best Seller List* by Vin Packer, published four years after *Peyton Place*, which told the story of a small-town housewife who wrote an unexpected and lurid bestseller. (Packer was the pseudonym of Patricia Highsmith's girlfriend Marijane Meaker. Highsmith wrote *The Talented Mr. Ripley* and *The Price of Salt*, which was recently adapted for the screen as *Carol*, and Meaker wrote groundbreaking young adult fiction and lesbian pulp in addition to whodunits like *The Girl on the Best Seller List*.) In a pinup–style riff on "Pandora in Blue Jeans" for the cover of Packer's book, the illustrator tried to pretty Pandora back up, putting her on a diet, shrinking and cropping her jeans, unbuttoning her plaid shirt and tying it tight above the waist, and sliding some bracelets over her bare wrist. This made-over authoress ignores her typewriter and looks straight at the viewer, holding a pencil close to her parted lips and languidly stretching her other arm over the back of the chair so her body is open to us. It's an infinitely sexier image, but it looks like a million pictures we've seen before.

In Packer's book, the Metalious character, renamed Gloria, is universally loathed, and (spoiler alert!) has possibly been poisoned by her agent, who finds her exceedingly difficult to edit. ("I remember how hard it was to get Gloria to make a change," he muses somewhat menacingly to a new client.) Meanwhile the real-life Metalious struggled to reconcile the roles of "bland housewife," as she was dismissively labeled, and bestselling superstar. What made it especially hard for her is that she was never actually able to be the woman in the picture, self-sufficiently sitting at her typewriter. Her writing life was troubled from the start.

"During the long year of editorial revisions," Cameron writes, "Grace turned into a difficult author, insecure, needy, and emotionally unstable." After the book came out she had an affair with a DJ, divorced her husband, broke up with the DJ, remarried her husband, and squandered a staggering amount of cash. She was Grace Metalious, not Pandora in Blue Jeans, and she wanted sex, liquor, love, and money, not just writing and more writing and yet more writing. In the end, she dissolved in alcohol, disintegrating like the picture of Dorian Gray, and dying at thirty-nine, only seven years older than her most famous portrait.

It would be nice if immersive work were a way to experience the drive of desire without its difficulty, and if writing were a way to escape the demand to be vulnerable, available, and easy to love. But unfortunately it's apparently impossible to stare into typewritten sentences forever and keep the world at bay. Still, for me this photograph offers an image of existence that's every bit as thrilling as lounging suggestively on chaises longues, or hurling thunderbolts, or buttoning up your shirt and channeling Hemingway, or unbuttoning your shirt and slowly lifting a phallic pencil to your parted lips. *Peyton Place* is an American cult classic that sold twelve million copies and is finding new life as a feminist text, but "Pandora in Blue Jeans" is the part of the Metalious legacy I prize the most: a rare iconic image of a woman dressed to unimpress, oblivious to viewers' expectations, deep in her work, absorbed in a world of her own making.

WE HAVE ALWAYS LIVED
IN THE VORTEX

LIKE GRACE METALIOUS, Shirley Jackson was a solidly built midcentury New England wife, mother, and writer of small-town horror stories who liked to hunch over a typewriter while wearing a plain plaid shirt. She too wrote books that touched nerves and climbed bestseller lists, and then died far too young as a result of addictive substances and stress. In the decades after her death, Jackson was sometimes dismissed as a one-hit wonder (she's still best known for her much-anthologized story "The Lottery," about a small New England town that practices random ritual human sacrifice), but her work is enjoying a much-deserved revival. In the last ten years, the Library of America published a new edition of her novels and stories; two of her children edited a collection of previously unpublished work from her archives in the Library of Congress; her atmospheric gothic novel about a family poisoned by arsenic, *We Have Always Lived in the Castle*, was adapted into a musical and a movie; Netflix made a TV version of her widely acclaimed ghost story, *The Haunting of Hill House*; and Ruth Franklin wrote a gorgeous and award-winning biography of her, *Shirley Jackson: A Rather Haunted Life*.

I first found Jackson on my grandmother's bookshelves when I was young, and then headed to the library to check out everything she wrote. Jackson's consummately crafted tales of horror and suspense are the basis of her current critical reputation, and I devoured them (I remember the particular dissonant thrill of reading shadowy neo-Victorian ghost stories on a bright summer day), but the Jackson books I liked the best were in a rather different genre: *Life Among the Savages* and *Raising Demons*, her hysterically funny memoirs about life with young children.

Though Jackson's dark domestic vision might have caused some single, childless readers to thank their lucky stars for their unentangled state (according to Ruth Franklin, one reviewer of *Raising Demons* complained that "impressionable girls reading her unvarnished recital of domestic life might take a vow of spinsterhood"), on me they had the opposite effect. Thanks to Jackson, throughout my teens and twenties I fantasized about living in the midst of a whirling cyclone of savage and demonic children in an old haunted house carpeted in clutter, with an emotionally remote and absentminded husband who would periodically knock me up.

Franklin's *New York Times* review of the new editions of Jackson's memoirs captures a lot of their appeal, but it makes them sound more straightforwardly aspirational than they actually are:

> At a moment when helicopter parenting is the norm, "free-range" parents are chastised for letting their children wander a few blocks alone, and the pressure feels greater than ever not only to "have it all" but to "be it all"—to manage both

to pursue a successful career and to produce homemade cupcakes for every birthday—Jackson's relaxed approach to child-rearing feels refreshingly sane.

I see what she means, but I would describe Jackson's approach to mothering as refreshingly insane—less an example of work-life balance than an unapologetic capitulation to an unbalanced life.

Jackson wrote about her home life as if it were enchanted—a sorcerer's apprentice fantasia from which she couldn't escape. The incantatory first lines of *Life Among the Savages* represent her domestic dystopia in oddly seductive terms, as a kind of irresistible entropy:

> Our house is old, and noisy, and full. When we moved into it we had two children and about five thousand books; I expect that when we finally overflow and move out again we will have perhaps twenty children and easily half a million books; we also own assorted beds and tables and chairs and rocking horses and lamps and doll dresses and ship models and paint brushes and literally thousands of socks. This is the way of life my husband and I have fallen into, inadvertently, as though we had fallen into a well.

If "Pandora in Blue Jeans" is an aspirational image of an auto-erotic relation to one's work, a world stripped down to a woman and her words, Jackson's authorial persona embodies a different kind of giving oneself over: to a life overridden, buried, submerged by intimate attachments. (In contrast to "Pandora in Blue Jeans," in which Metalious's three children are nowhere to be seen, Jackson's author photo for *Life Among the Savages* features all of her four children, but not Jackson herself; she is both multiplied and lost.)

Jackson's memoirs indulge in an aesthetic of uncontrollable excess, of overwhelming abundance and abundant demands, and one of her primary literary techniques is the list. "I believe that all women, but especially housewives, tend to think in lists," she writes, and proceeds to list some of them: cryptic to-do lists that are inscrutable to others ("peanut butter, evening paper, doz doughnuts, CALL PICTURE"); optimistic to-do lists of items that will never get done ("Mend fr coat" has been on a list in her dresser drawer for years, the missing "u" in fur a fleeting and inadequate attempt at efficiency); items she will never buy for a life she will never have (demitasse cups, tiny spoons, after-dinner liqueurs). Lists might seem linear and logical, but they are anything but: "You can start from any given point on a list and go off in all directions at once, the world being as full as it is," she observes, "and even though a list is a greatly satisfying thing to have, it is extraordinarily difficult to keep it focused on the subject at hand." Lists for Jackson are not a means to an end but an ongoing mode of existing in the world. Hilariously, Jackson refers to conversations between women as "double-listing," an intimate form I often find myself falling into with my friends as we try to keep our heads above water while deluged in things that must be done.

Jackson's love of excess is also evident in her adverbs, which ratchet up the emotional register of everyday life. Her young son requests money from his father "inexorably," she corrects her daughter's manners "vengefully," her children refuse to catch measles "diabolically," she reads aloud "grimly," her daughter speculates "direfully," she offers to carry her daughter "desperately." There's absurdity in all the out-of-proportion modifiers, but there's accuracy too: They capture the swirling undercurrents of familial intimacy, the chronic aggression and passive aggression and incomprehension and dread.

Though her memoirs were composed of pieces originally written for wholesome women's magazines such as *Good Housekeeping* and *Women's Home Companion*—publications that specialized in straightforwardly cheerful stories, and that sometimes rejected her writing for this reason—both *Life Among the Savages* and *Raising Demons* create a morbidly curious authorial persona who documents her children almost without guidance or interference, as if she were an anthropologist and they were members of a mysterious tribe. Jackson watches as her children play cowboys and cowgirls and die elaborate, ritualized deaths over and over. She witnesses them pretend to poison one another and die some more. And, like a witch who has summoned unknown evil spirits through the process of childbirth, Jackson loves her children most for their badly behaved imaginary friends who beat up their classmates or live at the bottom of the river. She revels in their casually callous attitudes toward her and one another, and in their amoral pleasure in a neighbor's house fire, which they see through enchanted eyes as a bonfire for giants.

Whereas other mothers might see their children as needy creatures to be tended and raised, targets of moral discipline and intellectual uplift, or objects of heroic parental effort, Jackson regards them as weird material for affectionately unsettling tales. She might work to write about her children, but she does not struggle to parent them. They are already complete and perfect in their strangeness and eerie unpredictability, which they share with all children everywhere. Jackson never seriously considers another way to be a mother. For her, the alternative to this bewitched and uncanny home life is not a different parenting style but a sterile, childless life in a hotel. And rather than fight to create order out of domestic chaos, Jackson succumbs to it. Every day, we assume, she sits at her typewriter to write stories like this one, and tries to tune out the curdling screams that surround her. But the screams also inspire her.

My desire for a twisted, Shirley Jackson–inspired version of the "having it all" dream was always pretty dark, and I'm not surprised that I was never able to get my boyfriends to share it. In many ways it is a very hard sell. Its appeal is almost impossible to explain to ordinary young men, especially the ones I dated, who preferred calm and sanity and a semblance of order. Nowadays the appeal is hard to explain even to myself. I've grown accustomed to other hopes, and when I reread Jackson in my peaceful, sunny, quiet apartment, the savages and demons seem impossibly distant. Reading between the lines of her books and in the lines of her biography, I catch painful glimpses of things I missed when I was young: her chronic anxiety; her resentment of her husband's habitual cheating; the agoraphobia that kept her confined to the house that she loved. I no longer aspire to the kind of life Jackson conjures up. But my desire for dark domesticity has never completely dissipated, even as the likelihood of attaining it has come to seem ever more out of reach and the fantasy of it ever farther away.

So maybe you can't ever leave your home, Jackson whispers to anxious wives and mothers and those who might become them, but maybe you don't want to. Is agoraphobia really so bad if you have everything, everything in the world, right here? Centuries of human history, in the chants and taunts that children have passed down from generation to generation. The riches of the nations, in your son's coin collection and your daughters' plundered piggy banks. A coffeepot for awakening. A typewriter for working. A wedding ring for rapping on the kitchen window, diamond on glass, to tell the children playing in the yard that it's time to come back inside.

DEAR OCTOPUS

The family—that dear octopus from whose tentacles we never quite escape, nor, in our inmost hearts, ever quite wish to.
—*DODIE SMITH*, DEAR OCTOPUS

It's a compound, or multiple, love story, pure and complicated.
—*J. D. SALINGER*, FRANNY AND ZOOEY

THERE IS a form of intimacy that consists of being harangued by someone in a bathrobe. A brother. He might be standing and pacing and you might be lying down on a couch under an afghan. He is exasperated in a way that tends toward escalating energy, and he intermittently throws off or elicits sparks, like a grindstone, like a rasp, like a pronged plug in proximity to a faulty socket. The stakes are high for him. He suspects that your way of thinking is suspect. You suspect that he might be right. You further suspect that it is not just your way of thinking that he finds dubious but the person you have turned out to be.

You find yourself arranged together in this way—pacing, bathrobe; reclining, afghan—because you share a home. In other words, you share a domestic space in which seriousness does not depend on dignified dress or ordinary standards of civility. In this home, certain protective coverings (shirts and pants) can be dispensed with, while other kinds of protective coverings (afghans) can be piled on or, in particularly tense moments, pulled over one's face and supine body like a shroud of surrender. But it is never really surrender: just a way to collect yourself and breathe warm condensation breaths under the wool while presenting an implacable surface to the man who is talking. You are biding your time until it is your turn to speak.

And you will inevitably speak. You will always have your say. You are arranged this way, after all, because you are brother and sister, tumbled together since childhood like agates in a rock polisher, generating your own conversational grit ever since you first had enough shared language to talk.

∾

I lived in the thick of my family of origin longer than most. I started out with a couple decades' worth of constant drama and chatter, hordes of siblings casually sitting on one another's laps or draping themselves against one another, giving voice to anything and everything they thought or felt, constantly bursting into song or tears or insults or puns or mimicry or self-deprecation or prayer. After an upbringing like ours, as my youngest sister says, a bathroom with one person in it feels somehow empty: At all times one expects there to be a sister in the shower, a sister on the toilet, a sister at the sink, and a brother bellowing outside the door that you have been in there forever. Your space and self are never your own. At any moment, in the bathroom or elsewhere, you may be denounced, serenaded, satirized, or called to account.

A running record of my siblings' smart and stupid sayings, as determined by ourselves, is collectively kept on a construction paper quote board in the kitchen. Our words don't disappear—they linger for decades.

The operating assumption for sibling conversation in our family is that we know far more about our siblings than they know about themselves, and certainly more than anyone outside the family knows about them. Others may be taken in, but we see right through them.

The rules of engagement between us are that nothing is off-limits. Though every sibling is fair game to every other sibling, each of us may have one sibling who is our particular concern: the one with whom we share a brain, or the one with whom we definitely *don't*.

For me, that sibling was my only brother.

≈

For the first twelve or fourteen years of our lives my brother and I were enemies, fighting physically until he got too big for me to ever win, whereupon he became my first best friend. We kept on fighting, but with words; argument became our affection. The point of doing anything was to debate it afterward, or during. When we weren't debating each other, we argued as a debate team with imaginary others: the misguided people who were wrong about Rita Hayworth, Spike Lee, the theological doctrine of predestination.

Sometimes—often—we would simply hold forth, with each other as our chosen audience. There was an urgency to our talk. *How else will we determine the meaning of anything if we do not hammer it out here?*

As formerly homeschooled children of religious hippies, we arrived at adolescence as anachronistic freaks, largely sheltered from TV (except the Olympics and State of the Union addresses), movies (except adaptations of Shakespeare or Dickens), radio (except NPR), and sugar (except honey and blackstrap molasses). We shared a unique set of cultural references, or perhaps a unique lack of them, which amounted to a secret language. We also had the fierce competitiveness borne of being bookworms less than two years apart. In high school we strove to rectify our pop-cultural ignorance together—going to see *Bamboozled* and *Dr. Strangelove* together on the big screen, watching 1940s noirs we checked out of the public library, playing Rolling Stones albums on the old Magnavox mahogany record player and radio cabinet in my room. We divided up expertise between us—he got STEM and foreign languages and most other things; I got English—though we both ended up majoring in history.

He liked high school and had many friends. I hated high school and had few friends, but I didn't need them; I had him.

One summer in our late teens we traveled together through England and Scotland, sometimes sleeping rough, in parks, on streets, huddled together for warmth. We woke from one of those nights with pound coins pressed in our palms—gifts from a passerby. We took a ferry to the Isle of Mull and talked about living together there one day in a ruined cottage.

I had a black bomber jacket I wore all through high school like armor, and at some point, maybe during that trip, I lent it to him and it became his. On me it had been grunge. On him it was classic, like a World War II photograph come to life.

During those years I read and reread *Franny and Zooey*, a set of brother-sister stories that make up the second volume in J. D. Salinger's trilogy about the seven hyperverbal Glass siblings. The siblings are all former child-prodigy radio stars who speak "a kind of esoteric, family language" developed by their oldest brother, Seymour, who subjected them all to a rigorous religious training involving rituals, renunciations, and an extensive recommended reading list. In "Franny," the college-aged Glass sister of that name has a religious crisis at a restaurant and feels intolerably distant from the man she's dating, who is not only wrong for her but also just generally wrong. In "Zooey," she returns to her family home to lie on the couch in the living room under a pale blue blanket and be harangued *ad nauseum* (almost literally) by her brother Zooey, first in person and then over the phone, as he tries to prevent her from straying from the proper spiritual path. Zooey attempts this intervention by, among other things, invoking their sainted brother Seymour, who died by suicide, and impersonating their living brother Buddy, who teaches college writing. It is a very brotherly book.

Like me and my brother, Franny and Zooey were a dyad amidst a horde. And my teenage love for them probably partook of some of the same smug self-love that caused my brother and me to watch and quote *The Royal Tenenbaums*. We felt an instinctive kinship with strange large families who were a cult unto themselves and lived in quaint set-designed dwellings full of anachronistic technology like my mahogany Magnavox Hi-Fi. (Franny and Zooey have three old radios in their living room that would be right at home in a Wes Anderson film.) But with *Franny and Zooey* my identification went much deeper.

This was partly because of the book's conversational form, which so closely mirrored our own. I recognized our postures and purposes, our inflections and allusions; the only discernible difference was the color of the afghan. Zooey's unseemly pleasure in the sound of his own voice and his uncanny talent for mimicry seemed like an exact echo of my brother's. Like Zooey's compulsive exhibitions as a "verbal stunt pilot," my brother's virtuosic verbal performances were known to produce both appreciation and exasperation. (He used to fall into extended monologues-in-character—a Latin lover, a Tammany Hall politician, a Church of England preacher—and refuse to snap out of them. Once, at her wits' end, my mom pulled the car over to the side of the road and refused to keep driving until he became himself again.)

I also kept returning to *Franny and Zooey* because its language is insistently Christian, but still different enough from the religious language I was used to that it seemed to open up a certain unprecedented realm of possibility. Franny keeps repeating an Eastern Orthodox prayer known as "the Jesus Prayer"; Zooey cites Seymour admonishing him to "shine his shoes for the Fat Lady"—i.e., to rise to the occasion and perform for an imaginary idealized audience member who stands in for everyone, and who is also, we learn, "Christ Himself." Despite the narrator's defensive disavowal of this being "a mystical story, a religiously mystifying story, at all," the book nevertheless seemed to invite me to read it as a semisacred text: if not scripture then adjacent to it. Religious texts were what my siblings and I had been trained to read, and I was always looking for some new ones to supplement the rigid recommended reading list I'd been brought up with. In its extensive discussion of what it might mean to approach stage and screen acting as a religious practice, *Franny and Zooey* seemed to open up the possibility of having a secular professional life without having to renounce either your faith or your family.

In addition to the pleasures of conversation with someone with whom you share so much history—the efficient shorthand, the rich allusiveness, the infinite opportunities for pointed teasing—there is a particular pleasure in sharing a sense of the truth. For a long time my brother and I shared a religious language. Though we might fight about some of the particulars of our faith, we agreed on the fundamentals. For this reason, my long-term relationship with my college boyfriend didn't affect my closeness with my brother. For one thing, he was religious enough to meet with my brother's approval. For another, he didn't talk much, so I still depended on my brother for that.

≈

The close-knit and combative religious community my siblings and I were brought up in was as wordy, cultish, and flagrantly esoteric as a set of Salinger siblings. At our church, sermons lasted forty-five minutes each, and there were two every Sunday, morning and evening, usually self-congratulatory arguments against false teaching. The pastor had a PhD from a medieval university in Scotland and a library full of centuries-old books, and he did not believe in dumbing things down. Doctrinal debate was the most socially and spiritually prestigious activity in our religious subculture, but it was one from which women and girls were utterly excluded. It was unthinkable that a woman would ever be in a position of equality to a man, or even a boy: In any mixed-gender situation, a woman's calling was to submit to men. Women preachers were heresy, and the only way a woman could speak in church was if she were confessing her sin of fornication to the congregation. Meanwhile groups of men would get together socially to discuss doctrine over liquor and cigars, and their wives would cook for them and stay out of their way.

For years my long conversation with my brother was a necessary and soul-sustaining reprieve from the divinely ordained gender segregation of church and school that told me in so many words that my brain was wasted on me and my voice was not welcome. With my brother I felt like I could verbally battle and tangle and form righteous alliances as an unquestioned equal. We trusted and respected each other. Our verbal world was a space of freedom.

But then things changed, or rather I changed. In a way, I betrayed him. And after that, instead of being a reprieve from the religious world of my youth, he came to represent it.

∼

I betrayed and lost my brother when I was twenty-four and decided it was fine for me to date an atheist. My brother grasped my hands across the table and told me, with tears in his eyes, that until I broke up with my boyfriend I was turning away from God, and also away from him.

Or I lost my brother when I was thirty and headed to a theologically liberal divinity school. He wrote me a long email out of the blue to tell me that I was becoming more dangerous than unbelievers, because I was training to be a false teacher: a whited sepulcher.

Or I lost him when I was thirty-two and he showed up in the comments section of my second published article to challenge my account of evangelical sexual hypocrisy, referring to me as "Ms. Hopper."

Or I lost him when I was thirty-three and he was staying with me after our grandfather's funeral, crashing on the floor of my room. I had to teach the next day, but he wouldn't stop explaining to me why my biblical hermeneutic was illogical and inadequate. I was practically weeping from tiredness, and finally turned out the light on him like he was a parrot I could throw a dark cloth over, but he still wouldn't stop.

Or I lost him when I was thirty-six and we were sitting in his house together on a Sunday morning while his toddler daughter played happily next to us on the living room rug. He told me that my conception of faith was too weak, and if his faith ever became as strong as he believed it one day could, it wouldn't matter if his daughter died because he could raise her from the dead.

Actually, that's a false narrative; there were no doubts or increments. I lost him forever at twenty-four. But these other moments still matter because they were times when he kept reaching out to try to bring me back in—to return us once more to our ancient mode of haranguer and haranguee or endlessly tumbling rocks, presuming a shared language that no longer existed. I always resisted. Though we still spent time together and mutually tried to keep up a kind of connection, I didn't know how to respond to his attempts at argument except by holding them at bay. To engage with him open-mindedly would have required me to make my right to love and work and take communion into something precarious and contingent and up for debate—or rather into something that I must be willing to sacrifice at the outset. I couldn't afford to do that, and I couldn't accept that he expected me to. There was no point in trying to talk; we didn't have enough common ground.

He was so stubborn, so hopeful, in trying to override my defenses, and attempting to mend the breach caused by conflict with yet more conflict. Until, at last, he stopped trying.

$\sim$

He might say: I lost her when she chose sex and the world over the things that really matter.

He might say: As her brother in Christ, it was my responsibility to try to save her when I saw her going astray.

He might say: I lost her when she told me to stop talking to her about politics and religion, and I refused to settle for such a superficial relationship.

He might say: I lost her when she stopped speaking my language, and I kept trying to figure out the new grammar, but everything I said got garbled and distorted.

He might say: She lost me because she started treating me like she didn't respect me; because she refused to meet my reasoned arguments with reasoned counterarguments, and instead flatly dismissed them; because she let all my words flow off her without touching her, like she had sealed and steeled herself against them, like I was a sound machine and they were just sound.

~

I left my family of origin when I was twenty-three, and have lived thousands of miles away ever since. Before I left, I made color copies of all the family quote-boards to bring with me to grad school, but kept them hidden in a poster tube in my closet. My ability to figure out a life apart from evangelical expectations seemed to depend upon distance, and I sometimes went for years without returning home. My siblings and parents occasionally came to see me, but for a long time I tried not to visit them without a friend or boyfriend for backup. Later, when my ragged edge had begun to mend, I could afford to go back alone.

Since then things have been relatively (pun!) quiet and distant, and at times I've gone days without talking to another person, and months without touching one. Sometime in my twenties, I realized I was not going to have my own legal family soon, or maybe ever, so I began to cultivate a family of choice.

"Family of choice" isn't quite the right phrase, since I have mostly fallen into families rather than chosen them. Over the years I've fallen into family with my godfamily (my goddaughter and her parents and siblings); with a close grad school friend and her husband, who made our familial status official by buying a toothbrush for me to keep in their toothbrush holder; with a gay friend who called himself the sister I never had; with a care team that formed around a friend from divinity school; and with many others, too numerous to name. Some of these families still exist and still surround me. Others have combusted or melted away.

Armistead Maupin, the chronicler of the legendary queer family saga *Tales of the City*, calls families found in adulthood "logical." "Sooner or later," he writes, "no matter where in the world we live, we must join the diaspora, venturing beyond our biological family to find our logical one, the one that actually makes sense for us." I understand what he means. At the same time, in my experience all families are fairly illogical, and all of them (even biological ones) have their own crazy logic. A term I sometimes use instead is "invented family," because it implies the work of creation. It is family as a mutually agreed upon fiction. But then all families are invented, even biological ones. A family is not reducible to legal status or DNA; it is also a provisional hypothesis constructed from the surviving documents; a collection of dissonant or harmonizing stories. Perhaps the best phrase for my purposes is "found family." It evokes something of the feeling of lost or cast-out sheep who find themselves once again safe in the fold.

What I love about found family is that it can accommodate all the love and meals and holidays and hospital visits of any other family—all the true confessions and late-night conversations and child chaos and quotidian mess and hugs and endearments and quantity time; and yet it is often kinder than original family, and more miraculous, because it is a gift given when you are old enough to appreciate it, a commitment continuously made when you know what that commitment costs and means. A family found in adulthood can never attain the involuntary intimacy of the siblings who have known you since birth, and squabbled with you in bathrooms and at breakfast tables from time immemorial. But sometimes, perhaps for this reason, a found family can know and love you for who you are—not for who you once were, or who you never were.

~

"Love circle" is a scornful term invented by one of my sisters to describe what she sees as the uncritical and frictionless mode of conversation practiced by most of my friends. (Once, after tearing apart one of my comments on Facebook, she told me that if I couldn't handle her criticism I could always go back to my love circle for comfort. The term has stuck.) Most of my friends communicate differently enough from my family of origin that to my siblings the love I have with my friends is not always recognizable as love. It seems too milquetoast; too lukewarm bubble bath; too much like vapid and effortless blanket approval. Meanwhile my conversations with my siblings don't always look like love to my friends. Sometimes after one of my siblings casually launches a grenade onto my Facebook thread, my inbox fills up with friends asking if I'm OK.

In these moments I feel a surge of defensiveness that swells in both directions. I am adamant that the love I've found in my love circles is real love. I am adamant that the form of love I was forged in is real love too. Still, I've had to execute complex feats of emotional engineering to keep from being overwhelmed by it.

At some point in my twenties I came to associate *Franny and Zooey* with a particular kind of harsh language and gendered judgment I needed to guard against, perhaps especially because its very harshness seemed to be presented as proof of familial love. It seemed significant that Zooey repeatedly calls his mother fat and stupid, going so far as to address her as "Fatty"; that he tells his sister she looks like hell, asks her why she has to be so damned dense, and describes her religious behavior as snotty and stinking; and that at different times both his mother and his sister call his verbal style "abusive." "If there's one thing I never am," he responds airily, "it's abusive." (He does eventually apologize and experience anxiety—though not, we are told, guilt or contrition—when Franny starts to sob in anguish, her body distorted in a "wretched, prostrate, face-down position." His next attempt at communication with her is more gentle.)

Memoirs by Salinger's daughter and by his former girlfriend, whom he wooed when she was a Franny-aged college student and he was decades older, contend that his relationships with women depended on gendered power imbalances and habitual callousness. It eventually became hard for me not to see Zooey's lovingly transcribed and brutal speech as an expression and defense of his creator's misogyny. What troubled me even more was that its stance of spiritual superiority increasingly seemed to be of a piece with the patriarchal and soul-threatening abusiveness of the religious elders who ruled my youth.

Despite its depictions of verbal damage, some have seen *Franny and Zooey*'s primary problem as not too much harsh criticism but too little. In a review in *Harper's* called "J.D. Salinger's Closed Circuit," Mary McCarthy dismisses Salinger (in a scornful and condescending semi-sisterly way) as the ultimate love circler, presiding over an invented family that is merely a mutual admiration society—or, worse, a self-admiration society. "The theme is the good people against the stupid phonies," she argues, "and the good is still all in the family, like a family-owned 'closed' corporation." McCarthy does not distinguish between Salinger and his characters ("Who are these wonder kids but Salinger himself, splitting and multiplying like the original amoeba? . . . To be confronted with the seven faces of Salinger, all wise and lovable and simple, is to gaze into a terrifying narcissus pool"), and she sees the books' chorus of fraternal affection as a vain attempt to drown out a note of doom: "Yet below this self-loving barbershop harmony a chord of terror is struck from time to time, like a judgment. Seymour's suicide suggests that Salinger guesses intermittently or fears intermittently that there may be something wrong somewhere." For McCarthy, the loss of a beloved brother is not the foundational myth that shores up the family's religious system; it is the warning sign that shows how it all might unravel.

Unlike McCarthy and my younger self, I'm no longer sure I need to identify Salinger with the Glass brothers, or to hear the voice of the books as the voice of their characters. I also no longer feel obliged to read the books in relation to the way I think they want to be read. As a result, in my most recent rereading of *Franny and Zooey*, after many years away from it, I was able to appreciate it with painful pleasure as an unparalleled portrait of family glamour, and as a deep-diving exploration of the way family can come to paralyze people in its many-armed embrace. I now think of Salinger as a writer who both conveys the seductiveness of familial suffocation and inspires the impulse to escape it. After all, as Zooey reminds Franny in her time of trouble, "*You came home. You not only came home* but you went into a goddam collapse." Franny returns home, but is it the welcome return of a Prodigal Daughter, or a kind of defeat? And at the end of the book, when she hangs up the phone after her conversation with Zooey and crawls into her parents' bed to fall asleep, is she purposeful and at peace, or just bludgeoned into temporary unconsciousness, trapped in the place where she was made?

I can't survive for long in my original family circle anymore, with its Wall of Words, like Phil Spector's Wall of Sound. But I can't survive forever without it either. On the rare occasions since my break with my brother that I've participated in brother-sister dynamics, either with him or with others—the harangues, the diktats, the rage, the scorn, the implacable judgments that bruise like a blow, the loving teasing with a serrated edge—I've been almost undone by how consoling and intolerable I've found it all to be.

≈

For octopi, ink is a defense mechanism, a means of escape. It is for me as well. Octopi surround themselves with clouds of ink in order to disappear before the clouds dissipate. Sometimes they also create hovering blots of ink that mimic their own shape, so predators will attack the ink and not them. Every time I write about my family, I instinctively obscure the truth with a cloud of self-protection, and invent versions of my life that give me a chance to evade the attacks I dread. The only way I know to get past the sense of threat is to go ahead and release the ink and then slowly wait for the cloud to clear. That might mean revision. It might mean time. It might mean a lifetime of time.

George Eliot, one of five siblings, was closest to her brother Isaac. When he learned she was living in sin with a married man, he cut off communication with her. Ten years after their break, when she was around forty, she wrote *The Mill on the Floss*, the story of Maggie and Tom Tulliver, a passionately close and then painfully estranged brother and sister who are finally reunited in the midst of a rising flood when Maggie sets out in a boat to find and save Tom. The siblings have just enough time to reconcile before drowning in each other's arms. Eliot can't imagine them living in peace, but she can't imagine them dying unreconciled. Ten years later she returned to the rift with yet more ink, writing a sonnet sequence about an estranged brother and sister whose spirits had mingled in their youth. Eliot and her brother were finally reconciled in their sixties, a couple of years after her longtime partner's death; he wrote to congratulate her when she finally got married to someone else. She died seven months later.

What awes me about families of blood and law is their visceral centripetal force, fierce as the flood in *The Mill on the Floss*. In the words of the novel's elegiac epigraph, "in their death they were not divided." I am not immune to these fierce forces, and like Eliot, I don't believe that the sibling soul-mingling of youth can ever be undone, not even after thirty years of silence. But that doesn't mean it can be sustained.

These days my brother and I text a few times a year. Birthday wishes, anniversary wishes, pictures of his children. I text him to ask where to mail their Christmas presents: a baby board book *Don Quixote*, a baby board book *Moby-Dick*. He texted me when he heard Mick Jagger singing "Angie" on the radio and was transported back to our teens. We both teach college, and we are both good teachers; it's possible we taught each other to teach. I texted him when my mom sent me a picture of a hilarious tribute his students made for him—a poster-board "Pyramid of Greatness" celebrating his various enthusiasms (for Freedom, for Family, for Logic, for Rain)—that confirmed that the brother I knew twenty years ago lives on in the teacher they know now.

My brother still wears the leather jacket I gave him. He often gets compliments on it, and he always tells people it was a gift from his sister. For my birthday he sent me a bottle of cloudy blue ink to fill my pen, dark enough to hide in. I am writing with it now.

REMEMBERING HOW IT FELT
TO BURN

THE SUMMER I was seventeen, I moved into a cheap old apartment in downtown Tacoma with my high school best friend. We were an attraction of opposites. She was an honor student; I was a two-time dropout who had started high school far too early and then finally finished on the third try. She had a scholarship to a Christian college in California in the fall; I was convinced I was done with formal education forever. She shampooed with Herbal Essences and washed her face with Noxzema; I dipped my hair in undiluted Clorox and covered my arm with self-inflicted third-degree cigarette burns. She was the good girl and I was the bad girl, or so it seemed. We needed each other: I provided the impetus for our experiment in independence, and she provided the even-keeled good-kid cred that made our parents feel like they could let us go.

I suspect we always secretly scorned each other for our differences, at least a little. I was proud of being a pariah, and assumed she was simply too afraid to be one too. It never occurred to me that she might genuinely prefer to be liked. But we were united by our loyalty to Sub Pop Records and

Pendleton shirts, and by our desire for an apartment of our own where we could finally live the way we wanted after being raised in a patriarchal, puritanical evangelical subculture. We'd first bonded during our sophomore and junior years at a tiny Christian high school located in a church basement, rolling our eyes and passing notes during the compulsory chapel sermons on the importance of sexual purity and the evils of masturbation. After graduation we got five-dollar-an-hour jobs working at espresso stands in seedy locations—the downtown bus station and YMCA—and we found a one-bedroom apartment we could just about afford if we lived on potatoes and free coffee. What I wanted more than anything that summer was a quiet place to read and write, free from the chaos of my five noisy siblings and the suffocating pressure of my anxious, God-obsessed parents. I didn't know what she wanted, but I soon found out.

Our very first night in the apartment, she brought home a man she met at the bus stop, a homeless gang member and IV drug user (*former* gang member and IV drug user, she assured me) whose hobbies included tagging, petty theft, and misogynistic fury. It soon became clear he was never going to leave, and she didn't seem to want him to. They fell into a rhythm: He would get paranoid and jealous, destroy things, shout, sulk. She would apologize and explain until he let his anger subside to a simmer, and the next day they would do it all again.

Sometimes he would search her belongings while she was at work, looking for a reason to rage. Once he found her male co-worker's phone number on a scrap of paper, and she came home to find he had written BITCH on every book she owned, every CD, every page of her calendar, with his fat tagging marker. Once he asked me what her favorite possession was; thinking he was having a rare sentimental moment, I told him it was the tea set she'd inherited from her grandmother. A few minutes later he was outside smashing it to smithereens on the sidewalk. Once he stormed out of the building early in the morning after one of their fights, and she chased him down the street wearing nothing but a T-shirt, calling his name and begging him to come back. Once he got into a fistfight with her ex-boyfriend in our living room, and afterward I found a bloody tooth on the floor next to a packet of powder. Once I opened the closet door to find him crouched in the dark, holding a knife, waiting. I don't know if he ever physically hurt her, but I know I was terrified all the time.

Before my friend and I moved in together I'd suggested some house rules (no live-in boyfriends, no hard drugs), and she'd agreed to them with the same easy insincerity with which she'd signed the Christian college's behavioral code (no drinking, no dancing, no gambling, no porn). When she broke our rules I felt betrayed. Now that I'm older and know more about the psychology of abusive relationships, I can cultivate empathy for her, but at the time I didn't feel a particle of pity. All I felt was fear and resentment that she'd brought this terror into our home. I resented her even more intensely because I could feel that on some level the terror thrilled her. The threat of violence infused our otherwise ordinary summer with the racing pace and pulse of melodrama. She felt heat, but I felt dread.

We both resorted to terrible measures to placate him. Holding a knife, he once asked me to become his blood sister by slicing our fingers and pressing them together, and with my adolescent's futureless brain and my immediate drive to survive, I agreed. I thought about AIDS the whole time our fingers were pressed together and for years afterward, but I was scared of what he would do if I said no. I don't know all she did to appease him, but I'm sure it was much worse. Then he began talking obsessively about guns.

I lasted until late July—not even two months. I waited until they were out of the apartment and then I called my parents for help and they moved me back home. By the end of the summer, she was pregnant and keeping the baby and had lost her Christian college scholarship, and I'd decided to go to community college after all, to try to plot a new escape from home through the long slow route of school. Now, decades later, one of us is a grandmother and still living in our hometown (or so I've heard; we haven't talked in twenty years), and one of us is still trying to be a writer, still living with roommates in a cheap old apartment in another gritty post-industrial city.

We both survived; we both grew up and made lives for ourselves. But I still can't bear to think about that summer. We could have died so many times.

$$\approx$$

Robin Wasserman's novel *Girls on Fire* is as intense as adolescence and as dark as a dream. Like a half-repressed memory, it altered the atmosphere of my days during the summer I read it, causing the air around me to shimmer with menace like heat waves on a highway. It's the closest I've come to feeling like a teenage girl since I actually was one, and it pushed me past my limits the way my own adolescence did, setting me on an inexorable track beyond my control and then flooding me with feeling. When I was reading it I couldn't put it down, and in between bouts of reading I was scared to pick it up. I'm apparently not the only reviewer who had to move it out of the bedroom in order to sleep at night. I've never made peace with the pleasures of terror.

Girls on Fire is a mystery and a tangled love triangle and a sharp, ruthless thriller, and on all these levels it's both satisfying and troubling. It's also an evocative and non-nostalgic novel about the 1990s, a time before Beyoncé united us all, when certain genres of popular music demanded ritual practices of alienation, and stardom sometimes looked like Kurt Cobain. But its most unsettling aspect is the utter relatability and ubiquity of its characters: "Girls, everywhere," in the words of the epilogue, "[i]mpossible not to see them, not to remember what it was like, when it was like that."

Like all good gothic, *Girls on Fire* reveals the unknown terrors of the already known. Specifically, it dramatizes the unpredictable horror stories latent in predictable patterns of female friendship and enmity, in this case in the fraught alliance between good girl Dex and bad girl Lacey and their ongoing feud with popular girl Nikki. The plot takes these ordinary high school dynamics to forbidden places, tracing the girls' various convergences and triangulations before and after the death of Nikki's boyfriend, Craig, who is found in the woods, shot through the head. His body is like a snake in the garden, foreshadowing their friendship's entwinement with the specter of decay.

Girls on Fire came out the same summer as Emma Cline's *The Girls*, which is based on the Manson family romance, and the books were often discussed together. They are both haunting historical novels about the potentially lethal dangers of adolescent female friendship. But unlike Cline's novel, Wasserman's is not made safe by its status as an aestheticization of a world-historical crime that has long served as an allegory for the end of a distant and golden era. Despite its nineties setting, it never feels like a period piece. Neither does it try to transcend time. Instead, the dangers it describes are as imminent and up-to-date as cyberbullying and campus rape. In occasionally anachronistic ways—at one point it uses the antiquated technology of a VHS tape to approximate the lethal effects of a viral video—*Girls on Fire* takes the classic and contemporary teen ingredients of peer pressure and rape culture and compulsive photo-documentation and still-legal-in-most-states conversion therapy, and turns them into a tale that will horrify even the most blasé adult. It plays on the familiar fears we already have about the young people we love and think we know. It's a call coming from inside the house.

Recently I was at a dinner with an otherwise intelligent-seeming man who said he didn't understand why dystopian novels about teenagers are so popular when modern teens experience so little social or state repression. Teens' real problem, he posited, is growing up in a world with too much tolerance. This seemed like a stunningly strange statement to make, especially by someone who lives in a stop-and-frisk city, and especially during a week when bathroom bills were all over the news and conservative principals and parents were insisting that students live and piss according to the gender specified on their birth certificate.

My own sense is that modern adolescence is a time of becoming repressed in both old ways and new ones. It's a period in young people's lives when, already under scrutiny from parents and teachers and one another, they enter a high-stakes new phase of being profiled and policed in public, catcalled and categorized by a world that often perceives them not just as objects but as a potential threat. As has been made abundantly clear, the burden of this surveillance falls dispro-portionately and heavily on people of color, but any teenage girl who has walked down a sidewalk or a school hallway has known what it's like to bear the weight of a gaze. In much modern fiction, white girls' experience of this heightened scrutiny is transformed into allegory (A vampire is watching you while you sleep! You are fighting for your life on reality TV!). In *Girls on Fire*, the problem of surveillance is more literal, even banal, but less absolute: Everyone is watching, from cops and concerned parents to fellow teenagers with video cameras; but when it matters most, no one is watching closely enough.

Readers are forced to watch too. Like my favorite 1940s noirs, *Girls on Fire* is narrated in a haunted voice-over of recrimination and regret—the kind of noir narration that helplessly, compulsively tells a tale of woe after the worst has occurred, to an audience that is sometimes a lost love or a co-conspirator, sometimes an imagined jury or confessor, and sometimes an unacknowledged audience of moviegoers or readers who, in listening, become accessories after the fact. The long sections marked US, narrated in breathless first-person by Dex and Lacey, are interspersed with short sections marked THEM, written in detached third-person from the perspective of their parents—sections that provide a brief reprieve from the hot and sometimes stifling adolescent perspective of the US chapters and help explain why this is classified as a book for adults. (All the uncensored sex and violence are doubtless part of the adult marketing too.)

But unlike the multiple unreliable female narrators of the bestselling thriller *The Girl on the Train*, an exhilarating exercise in wish-fulfillment in which the women's separate stories ultimately merge to become a kind of righteous feminist truth united against the threat of male violence, the narrators of *Girls on Fire* remain unreliable and unsettled until the end, because the danger is not just outside them but within them. Even as the mystery is revealed and the plot rushes to a climax, these girls remain fundamentally inscrutable to themselves and to us, as adolescents often are. Their story is spun smoothly and skillfully at a fiendish speed, with suspenseful alternations between taut and slack, but the girls' motives and feelings remain appropriately torn and tangled. No narrator, no matter how omniscient, could make order out of their roiling moods.

To me, the most horrifying parts of the book were not the many graphic accounts of vicious violence (though they saturate the pages) but the cringingly familiar depictions of youthful freedom and friendship attempted without knowledge or self-knowledge or empathy or limits. Living through a fraught, contingent time before their identities are fully fixed, these girls are utterly at the mercy of the destructiveness of intimacy, vulnerable to all the ways closeness can hurt you when you don't know its dangers, when you can't get out of your own head enough to imagine another person's perspective, when you can't imagine a future for yourself or anyone else, and when you haven't yet formed a strong enough sense of self to know when to stay and when to run. By the time they learn, it's too late.

It is this ragged edge, this blurriness of the teenage self, that makes *Girls on Fire* a more reliable guide to the lived dystopia of adolescence than the melting masochism of *Twilight* or the righteous fight of *The Hunger Games*. Because in my experience there is no clarity or meaning to be made of a misspent youth. Girlhood is there, and then it is gone. This is the poignancy and problem of the It Gets Better campaign, with its well-meaning adult attempts to send a message in a bottle to a painful adolescent past—because even if it gets better, it will get better not for the self who is suffering, but for the adult stranger they may eventually become. So much of adolescence is spent without a sense of consequences or hope because the future feels so distant it may as well not exist.

"Remember how good it felt to burn," Wasserman writes.

Twenty years ago I spent hours and afternoons burning melting messages in fire on my skin, making scar after scar, because I wanted to write my misspent youth on my body in a way it could never forget. I didn't want my future self to ever disavow how much I hurt in that moment. I didn't want to lose myself to happiness. But scars fade, and I consider it one of the great accomplishments of my life that I eventually broke faith with the girl I was and decided I owe her nothing. I traded in my Soundgarden CDs for NPR and my unfiltered Lucky Strikes for tea and therapy, and I can teach and care for teenagers today because there are so many things I do not allow myself to remember.

It's a purposeful forgetting: a necessary loss. But for a few days one summer, *Girls on Fire* helped me feel how thin the membrane might be that separates our present from our past, our adulthood from our girlhood, our selves from our selves.

COMING HOME TO THE BEST YEARS
OF OUR LIVES

S OME FILMS SEEM to script our heart's desires, or to
reveal them. When you're coming of age and starting to
crave forms of love before you've had a chance to feel them,
it can be hard to know which is which. Is this movie making
me, or is it uncovering me? Is there something about this
combination of images and sound that's causing me to want
something and keep on wanting it? Whether a film creates
our desires or merely finds them, it is certainly true that it
can wake them up.

There are some youthful scripts that we have to leave
behind, but others stay with us, writing our lives in ways
we might not even know. I don't fully understand why I've
lived the adult life I have—craving commitment, yet wary
of "Happily Ever After" stories; always the officiant, never
the bride—but I suspect the answer is somewhere in *The
Best Years of Our Lives*, and its haunting vision of marriage
and home.

∾

I used to say that *The Best Years of Our Lives* was like a religion to me. In college I watched it over and over again in times of duress—first hoping the fat double-tape set was at the library, which it always was, then bringing it home and sliding it into the VCR and sitting too close to the screen, not wanting any of my real life in my peripheral vision. There were moments in the film—often scenes with Dana Andrews or Teresa Wright—when I would reach out and touch the television's warm, gently curved surface, the static electricity turning the glass into something soft and almost alive, like sparks on velvet.

I may have loved it more than most, but I'm not the first person to hold this film in reverence. *The Best Years of Our Lives* is a certified American classic, a heartland epic about three veterans returning from World War II, and it is indeed pretty Best: It won eight Academy Awards, including Best Picture, Best Director, Best Actor, Best Supporting Actor, Best Screenplay, Best Score, and a special Oscar for disabled veteran Harold Russell for "bringing hope and courage to his fellow veterans." It ranks high on the list of the American Film Institute's Best American Movies, and it was one of the most commercially successful movies ever made.

It was also a deeply personal endeavor for director William Wyler, a veteran of combat in Europe who based many of the scenes on his own experiences. Like Fredric March's character Al Stephenson, Wyler was a middle-aged soldier who came home to a life with financial security, a loving family, and invisible damage. Like Dana Andrews's Fred Derry, he'd flown in bombing missions over Europe and lost a close comrade who was shot down. And like Harold Russell's

Homer Parrish, he came home physically disabled, though Wyler lost half his hearing, not both his hands.

The film is often praised for its documentary realism—it was partly shot on location in midwestern streetscapes and in army airfields, the actors wore little or no makeup and off-the-rack clothes, and Homer was played by a nonprofessional actor with a real disability. This ordinariness gives the film its step-through-the-screen immediacy. But I love the film just as much for its uncanniness, which is heightened by its veri-similitude. *Best Years* shows us an everyday reality that will never be the same again: a hometown that appears to be itself, but is forever changed; a homesickness that even home can't seem to cure. After the war, soldiers feel the aches of phantom limbs, and phantom selves as well.

As we are reminded again after every war, coming home is rarely simple and often sad. In the African American church, "homegoing" is a word for a memorial service: the idea being that in the end, you get home by leaving your home behind and encountering death. *The Best Years of Our Lives* applies a version of that paradoxical logic to veterans, only it seems that for them the war itself was a kind of home—it was maybe the best years of their lives—and now returning to the lives and loves they left behind is like facing death all over again.

∼

The film begins with Homer, Al, and Fred catching a flight back to their fictional midwestern hometown, Boone City. As they sit in the nose of the plane surrounded by glass, we see their panoramic view of America: ribbons of lit-up highway stretching beneath them like stars in the darkness, and then daybreak and bright clouds in front of them like the entrance to a celestial afterlife. But then they descend into an airfield ominously crowded with warplanes waiting to be scrapped, left behind like bodies on a battlefield, and it starts to seem like going home is actually a return to combat. As Al says as he prepares to reunite with his family, "I feel as if I were going in to hit a beach."

From the beginning, it is clear that the world is no longer safe, as new threats haunt old sites of security. This is true at a global level: On Al's first night home, his earnest teenage son asks him if he saw any signs of radiation sickness in the people in Hiroshima, and observes that in the future countries will have to get along "or else." The threat of nuclear holocaust is invoked again in a homey neighborhood bar when Homer tells his uncle Butch (perfectly played by songwriter Hoagy Carmichael) that his family can't get used to his prosthetic metal hooks. "Give 'em time, kid, they'll catch on," Butch drawls, sitting at the piano, to the accompaniment of soft legato chords. "You know, your folks will get used to you, and you'll get used to them, and everything will settle down nicely. Unless we have another war. Then none of us will have to worry 'cause we'll all be blown to bits the first day. So cheer up, huh?" In this strange new world, annihilation is offered as consolation.

This uncanniness is also manifest in smaller moments of self-estrangement or mistaken identity. Without hands, Homer has had to learn how to do everything as if for the first time: lighting a match, drinking lemonade. He has mostly mastered his hooks, but now every ordinary social encounter is a minefield of awkwardness, and he can't bring himself to touch his girlfriend, Wilma.

Meanwhile, on his first night home, a drunken Al dances with a wife he is too far gone to recognize. He falls into his habitual overseas seduction script, telling her: "You're a bewitching little creature. You know, you remind me of my wife." His wife, Milly (Myrna Loy, only slightly less sparkling than her perfect prewar wife, Nora Charles, in the *Thin Man* movies), gamely plays along: "But you never told me you were married!" After their strained reunion earlier in the day, Milly finally connects with Al by pretending to be one of the women he cheated on her with. The next morning, hungover, Al skeptically compares a glossy prewar photo of himself with the aging, disheveled man in the mirror. Later, when he goes back to work, he discovers that his time in the infantry has given him a social conscience that makes him unrecognizable, and sometimes unacceptable, to his fat-cat bosses at the bank.

Fred, who flew the highest, has the farthest to fall. Before the war, he was just a soda jerk from the wrong side of the tracks, but during the war, he was a dashing bomber pilot: "an officer and a gentleman," as he says bitterly in the bad British accent he adopts in ironic moments, who wooed and won a brassy blonde named Marie (Virginia Mayo, playing against her usual comic heroine type). Fred came home with "a whole ribbon counter on his chest," recurring nightmares, and the resolve to make something of himself. But as Al says, "It isn't easy for those Air Force glamour boys when they get grounded." Fred can't find a good job, and after months of struggle he eventually returns to the despised soda jerking, a metamorphosis Dana Andrews plays with pained restraint as Fred's "smooth operator" banter slowly turns into something defeated and self-lacerating. He's back in his white soda-fountain uniform as if nothing had ever happened, except now he's haunted by the knowledge of what he's capable of and what he's lost.

Marie refuses to recognize Fred in his civilian clothes, and insists that he change into his uniform when they go out: "Oh, now you look wonderful. You look like yourself! . . . Just as if nothing had ever happened. Just as if you'd never gone away." Fred burns with a pilot light of anger always ready to ignite, and it flares into flame as he tries to shake some sense into her: "Don't say that, Marie. We can never be back there again. We never want to be back there."

Marie won't acknowledge the extent of the war's damage. The film, on the other hand, won't let us look away. Mostly avoiding close-ups, it habitually shows its characters arranged in relation to each other, their moments of connection and alienation framed by their friends, family, and environment. There's a kind of respect and love in the sheer duration of its attention and deep focus: It's a long movie with sustained shots and slowly unspooling scenes that mire you in the shame of not having fingers or fists, the uphill battle of bureaucracy at the bank, the indignity of trying to survive on $32.50 a week. As the hours of the film unfold, we watch each of the men resort to macho military strategies that fail to work in the civilian world. Homer withdraws into solitary target practice interrupted by flashes of rage. Al turns to booze. Fred briefly regains a flash of flyboy glamour when he leaps over the soda fountain counter to punch a Nazi sympathizer, but it costs him his job. In postwar America, punching Nazis lands you in the unemployment line.

We are encouraged to empathize with the characters by the film's quiet melodic patience, the hours of deepening struggle set to a wistful soundtrack. But there is more to their appeal than that. We are also being educated in a new erotics of male vulnerability, a broken beloved masculinity that hints at the Method antiheroes of the decade to come. It's a vision of romance in which the men fall apart and the women keep it together. In a scene of utter vulnerability, Homer finally shows Wilma how to disarm him when she takes on the task of removing his prosthetic harness. Once it's off, he tells her, he can't smoke, put on his clothes, or open the door. Their marriage will depend on their acceptance of his dependence. She is ready when he is.

Al unsteadily walks the line between social drinker and alcoholic with a wry, wrecked charm. Milly watches her husband's compulsive self-medication, silently counting each drink and confiscating as many as she can. She seems to have given up any expectation that he will stop drinking, but she refuses to accept it all the same. Her anxiety is mostly covered by humor, and when she can she relaxes into moments of relief, pride, and the familiar physical intimacy that has lasted half their lives.

Marie's response to Fred's PTSD is to tell him, "Snap out of it! The war's over," which is how we know their marriage is doomed. When Fred hits the town with Al and Milly and their grown-up daughter, Peggy, played by the tough and thoughtful Teresa Wright, Peggy seems immune to his practiced patter. Later that night when Fred and Al both come home drop-dead drunk, Peggy matter-of-factly flops Fred on her frilly canopy bed, unbuckles his belt, loosens his tie, casually fends off his automatic attempt at a pass, and then goes to sleep on the couch. Later she is woken by his screams. She sits with him and holds him as he sweats and stares and watches his friend dying again before his eyes. The next morning is an approximation of a morning after. She cooks him breakfast, and Fred flirts: "Do you mind if I ask you a personal question? Where did you sleep last night?" She banters back. But they both know that what they shared was more intimate than sex.

This is the film's bracing view of romance, one in which men and women walk into love already embracing the worse, the poorer, the sickness of wedding vows. In the movie's most emotionally expressive speech, Milly sums up her relationship with Al as a series of difficult returns to the same familiar but often hard-to-find place: "How many times have I told you I hated you and believed it in my heart? How many times have you said you were sick and tired of me; that we were all washed up? How many times have we had to fall in love all over again?"

This kind of constantly reclaimed loss is the film's view of work as well: A good job is a return, a recycling, a repetition of the past but with a difference. Al is still a banker, but a better one, one who resists the system. And in one of the last scenes in the film, Fred finally finds a way forward when he heads back to the airfield of scrapped planes, fed up with Boone City and about to take the next flight out. He's sitting in the ruins of an old bomber, reliving war memories, when he meets a man who offers him a job turning scrap metal into prefabricated houses—salvaging homes from the wreckage of the war. Divorced, broke, and homeless, Fred decides to stay and work.

At Homer's wedding, Fred runs into Peggy, after months of keeping his distance during the protracted death of his marriage. "Dad told me he heard you were in some kind of building work," she says. He replies, with guarded self-deprecation, "Well, that's a hopeful way of putting it. I'm really in the junk business." The film leaves us with this image of hopeful wreckage, with Wilma grasping Homer's metal hand as they say their vows, and finally with Fred's ragged marriage proposal, more a warning than a promise, which also serves as the film's last words: "You know what it'll be, don't you, Peggy? It may take us years to get anywhere. We'll have no money, no decent place to live. We'll have to work, get kicked around . . ." The offer is broken enough to be believable. The joy hurts enough to feel real.

In his classic antisentimental essay "Everybody's Protest Novel," James Baldwin puts *The Best Years of Our Lives* on a list of infamy along with *Little Women*, *Gentleman's Agreement*, and *Uncle Tom's Cabin*. According to Baldwin, they are all failed feel-good liberal art. He is only partly right. Yes, *The Best Years of Our Lives* is a popular straight white romance, and if it weren't for its melancholic score and ironic dialogue, its war-haunted performances and unfinished ending, it could be summarized as some kind of pat statement about democracy and the love of a good woman. But its sentimentality is mitigated and messy and tarnished enough that at the end of the film I am always ready to say Yes.

Yes: Work is hopeful junkyard salvage, and love is enduring struggle, and it may take us years to get anywhere, but yes, *this*. It's what I once tried to touch, my hand on the screen—the hope and the struggle, if I could only find my way home to it.

The Best Years of Our Lives has stayed with me. At times I have measured my relationships by it and found them wanting, and realized I needed to let them go. At other times it has helped me summon the strength to keep on loving when love is increasingly hard. I watch it less now than I used to, but it's one of the movies that I've made friends and boyfriends watch, and some of my little sisters have gotten hooked on it as well (one says Fred Derry's marriage proposal is her "daily mirror affirmation"). The film can still be religion as needed, and even elegy. Eight years ago I watched it with a new friend who was in the midst of a long and courageous struggle with mental illness, and two years later I read some of its restless, uncanny dialogue at her scattering-of-ashes service:

"I had a dream. I dreamed I was home. I've had that same dream hundreds of times before. This time I wanted to find out if it's true. Am I really home?"

ACQUAINTED WITH GRIEF

M Y FRIEND'S SISTER'S story isn't mine to tell. All I can say is that she lived in the city I live in, and she died here the year before I moved here. Though I never knew her, I have never known this city without the thought of her, and I have never walked here except in her steps. Every new year when I buy a new calendar, the first thing I write is the day of her death. On the first anniversary that I was here, my friend asked me to bring flowers to the site of her shrine. Ever since then I have wanted never to forget to bring her flowers, and I have wanted never to need to be reminded.

I want to share some of the involuntary labor of a mourner's memory, and to feel some of the force of the tide that turns on anniversaries with inexorable force. I want my body clock to be set to the dates of her life like an alarm that can't be silenced. I want the melting weather of early spring to always feel hard as well as welcome. I want to bear some of the burden of the season of her loss with my friend who loved and loves her.

But I am a mourner at one remove. Every night before the anniversary I always have to write my friend's sister's name in marker on my hand, because even after all these years there is still a chance I might forget. Friendship is writing a name on your hand to remember. Grief is not being able to forget, however much you might want to.

In the wake of a death at one remove there are many temptations and attempts to make an irreplaceable person into someone replaceable.

There is the illicit but almost irresistible lure of mental substitution—a desire to appropriate another's real griefs as a portal to our own imagined ones, and to turn someone else's sorrow into a preview of our own; or worse, to use it as a confirmation of our own relative well-being, a reminder of our own completeness and luck.

There is also the loving but futile desire to restore what can never be restored. When my friend's sister died almost a decade ago and left my friend without a living sibling, it was the first time I felt a friendship stretching into the future for the entire duration, for the whole remainder of our days. I felt a vow forming inside me that I didn't confess to my friend for years, a vow that I would be present in her life as long as she needed me, as loyal to her as I am to my sisters, and sometimes even more, because they have each other. I have kept that vow to the best of my ability, and I always will. But as much as I might wish it otherwise, it is not possible for any friend to be as present to my friend as her sister is absent.

Some replacements are beyond the pale of possibility. Some lost people can never be found again, and the hard work of mourning cannot be delegated. I can't ever stand in for my friend's lost sister, no matter how much I wish I could. And no matter how tired my friend is of grieving, I can't volunteer to cover her shift while she rests. But though I can never stand in for my friend, I can still stand beside her. I don't know what it's like to lose a sister, but I know what it's like to love a sister, so I will remember my friend's sister for her sake.

I will buy some flowers every year, and I will bring them. I will go back to the Walgreens on the corner once more, and choose the brightest bouquet from the fridge by the door. I will find a new card from the "Sisters" section, and I will write in it again, as if hearing and transcribing my friend's fervent voice: *Mila, you are loved. You are remembered. You are missed.*

HOARDING

Lay not up for yourselves treasures upon earth, where moth and rust doth corrupt, and where thieves break through and steal: But lay up for yourselves treasures in heaven, where neither moth nor rust doth corrupt, and where thieves do not break through nor steal: For where your treasure is, there will your heart be also.

MATTHEW 6:19–21

M Y STORAGE UNIT is located in the Puyallup Valley in Western Washington, a place where future catastrophes converge.

On an earthquake map, the valley lies in a strip of red that designates the region's most treacherous ground. When the Cascadia earthquake finally hits, the deep-buried water in the Puyallup River basin will seep to the surface and suspend the moist soil. The earth will get viscous and act like a liquid. The whole of the valley will flood from below. Water and sand will erupt from the ground, and man-made structures will crack and sink.

But an earthquake is not all that lies in store. When Mount Rainier finally blows, a fast lahar will flow through the valley like a concrete tsunami, a tall molten wall of magma and mud. The wall will bury all that it finds. It will be judge, executioner, gravedigger, and grave.

Nobody knows which fate will come first. The volcano could blow at any time, and the quake is a century overdue. But one day, one way or another, the miscellaneous contents of Fife You Store It Unit B-77 will finally meet their natural end.

If the quake comes first, which it may without warning, my boxed-up childhood library will swell with the flood. Each book will become a stratified sponge; each page will return to the pulp from whence it came. The dresses and coats I wore in college will tremble on their metal rack and billow and stain in the rising tide. The furs, long dead, will finally drown. The hope chest holding my grandmother's china, each teacup wrapped in crumpled newsprint, will look deceptively like a dead pirate's treasure—sodden, swollen, sunk, submerged—but no one will see it except a few salmon. The cloth and leather will disintegrate first. The wood and metal will last much longer. When the muddy water finally recedes, even if the unreinforced masonry structure miraculously still stands, the mold and rust will have claimed almost everything.

Alternatively, in the event of an eruption, the igneous flow will trap my relics like spiders in amber. The unit will become a Vesuvian tableau. In the absence of air, it will all last forever, suffocated under a sheet of rock. The fabric won't fade; the boxes won't fall; each word on the pages will remain; each follicle of fur will be preserved.

Whether it's a river of rock or a vast valley of water, the unpredictable moods of Northwest geology will turn my hoard into a lost still life.

Or maybe instead, sometime between now and the apocalypse, I'll spend a day at the storage unit with a Sharpie and Post-its and systematically sort through it all. I'll ship some of the stuff and sell some of the stuff and donate the rest to the Tacoma Goodwill. I'll sweep the space clean and return my key.

It could happen, I suppose. Anything is possible.

~

I first found out about the existence of my storage unit seven years ago. I'd moved out of my parents' house almost a decade earlier, or perhaps it would be more accurate to say I'd moved *away*. I left behind a hundred boxes in their attic, plus clothes racks and hatboxes and old steamer trunks, the manifestation of a youth misspent in thrift stores. None of these possessions seemed necessary to bring along with me to my new life as an East Coast grad student, but none of them seemed ripe for letting go. I needed to keep them, and I needed to leave them behind.

I took a deep pleasure in packing up my things that long-ago summer after college. My things had built me, equipped me, and gotten me ready. I had enlarged my vocabulary in order to comprehend the books, and dieted to fit into the dresses; I had submitted my mind and body to their rigor. Now I was ready to take what they'd taught me to another

region, another era. I knew that I would likely go for years
without seeing them, but they were all filed away in the folds
of my brain, cross-indexed by memories and associations, an
external hard drive for my first couple of decades, a mnemonic
device, a tangible past.

PARTIAL INVENTORY OF THINGS I LEFT IN MY PARENTS' ATTIC, SUMMER 2001

Item #1. Checkers, a threadbare corduroy cocker spaniel with button eyes and yarn ears (located in the tray of the tan steamer trunk). My East Coast Republican grandma, Bette, made him for my dad in 1952 and named him after the cocker spaniel in a famous Richard Nixon speech about emoluments and bribes. Checkers was my first comfort object. As a five-year-old I worried that I loved him more than God. I knew it was wrong but I couldn't help it. When my Sunday school teacher talked about the sin of idolatry, I thought about Checkers and trembled.

Filed under: Stuffed Animals; Grandmothers; Richard Nixon; Idolatry.

Item #57. A set of sexy lobby-card movie stills featuring blacklisted actor John Garfield, who died of a broken heart (located in a tattered portfolio in the striped canvas suitcase with the clear Bakelite handle). I started loving John Garfield because he was a beautiful talker with good hair, and I kept on loving him because he refused to name names to the House

Un-American Activities Committee and then died of a heart attack at thirty-nine. I managed to track down these lobby cards in my late teens, before the days of eBay and Google, by frequenting a cinema bookshop near the British Museum run by a very camp man with a very large parrot. I was working in a cafeteria at the time and being paid a pittance, but I spent all my spare pennies on my John Garfield shrine. John Garfield playing the violin. John Garfield boxing. John Garfield picking up Lana Turner's dropped lipstick. A perfect triptych.

Filed under: Idolatry; England; Parrots; John Garfield.

Item #733. A 1940s tortoiseshell "flapjack" compact (located in the turquoise train case). A perfect pancake-sized mirror for applying perfect pancake makeup. I bought it for a dollar at the Catholic thrift store St. Vincent de Paul (known in my family as St. Vinnie's). Where the powder had once been I put a John Garfield quote from his hottest movie, *Humoresque*: "I can do anything a brainless man can do, and I can do it better." Every time I opened the compact and looked in the mirror I made a vow to one day be worthy of him.

Filed under: John Garfield; Tortoiseshell; Solemn Vows; My Face.

I arrived at Princeton with only a backpack and a duffel bag and felt exhilarated and light, and then I proceeded to fill my life with a thousand new things.

In the years after I abandoned Checkers and John Garfield in the attic, some of my sisters scattered from coast to coast, but thanks to ill health, a shaky economy, and the high cost of college, others were still stuck like barnacles to our childhood home. Perhaps because my restless parents couldn't yet fully empty their nest, they decided they would at least evict the daughters who had already left. So one day, out of the blue, eight years after I'd left, my mom called and told me that she and my dad had decided to relocate my personal archive. My credit card number was required for auto-debit purposes. I was now the legal tenant of my own storage unit.

≈

The year I got evicted from my parents' attic was a particularly hard one. I had gotten a PhD but couldn't get a job: There was a nationwide hiring freeze in the wake of the global financial crash. I had begun retraining to be a minister, but in the meantime I couldn't make ends meet. I was taking a full load of classes and taking out a maximum load of loans and teaching Dickens and American Studies and creative writing to college students and leading worship at the chapel on Sunday mornings and prayer services on Wednesday nights and tutoring on other nights and publishing essays when I could and sleeping almost not at all, and my old car was always breaking down in the snow, and the winter that year seemed like it would never end. And what was sometimes the hardest to handle: After most of a decade of having my own home and life, I was living precariously on the edge of a friend's.

I was renting a room from my beloved friend Cathy. Cathy and I had fallen into instant friendship years before when we were visiting grad schools—rapturously running into each other on consecutive prospective students' weekends in Berkeley and Philly—and when we met we were on uncannily parallel tracks. We were both living in England, both in long-term long-distance romantic relationships, both about to start PhDs in the New Jersey Transit/SEPTA region, both trying to make sense of our intense religious upbringings (she was the daughter of a devout ex-nun; I was the daughter of devout Calvinist converts), and both fond of *Sex and the City*, hazelnut gelato, and the novels of E. F. Benson. Our friendship seemed predestined.

But I gravitated to Cathy because of our differences as much as our convergences. From the beginning, Cathy's way of being often seemed both admirable and unattainable to me: objectively better and fundamentally foreign. I was fascinated by the ways we seemed to represent two contrasting temperamental responses to the same essential traits. We were both anxious perfectionists, but I externalized my stress—crying in professors' offices and scattering my room with the scribbled-on drafts of my latest writing project (and, much later, complaining hyperbolically on social media, which hadn't yet been invented). She turned her worries inward, berating herself in private while presenting a polished professional persona to the world. I dreaded deadlines, unsure whether I would meet them; she welcomed them, knowing she would. We were both hyperverbal, but though I reveled in private conversations, I often felt tongue-tied in public and blocked on the page. I especially loved Cathy's sparkly and intimate ways with words: the way she seemed to light up with language whenever she talked, fearless and shining, whether she was sitting in a living room with me or standing in a lecture hall full of strangers; the way she couldn't help whispering to herself when she wrote.

We took an idyllic trip to Positano the first summer we knew each other, and for a long time our friendship kept that honeymoon quality. It helped that for years we lived a couple of hours away from each other, which meant that we saw each other often but never every day, so our time together was always set apart. When we were in different places we separately slogged through the anxious and tedious parts of our daily routines, but when we were together we spent long leisurely days reading across the table from each other in coffee shops, and then stayed up late talking about God and love. Even our difficult conversations seemed to exist in a charmed safe space. For years we could comfortably dump our direst, most undiluted fears and needs onto each other, because our lives were still separated by state lines, and we knew that when we hung up the phone or caught the train home the hardest parts of empathy and identification would be tempered with distance.

Our friendship flourished in this intimate middle distance as we spent our twenties learning how to be teachers and scholars. We wrote an academic talk on religion together; we took a seminar on Melville together; we went to hear Edward Albee speak and passed notes back and forth. (I was so proud of Cathy during the Q&A when she confidently challenged Albee's take on Samuel Beckett to his face. Albee thought Beckett was warm and affirming; Cathy insisted he was bleak.)

We were each other's first adult friends: the first friends we'd made as adults, and the first friends we measured our adult lives by, like parallel penciled growth marks on a closet door.

Our lives began to diverge a few years into our friendship when Cathy married the love of her life the same month that I was dumped by the love of mine, but we still stayed close. I was in her wedding; I was her daughter's godmother. She supported me through my breakup; I supported her through her postpartum depression; we supported each other through the end of grad school and the job market. She read my dissertation readers' reports before I did to make sure they were OK (they were!), and I traveled up from Princeton to babysit her six-month-old daughter during her multiday on-campus job interview at Yale (Cathy had to keep rushing back to our hotel room to nurse between high-stakes talks and meetings; we handed baby Miriam back and forth like a baton).

And then, suddenly, things changed.

Seven years into our friendship, we found ourselves living in the same city for the first time, but on totally different planes: She was a tenure-track professor with a husband and a kid and a four-bedroom house, and I was a single, childless, broke divinity student living in a dilapidated dormitory apartment, struggling to pay my bills. My first year in New Haven I felt like the earth was shaking and melting beneath me, while she seemed to be living on solid ground. I realized I couldn't afford to live alone anymore, and I preferred to live with someone I loved. When I asked if I could move in with her, she said yes.

Taking me in was no small thing (and not just because, unbeknownst to me, Cathy was already thinking about our new living arrangement as more of a rescue mission than a standard housemates scenario). At that point I'd spent most of a decade frequenting thrift stores and furnishing apartments in and around central Jersey, and I'd accumulated an apartment's worth of stuff that I proceeded to store in Cathy's attic, basement, and garage—an avalanche of bagged clothes in the attic, a pyramid of boxed books in the garage, plus assorted domestic miscellany. (Cathy was particularly amused that my stash of housewares included two whole boxes of spice racks. I'd tried to stock my kitchen with spices for every letter of the alphabet, from Aniseed to Zest.)

If storing my stuff after college felt like freedom, storing it after grad school felt like hibernation at best, and burial at worst. Confining my life to a small spare room in someone else's house meant saying good-bye for a while or forever to the parts of myself that hosted weekly gin nights and kept a complete collection of Agatha Christie in the living room and had friends over for impromptu home-cooked meals served at my kitchen table (a 1940s metal-topped expandable wooden table from the Trenton Goodwill that was the twin of one in Luke's Diner in *Gilmore Girls*). I'd already lost my romantic self and my scholarly self; now I was losing my social self, my domestic self, my generous and hospitable self. I was trying hard to hold on to my teaching, preaching, and writing selves: I couldn't afford to let them go.

I didn't always feel like I had a present or a future that year, but I still had a past—even if half of it was stored in my friend's attic, basement, and garage, and the other half was housed in a faraway cinderblock storage unit in a volcanic earthquake zone. Somewhere in all those boxes was everything I'd ever been or hoped to be. I had barely any disposable income, but I felt I had no choice but to maintain my Tacoma time capsule and wait for the day I was ready to face it. I've been paying to preserve it ever since.

~

I come from a family of hoarders. My mother's generation of four sisters and their mother before them are all on the hoarding spectrum. They gather things and then can't let go.

They brake for yard sales and estate sales—literally. (I remember the precise feeling of being in the car when my mother sees a yard sale sign and suddenly slows down.)

Their mental map of their hometown consists of monuments to thrifting: the 38th Street Goodwill, the 72nd Street Goodwill, the South Tacoma Goodwill, the Thrift Center, Thrift City, Bargain World, the Second Closet, the American Cancer Society Shop, the Salvation Army, St. Vinnie's, and Value Village (sometimes pronounced fake French-ly: *VallOO VillAHHJ*).

They have memorized the rummage sale schedules of local churches. They know which weekends to head over to the Methodist church basement and when to stop by the Lutheran church fellowship room and when to hit the Episcopal church parish hall. In all cases it is customary to arrive early, before things get too picked over.

They are connoisseurs of what Barbara Pym in *Excellent Women* calls "jumble in all its glory"—the flotsam and jetsam of items donated and bought by church ladies. Jumble (or, as it is known in the United States, "rummage") has not changed all that much since the parish jumble sales of Pym's novels. Most of a century later, my mother and aunts are still rummaging through what Pym summed up as "worn garments, stuffed birds, old shoes, golf clubs, theological books, popular dance tunes of the 'thirties, fenders and photograph frames." Like pearl divers, they plunge into the depths, hoping to emerge with something precious.

They have a devout and capacious sense of family heirlooms. I remember as a child being asked by my grandma to mend a tortoiseshell comb that had belonged to her own grandmother. I spent an hour reverently and precisely reattaching the brittle broken teeth, and then gently laid the comb on a cushion to rest as the glue slowly dried. I remember my mother giving me, as a blessing for my first apartment, the bottom part of an unremarkable clouded glass butterdish that had once lived on my great-grandma's kitchen table. The cover had broken, which in another family might have made the dish worthless, but in ours made it doubly precious, since it was all that was left.

The houses of my mother and grandmother and aunts have a family resemblance, and range from full to overflowing. Some (including their inhabitants, at times) experience these dwellings as warm and welcoming. Others (including their inhabitants, at times) find them overwhelming. They are certainly unwieldy to live in and maintain.

To me, they are home. And learning how to make a home along these lines has been my matrilineal legacy.

THE HOARDER'S GUIDE TO HOUSE-KEEPING: OR, HOW TO KEEP A HOUSE WHERE EVERYTHING IS KEPT

FIRST: Find a house, ideally one built in the late nineteenth or early twentieth century with an attic and a basement and lots of built-in corner cupboards and china cabinets. The house should have good bones and discernible "character," but its surfaces may be imperfect or provisional. If the fridge door is streaked with rust, cover it with a sheet of brown paper held on with mismatched magnets. Duct tape is an adequate substitute for window trim: one of many temporary measures that can last for decades.

SECOND: Fill the house with furniture that might be described as somewhere between shabby chic and scabby chic: an old oak sideboard that sports nylon bootlaces as makeshift handles; a scarred but handsome dining table that expands to seat a dozen uncomfortable people, who must all remember to sit in such a way that they do not gouge their thighs on its sharply angled underpinnings; and a lovely dignified secretary-style writing desk that can't be written on because its writing surface slopes and sags alarmingly.

THIRD: Alter your habits and posture as necessary to suit your furniture.

FOURTH: Cover all horizontal surfaces with chipped china lamps, origami animals, pincushions, stopped clocks, Danish butter cookie tins full of tangled spools of thread, stacks of discarded library books with yellowed cellophane jackets, matchbox cars, rag rugs, saucers of sea glass, and similar.

FIFTH: Cover all vertical surfaces with posters, paintings, photographs, lithographs, folk art, toddler art, postcards, Christmas cards, corkboards, chalkboards, grocery lists, to-do lists, Post-it Note admonishments, and taped-up pages torn from *National Geographic* and *Sunset*.

SIXTH: Don't neglect the nooks and crannies. Drawers must be full enough that they require at least two tries to open or close. Shoeboxes full of things other than shoes should undergird the beds. Several steps of the staircase should support milk crates full of things that are on their way up or down or settling in for a long rest.

It's great that your books are double-stacked. But are there books *on top* of your bookshelves? Can you fit *more* books on top of your bookshelves?

Don't be afraid to be creative. For example, when I ran out of room for cake pans in the kitchen I started storing them underneath the love seat.

SEVENTH: In moments of aimlessness, energy, hope, or despair, turn once again to your possessions. Move, mend, sift, sort, repair, restore, refinish, polish, purge, or replenish them. Or simply stare at them wordlessly, helplessly, in paralysis and awe.

EIGHTH: This process does not have an end. Continue to repeat steps two through seven until you die.

None of the women in my family would qualify for hoarding horror shows like *Hoarders* or *Hoarding: Buried Alive*. I do not worry about our being literally buried by newspapers or befriended by indoor raccoons. We are, in general, more than averagely hospitable people whose homes pose no unusual health hazards. Many of us are even used to hearing compliments and delighted exclamations when guests come over and are greeted by, e.g., a bevy of burnished brass candelabras in the living room and a row of brightly colored Art Deco teapots in the kitchen, as if in a nonanthropomorphic *Beauty and the Beast*. "More is more" can be a nice place to visit and, often, a nice place to live.

But psychologically speaking, several of us would probably place ourselves—or be placed by others—somewhere in what the latest edition of the *Diagnostic and Statistical Manual of Mental Disorders* would diagnose as hoarding disorder territory. I recognize us in the *DSM*-based self-diagnostic rubric spelled out by the psychiatrist David F. Tolin, the psychologist Randy O. Frost, and the social worker Gail Steketee in *Buried in Treasures: Help for Compulsive Acquiring, Saving, and Hoarding*, 2nd ed. (Oxford University Press, 2014). To varying degrees, many women in my family experience what Tolin, Frost, and Steketee characterize as "difficulty," "distress," or "impairment" when faced with the prospect of getting rid of our things or ceasing to collect them. We can't easily downsize or stop shopping, even when we or the people around us wish we could. And the psychological patterns these experts list in the sections on "Hoarding in Your Thoughts" and "Hoarding in Your Emotions" sound suspiciously like our habitual modes of magical thinking about objects:

"**Overly Creative Thinking**" ("When a person who hoards holds an item in his or her hands, all kinds of wonderful ideas and opportunities come to mind");

"**Sentimental Attachment**" ("For some people, these items serve as a tangible record of their lives; throwing them away feels like losing that part of their lives");

"**Feelings of Identity**" ("the items give them a sense of self, as they are defined by what they own");

"**Feelings of Safety, Security, and Control**" ("We have met people who described their possessions as a 'nest' or 'cocoon' that makes them feel protected from what they perceive to be a dangerous world");

and "**Positive Feelings**" ("many people with hoarding experience strong positive feelings—excitement, joy, wonder, pleasure—when they see new things they'd like to acquire or find things they had forgotten about").

Sometimes our thoughts verge on animism. We believe that we have an ethical responsibility to our own or others' objects that involves rescue, restoration, and ongoing care. We believe that objects have a kind of life.

As a product of my material-girl upbringing, and as a citizen of the shopping-and-decluttering-and-hoarding-obsessed modern USA, I gravitate to hoarding and organizing self-help lit, and read it with alternating flashes of recognition and resistance. When I encounter psychological definitions of hoarders, I can't help but feel that these are my people. I experience the ambivalent comfort of being known and named (even if that name is also a stigmatized medical diagnosis), and I crave the contradictory consolation of the psychologists' contrasting premises that hoarding is a neurological quirk (possibly built into our genes) as well as a set of behaviors that can be modified (and thus potentially manageable, malleable, and under control). It's reassuring to feel like my eBay addiction connects me with my mother, aunts, and grandmother at the level of our DNA. It's also reassuring to think that we could train ourselves to steer clear of yard sales and reinvent ourselves as sleek, uncluttered midcentury modernists if we ever wanted to.

But as tempting as it is in some ways to accept the most up-to-date psychological story about hoarding disorder, I know that it will never fully work for me. The problem is that it pathologizes an entire deep-rooted orientation toward the material world, an orientation that constitutes my lifelong experiences of creativity, attachment, identity, safety, and joy, as well as every other feeling. And it defines recovery from hoarding disorder not as order or tidiness but as the process of learning to demystify and disenchant one's relationship to material things and to disentangle things from emotions. ("Decluttering your home will be part of the program, but changing the way you relate to possessions is what will make this approach successful.") This kind of disenchantment seems to me both unrealistic and undesirable. As a result, the workbook section of *Buried in Treasures* brings out the surly and recalcitrant teenager in me:

Are you keeping it for sentimental reasons? If so, does it truly make you happy to have it? *If my criterion for whether to do something was whether it truly made me happy, I wouldn't do anything except take bubble baths. Next!*

Are you keeping it as a way of remembering good times or a special person? If so, is keeping it the best way to remember? *Yes I am, and yes it is. I know you want me to prefer a pixelated photo that takes up no space, but pixels can't hold me close like a rough wool sweater, or spur me to work like a pen between my fingers.*

Do you keep this for emotional comfort or to make you feel less vulnerable? If so, does it really protect you? *We live in a world of nuclear weapons and mass shootings and environmental toxins. Nothing really protects us. Not guard dogs, not armies, not the love of a good man. But since you ask, arranging these small items on my desk before I write does indeed make me feel less vulnerable. Charles Dickens couldn't write without a tiny*

china monkey on his desk, and if OCD desk charms were good
enough for Dickens, they're good enough for me.

If psychologists seem overly optimistic about the prospect
of rewiring hoarders' emotional orientations, organizers often
seem to presume that their readers have a fairly unfraught
relationship with their possessions in the first place. I remember
being horrified as a kid by the bossy, no-nonsense organizing
books that my intermittently overwhelmed mother checked
out of our local library. The books had militant titles like
Clutter's Last Stand, and they recommended that every house-
hold furnishing be chosen solely based on how easy it was
to clean. (Wall-to-wall carpet: always! Chandeliers: never!)
This kind of thinking was clearly never going to fly with us,
given that our house was lit with dusty sconces and chandeliers lovingly salvaged from my mother's childhood home.
One time a traveling salesman came to our door and demonstrated the effectiveness of his cleaning products by scrubbing the patina off the old brass doorknocker without asking
for permission. My mother mourned the lost tarnish for
months.

Even Marie Kondo, the world-famous organizing expert
who unapologetically uses the language of magic to talk about
possessions, expects her readers to have a mostly disenchanted,
emotionally disengaged relationship to most objects. In *The
Life-Changing Magic of Tidying Up*, Kondo tells us to hold each
item we possess and ask: Does this spark joy? If it doesn't, we
need to let it go. When Kondo asks herself this question, she
ends up living in a spare and stark minimalist paradise, and

she assumes that we, like her, will experience more fizzle than spark.

But what if you had an attic and basement and garage and storage unit full of objects, and they all sparked joy? What if they all lit you up like the northern lights? Would you really want the joy to stop?

~

Maybe because I'm not really in search of a cure, my favorite books about hoarding are not written by organizers or psychologists. I especially love Scott Herring's *The Hoarders: Material Deviance in Modern American Culture* and the classic canon of hoarders he describes: the Collyer Brothers of Harlem; the Big and Little Edies of *Grey Gardens*; Andy Warhol. Herring writes about hoarders with empathy and humor, but he is as interested in the popular discourse about hoarding as he is in hoarders themselves. He is troubled by the recent attempts to diagnose hoarding as a disease and to track its neural traces in brain scans. Instead, he sees hoarders as a social phenomenon, arguing that they fill a role in our culture similar to witches in old Salem: They are scary "folk devils" onto whom others project their fears.

Herring wants to understand hoarding from the outside as a form of mass panic. I want to understand hoarding from the inside as a logic of love. I am fascinated by the way hoarding allows human relationships to be mediated and commemorated through objects, and the way it allows for the maintenance of lost and supplemental and prosthetic selves. I am moved by the ways that hoarding can accommodate and deny the inevitability of decay. Above all, I see hoarding as a way to accept loss by denying it: to hold on and let go at the same time.

So much of my favorite writing could be characterized as hoarding literature, not necessarily because it depends on depictions of *DSM*-certified hoarding (often it doesn't), but because it stages precise verbal reenactments of hoarding's logic: the compulsive reliance on seemingly random collections of ordinary objects as a primary way of making meaning in the world.

The first and best hoarding novelist was Dickens, who crammed his big books with all the details they could hold, and created an unparalleled hoarder portrait in Miss Havisham of *Great Expectations*, who keeps every object as it was at the hour she was jilted. She has worn her wedding dress ever since, and her room is preserved like a messy mummy's tomb. Thanks to her stopped clocks and raveling yellowing silk, she is forever remembering her hour of loss, and forever getting ready for her day of love. Miss Havisham is one in a long line of women who use the logic of hoarding to try to make sense of the past.

By all accounts Joan Didion's homes are immaculate, but she writes like a hoarder. Her grief memoir *The Year of Magical Thinking* famously describes her enchanted relationship to her lost husband's possessions, which she cannot bear to give away, but by the time she wrote it she had already been writing about hoarding logic for over half a century. Her classic essay "On Keeping a Notebook" is a reflection on her lifelong habit of collecting cryptic scraps of words and phrases, a practice she doesn't fully understand yet can't do without. In "On Going Home," an account of a visit to her parents' house, she deals with a bout of emotional disorientation as any hoarder would, by exploring a drawer:

> Paralyzed by the neurotic lassitude engendered by meeting one's past at every turn, around every corner, inside every cupboard, I go aimlessly from room to room. I decide to meet it head-on and clear out a drawer, and I spread the contents on the bed. A bathing suit I wore the summer I was seventeen. A letter of rejection from *The Nation*, an aerial photograph of the site for a shopping center my father did not build in 1954. Three teacups hand-painted with cabbage roses and signed "E.M.," my grandmother's initials. There is no final solution for letters of rejection from *The Nation* and teacups hand-painted in 1900. Nor is there any answer to snapshots of one's grandfather as a young man on skis, surveying around Donner Pass in the year 1910. I smooth out the snapshot and look into his face, and do and do not see my own. I close the drawer, and have another cup of coffee with my mother. We get along very well, veterans of a guerilla war we never understood.

Amid the unquiet ghosts of global and local history (the Holocaust darkness of the "final solution"; the cannibalistic aftertaste of Donner Pass), Didion evokes a family history of building and publishing left undone; of a bathing-suit body that is no longer seventeen; of the brittleness of the teacups, odd-numbered, implying that one or more has already broken. Didion is at a loss, but the drawer's small hoard enables her to face her family and her past head-on, as a question that can't be answered and a problem that can't be solved. Her tactile encounter with the photographed face that both is and is not her own (her smoothing of the snapshot is almost self-care) is an uncanny self-confrontation that allows her to eventually return to the world.

The drawer, we presume, remains uncleared at the end of the paragraph. The items are either back inside it, or still spread out across the bed. But they have served their purpose as a prompt to connection and creativity. In the immediate moment, Didion's time with the hoard propels her toward her mother and their shared coffee and incomprehension. Later, this same hoard is presumably part of what prompts her to write "On Going Home."

For Marilynne Robinson, the logic of hoarding provides not just an encounter with the past but a way of imagining a future. My favorite hoarding novel is *Housekeeping*, in which Ruth and Lucille, bereft sisters who have lost their mother to suicide and their grandmother to old age, open a different hoarder's drawer and reflect on the things that are left:

My grandmother had kept, in the bottom drawer of the chest of drawers, a collection of things, memorabilia, balls of twine, Christmas candles, and odd socks. Lucille and I used to delve in this drawer. Its contents were so randomly assorted, yet so neatly arranged, that we felt some large significance might be behind the collection as a whole. We noted that the socks, for example, all appeared unworn. There was a shot glass with two brass buttons in it, and that seemed proper. There was a faded wax angel that smelled of bayberry, and a black velvet pincushion in the shape of a heart, in a box with a San Francisco jeweler's name on it. There was a shoebox full of old photos, each with four patches of black, felty paper on the back. These had clearly been taken from a photograph album, because they were especially significant or because they were not especially significant.

Like Didion, Ruth and Lucille are looking for clues to their family's past, and above all to their mother's drowning in the depths of the lake, but unlike Didion they find a kind of resolution. In the shoebox Ruth discovers a religious brochure imprinted "I will make you fishers of men," and this reassuring verse prompts her to imagine a heavenly net that will dredge every lost person and thing from the depths, each one present, gathered, redeemed, restored: "There would be a general reclaiming of fallen buttons and misplaced spectacles, of neighbors and kin, till time and error and accident were undone, and the world became comprehensible and whole." The very randomness of fragments seems to call forth a satisfying answer, a "general rescue": for "What are all these fragments for, if not to be knit up finally?" This is the logic of hoarding as religious resurrection. Consoling narratives must be constructed from the shards of loss.

Writing like Dickens's, Didion's, and Robinson's blurs the distinction between loving people and loving things—between dresses and lovers, photographs and grandfathers, misplaced spectacles and lost mothers. It also draws a close connection between hoarding and narrative. I remember how my mother used to fill up our car every year with $5 brown paper grocery bags full of books from the library book sale: Somehow, through those sacks of stories, she was trying to give us a future. Meanwhile my cousin Ariel, a songwriter and singer, once wrote to me about her mother, my aunt:

> I have daydreams in which I rent a school gymnasium and empty out her house. Have all like objects placed with one another and then she can walk down the neat rows and reacquire what she wants . . . I'm rambling about clutter because we share a family of "collectors" so you know what I mean but perhaps I'm mostly blabbing on because I'm anxious about lyric writing and the impending recording that is coming in a month's time . . . As I write this I see my mother's object clutter mirrored in my creative messy attic. It's a revelation.

Like my cousin, I think about writing and hoarding together. To make an essay or a song, so much must be serendipitously discovered and rediscovered and collected and stored. First there is the long, meandering, seemingly random work of gathering, and then there is the moment of critical mass, followed by the laborious grouping of like with like, and the time-consuming selection and arrangement of each arbitrarily precious mental object. So much of the work of writing is saying to oneself: Here I am, holding this mysterious or familiar thing. It is either especially significant or not especially significant. Why did I pick it up in the first place? And what should I do with it now?

Like hoarding, writing is a compulsion and a burden, but it's also an archive, a hope chest, an endless reserve.

∾

These days I try to channel most of my hoarding impulses into writing, not housekeeping, but I can't help but experience the world with a hoarder's mind and memory. I can narrate the provenance of every item I own, and I feel emotionally responsible for inanimate objects. I walk by an old house being remodeled and, seeing century-old windows propped against a dumpster, poignant in their drafty inefficiency, want to gather them into my arms. But I don't. I know how hard it can be to love things too much.

Still, I want to hold on to almost everything. "You have a hard time letting go," my therapist told me, and it is universally true. I never get over exes; I'm unwisely tempted to revive dead friendships; I like to imagine that one day I will mend all the moth holes, and find a cobbler who will resole all my broken-in boots. Even my body hoards. I am incapable of making myself throw up; I can't even purge when I've had a bad oyster.

I mostly manage to keep chaos at bay. My apartment is nearly always company-ready, and though my bedroom's tidiness ebbs and flows with my moods, there is a place for everything, and everything is often in its place.

There have been only two years when my living space swirled into unremitting chaos. One of them was my first year in

New Haven, when I was so homesick for the life I'd left behind in New Jersey that I never bothered to finish unpacking. The other was the following year: the year I lived with Cathy.

≈

For most of a decade afterward, Cathy and I never spoke about that year. We might occasionally venture a cautious and partial reminiscence (Do you remember how Miriam always used to help me make coffee in the morning? Do you remember the time all your sisters came over for an impromptu slumber party?), but then we would quickly back away, retreating toward the extensive common ground of all the other years we'd shared.

In the aftermath, immediate and otherwise, we continued to be close, writing together, working together, sharing holidays and hopes and meals and jokes, still friends for a lifetime, friends without end. Our bond was stronger for having survived the kiln-hot crucible of cohabitation.

But every so often, in the private vaults of our hearts, we would return to our memories of that year with relentless resentment. We would gather and cling to implacable grudges; we would stockpile unspeakable accusations; we would silently sift through old bitterness and hurt. And we would always arrive at opposite answers to the year's burning questions:

Who was the injured one? Who was the crazy one? Who was the one who deprived the other of a home?

≈

Like many roommate stories and more than a few hoarder stories, ours was a kind of gothicomedy, with the comic aspects much easier to see in retrospect.

If I were telling the story, I suppose I would start with the onion, because it was the onion that led to the streaked mascara, and the streaked mascara was the fateful fact my friend Ash describes as "the one small thing that's out of control that indicates disaster to someone else."

It was an early evening in September. I'd moved into Cathy's house that summer, and I was making ratatouille and feeling fine: somewhat stressed, as always, about love and work, but otherwise OK. At some point in the process I cut up an onion, and it made me stream tears, and my mascara melted down my face. Cathy came in, took one look at my melted mascara, and (as I later learned) felt a surge of panic. She assumed I was having an emotional breakdown in her kitchen, complete with wild, unblotted rivers of tears. Cathy and her family don't do public emotional breakdowns (or at least they didn't before her dramatic second daughter, Ruthie, was born).

What she thought was: I can't live with someone like this. I've made a terrible mistake.

What she said was: "Your mascara's kind of runny. You might want to fix it before you go out."

I said, "Oh, thanks," and thought nothing of it. I assumed she knew that my mascara was runny because of the onion. But for months afterward she seemed distant, guarded, polite, remote, as if she had been body-snatched by a stranger, and I didn't know why.

Then there are the other stories I have hoarded. How her husband once slept in my bed without asking while I was out of town. (He'd been temporarily displaced by the squirmy toddler who'd climbed into their bed.) It didn't occur to him that I would mind, and I tried not to—I knew he was just exhausted and looking for the nearest place to crash—but afterward I couldn't help feeling like the room was permeable, and provisional, and not really mine. How I came to the unnerving realization that conversation inside the room was audible to people outside it, so from then on I always went outside to talk on the phone, which was a fairly bleak experience during the half of the year that Connecticut was below freezing. How the house was kept at a temperature that would have been perfectly comfortable if I'd been sharing my bed with a husband and a toddler, but, as it was, I was too cold to sleep.

I felt like I had no privacy, and I was uneasily aware that this meant they were probably feeling the lack of privacy on their side of the bedroom wall as well. I began to experience myself as I imagined they experienced me: at best, as a potential noise nuisance; at worst, as the parasite who was preventing them from having a normal private married life.

Meanwhile I was working twelve-to-fourteen-hour days, seven days a week. I had to keep rising to the occasion for students, for teachers, for editors, for congregants, and presumably for God.

Something had to give, and what gave was the room. Partly because I had no time to clean it, and spent barely any time in it. Partly because it didn't feel like it was actually mine in any of the ways I needed it to be. And partly because in my heart I was a hoarder, and so the consolations of hoarding were available to me.

The room became a vortex of chaos. The bed was never made. The floor was covered in deep drifts of clothes, books, and papers. There was no way to walk between distinct heaps of things; instead there was one large billowing heap that stretched from wall to wall, and one could only tramp over it or wade through it. I kept what I needed for teaching close to the bed, but everything else drifted and disappeared: library books, old love letters, a much-missed check from the IRS. The wooden chair I used as a bedside table got mired in the detritus, anchored in place by the clothes tangled around its legs like seaweed.

I took a weird pleasure in the room's untamed wildness. Since my previous dwellings had generally been ordered and beautiful even when they were crammed to the gills, the unremitting chaos of this room served as a necessary dissociation from my former life: a way to partially detach myself from what would otherwise have been too hard to bear, which was that I had nothing much to show for my adult life but friendships, and now even they seemed to be slipping away.

My moat of objects gave me a measure of protection. I was living inside a Didion drawer, or at the bottom of a lake. One day I might be dredged from the depths in a net of salvation, but in the meantime I reveled in the consolations of squalor. I felt like I could continue to keep it together, but only as long as my aggressively messy room reassured me of what I needed to believe:

This is and is not my home.

This is and is not my family.

This is and is not my life.

Every once in a while, I asked Cathy how everything was going from her perspective roommate-wise, and she said everything was fine. Because what could she say? It's not fine, I've made a terrible mistake, I can't do this, you're evicted?

Cathy had said yes to my request to be housemates in the hopes that our life together would involve pleasant family dinners and fun times with Miriam and maybe some dreamy conversations reminiscent of our honeymoon era. Instead I came home from work late at night when she was wrung out from a long day of teaching and parenting and had nothing left to give. My attempts to talk to her felt like an imposition; my retreats to my room seemed like sullenness.

She was always already anxious, and my presence that year added unbearable new worries to her hoard. It was hard enough worrying about her job, about her husband's job search, about how Miriam was doing in daycare, about whether she should have another baby. Now she had to worry about whether her best friend was having a full-on nervous breakdown under her roof. She'd gotten me my teaching assistant job in her department, so when I complained melodramatically that I didn't know how I was ever going to manage to read a thousand pages of *Bleak House* before class, she worried that I was going to fail as a teacher and drag her down with me. And my deepening debt and precarious financial future sent her into an anxious tailspin.

Above all, there was my room, a locus of horror. Its chronic chaos was not only irrefutable proof of my mental instability, it felt like a daily act of aggression toward her and her family. She had generously opened her home to me when I was in need, and instead of being grateful, I had trashed it. Cathy had visited my apartments before, and she knew I was capable of creating pleasant spaces. Why was I inflicting domestic bedlam on her? My infuriating insistence that I was OK and my room was OK, in willful defiance of the evidence, had to be either delusion or gaslighting—yet more proof of my insanity, my hostility, or both. (Denial is, in fact, one of the *DSM* symptoms of hoarding.)

Things came to a head in November when I told Cathy I was really ready for Thanksgiving break and she cautiously ventured, "Yes, I can tell you're kind of falling apart." I was shocked and hurt by her diagnosis: I felt like I was doing a heroic job of keeping it together. She brought up my kitchen-crying, and I explained about the onion. But the onion didn't reassure her: Even if I hadn't in fact been reduced to crying in public, my room remained damning evidence that I was a mess. But my room was far too fraught for us to discuss. Meanwhile I knew that no matter what Cathy said or thought, I simply could not afford to break down or to fall apart, or even to entertain the possibility of doing either of those things. Cathy's take on my life felt like a dark prophecy I needed to flee. After that conversation I knew I needed to move out of her house as soon as I could, but it took me until March to find a place I could afford.

That whole terrible year, Cathy felt like she had sacrificed her pleasant family life and her own peace of mind for the sake of our friendship, and it was all in vain. My room was a mess, the attic was a mess, I was a mess, and I resented her. Her generosity was utterly wasted on me, and her sacrifice was unappreciated.

Hoarders are very hard to love.

≈

That same November I got a student ticket to the Yale Rep to see *A Delicate Balance* by Edward Albee. It turned out to be about a couple who show up unannounced at their best friends' house and then refuse to leave. The couple claims they can't go home because they are in flight from existential dread. Their poor hosts come to view them as oppressive parasites, and eventually all the roommates are pushed to the brink of hysteria. The play explicitly dramatizes the limits of friend-ship, with the characters arguing about whether friendship is based on responsibilities and rights or on affection and love. Do the terrible uninvited guests have a *right* to make such an extreme demand on their long-suffering friends? Perhaps they do. But their presence is still appalling and unendurable. In the end, the parasites finally leave.

In an attempt to bridge our chasm with humor, I came home and told Cathy, "OMG Edward Albee wrote a play for us!" and summarized the plot, hoping we could somehow laugh about it together. She didn't think it was funny. To be fair, it wasn't. Not then. And not for a long time.

≈

It took us six years to finally acknowledge the lingering horror of that year. It happened because I posted a version of the onion story on Facebook, mentioning no names (the onion story remains one of my favorite friendship stories), and instantly all of Cathy's suppressed resentment came roaring back and burst the dam. Soon afterward, after our eons and epochs of silence on the subject, we found ourselves weeping openly together at a coffee shop, discussing all the old stock-piled feelings that had been taboo for so long: How much it hurt her to open her home and turn her life upside down in an effort to help me, and then to have me reject her help as oppressive. How much it hurt me to know that my closest friend thought I was failing at life, when I was doing my absolute damnedest not to. How painful it was for her to feel that simply by having a job and a family and a home, she symbolized everything I didn't have. How frustrated I was that even though we were both totally neurotic, she got to be the sane one, while I had to be the crazy one. Also: If she really cared about me and she thought I was weeping disconsolately into the ratatouille, why didn't she ask me if I was OK? Also: If I really cared about her and she was being driven batty by my clutter, why didn't I fucking clean my room?

Fifteen years after we'd met, there we were: two almost-forty-year-old women holding hands and crying in public.

After our cathartic conversation Cathy sent me an email reflecting on why our year as roommates was probably always destined to be doomed:

I am someone who copes with what feel like unmanage-able ambient anxieties with obsessive forms of tidiness. I'm a mediocre housekeeper at best when it comes to things like scrubbing toilets and dusting baseboards, but I sublimate my stress every morning by making the beds and vacuuming the toast crumbs off the dining room rug, and I get what feels like a drug-induced dopamine rush from replacing the wilted flowers on the dining room table with fresh ones from the yard. (You are not the only person who has suffered from this tendency: One of the central recurring tensions in my relationship with Miriam and Ruthie is that they regard a living room completely covered with bits and pieces of Playmobil as a haven for the weary, a spur to creativity, and a banquet for the senses; I find that it saps my will to live.) So our metaphors of home/security were probably on a collision course from the start: The consoling heaps of stuff that were the props of your emotional existence I experienced as looming threats to my teetering stability. (Do you think a propensity for self-dramatization is another one of the ties that bind us? Hmmm.)

Perhaps we were never meant to be roommates. But now, all these years later, I can finally afford to acknowledge what I couldn't admit to myself or Cathy at the time, which is that of course I needed saving, and of course she helped to save me. That was the year I preached my first sermon, and the year I got my first full-time job with a salary and benefits, a job that I loved. I started that year as Cathy's charity case, but I ended it as her colleague. Maybe I was breaking down, but I also broke through. Meanwhile Cathy decided to get pregnant again that fall partly because I brought home a tiny handmade blue jumper from a thrift store and gave it to her for her hypothetical second child. For some reason it was the catalyst she'd been waiting for. The following June, a few months after I fled the house, I came back to stay with Miriam while her little sister was being born. We were all truly and unequivocally family again, taking care of each other with joy.

In the end I never fully moved out of Cathy's house; I just moved away. In addition to leaving behind a reasonably tidy stack of stuff in the corner of her garage, I left a row of decorative enamel chinoiserie tins in the upstairs bathroom; a dozen brightly colored teacups hanging on the kitchen wall; and two old floral lithographs on the walls of the bedroom, along with an antique lamp. Cathy says she likes living with these remnants, the fragments salvaged from our year together. I think she means it.

≈

One night a couple summers ago, when I was in Tacoma visiting my parents and sisters, I got a call from the police. My storage unit was one of several that had been broken into, and they had confiscated some suspected stolen items from the thieves. Could I come down and identify my stuff?

The timing was uncanny. I'm almost always thousands of miles away, and that was the one time that year I happened to be close. It was also uncanny because my parents had just joked earlier that week that I didn't have to worry about anyone stealing my stuff, since it had sentimental value but no resale value.

I drove down to the deserted storage facility with my mom and we sat quietly in the car in the dark for a while, waiting for the police to arrive. When they finally did, they led us to the thieves' storage unit, and I saw, amid sinister objects like strangers' busted-open gun cases, the old trunk containing Checkers. The police released him into my custody right away. John Garfield, on the other hand, was entered into evidence. Later, during the criminal trial, when I was subpoenaed by the state of Washington and flown across the country to testify, I had to identify a photograph of the John Garfield shrine, and swear under oath that he was mine.

In her book *The Victorian Novel of Adulthood*, my friend Rebecca Rainof writes about George Eliot's novel *Silas Marner*, the story of a hoarder. Silas is a reclusive miser who suffered "cataclysmic disappointments" in his youth, including being jilted like Miss Havisham, and then spent sixteen years alone with a small hoard of gold. After his hoard is suddenly stolen, Silas rejoins the world, adopting a daughter and enjoying a long and meaningful life as a single parent. It would be easy to see his hoarding years as wasted time, but Rebecca argues that for Silas hoarding is "an activity that is at once stigmatized and yet, in its warped way, sustaining." She writes, "His sixteen years of miserhood may appear dehumanizing . . . but despite their bleakness, they allow for him to begin a new course of development: recuperation, configured as the literal work of pulling himself together."

When my Tacoma hoard was broken into I lost some things that I didn't get back, but I don't know what they are. I know they are gone because before the break-in the storage unit used to be full, and now it's not. I don't want to know what the lost things were, and I don't really need to know. I still don't ever want to let things go, but now I know that I can.

DEAR FLANNERY

written with Ashley Makar

I MET ASH at a party my very first month in New Haven. It was an awkward party, and I think we were both glad to find each other. We talked about writing, about how we'd ended up in divinity school, about making time for creativity in lives filled with other things. She was smart and hilarious, with a yoga mat slung across her back like a quiver and a slight Alabama drawl. I've found my first New Haven friend, I remember thinking. But our friendship took a while to ignite. We crossed paths at a few more parties and got lunch together once or twice, but we were both busy, and it took us two years to start to really get to know each other. By that time she had been diagnosed with Stage IV esophageal cancer.

It was her writing that brought us back together. I had been reading and rereading her essays online and I couldn't get over how gorgeous they were. I invited her to visit the class I was teaching, and she talked with my students about empathy, about ethics, about faith and doubt and detailed description and her favorite copper beech tree. Afterward she invited me to come and write with her during her four-hour chemo infusions at the Yale Heath Center, and that is where our lives began to converge. We got to know each other by writing in each other's company.

Becoming Ash's friend meant getting used to her way of invoking Flannery O'Connor: intimately, often, and on a first-name basis. When I asked if Flannery was like a saint to her, Ash said, "Not exactly. It's more that there's a holy fire to her that I want in my life, and she's able to put that fire into words." The second summer of our friendship, Ash and I took a road trip to Georgia to visit Flannery's farm, Andalusia. We spent time with the peacocks and marveled at Flannery's typewriter and crutches, and then sat and wrote out on the verandah. That winter, when we found out Flannery's prayer journal was being posthumously published, we decided to write about it together. The journal was written in the form of letters to God, so we wrote letters as well: to God, to Flannery, and to each other.

∾

Dear Bri,

Your gift sits on my writing desk. An illuminated manuscript you've made of Flannery's voice, inscribing afflicted bodies with rising life. It's as if she's speaking from the grave:

For me it is the virgin birth, the Incarnation, the resurrection
which are the true laws of the flesh and the physical.
Death, decay, destruction
are the suspension of these laws.

I am always astonished
at the emphasis the Church
puts on the body.
It is not the soul she says
that will rise
but the body, glorified.
—Flannery O'Connor, in a letter to Betty Hester, 1955

You've written me this, given me this, in a vintage sketch-book. I can almost see the shadow of your pen moving across the vellum-colored page: crossing *t*'s to loop into the shoe-lace tops of *h*'s, making *f*'s that look like infinity symbols standing upright, rounding out a cursive *s* in the shape of a bird's barreled chest.

The first period is like a tiny kite, no string. The second, a red dwarf becoming a star. The last, a little leaning cross. I didn't notice the shapes until I looked hard trying to describe the gift, trying to give the words all my attention. Now I see the *D* in *Death* like a treble clef, unraveling. I see *ASTON-ISHED* and *BODY* as an epitaph, magnifying. As if through a tear, brightly.

Simone Weil wrote that prayer is absolute, undivided attention. And that's what it takes to be a writer like Flannery, the kind of writers we want to be. I imagine prayerful writing to be a vigilant flame sustained and made into the words we need. But I keep looking away. I fail at writing every day. You and Flannery help me not to take myself too seriously. If I told you my self-loathing spiral of today you'd show me all the Christmas ornaments you polished while you were trying to write: the white globe with the red mallards, the iridescent rocking horse, the silver angel holding a candle. We'd laugh at that little blond angel face of forlorn piety. We'd light our own candle to try and write by.

In her prayer journal, Flannery tells God that it's at some insipid moment, when she's possibly thinking of floor wax or pigeon eggs, that the opening of a beautiful prayer may come and lead her to write something exalted. The prayer availing itself seems to be a gesture of the grace young Flannery is praying for. And her response to that action of grace is her work, her strain to give it undivided attention.

A pigeon egg hatches into a map of the universe, a peacock's tail. Another world unfurls. And yet, "How hard it is to keep any one intention, any one attitude toward a piece of work any one tone any one anything," she writes. "Dear God, I am so discouraged about my work." She's even discouraged about her prayer—how she's never been sorry for a sin because it hurt God. I bet Flannery's sins were pretty innocuous—"gluttony" for Scottish oatmeal cookies, "laziness" in writing and prayer. And yet she tried and worked so hard. She suffered much in her labors of fierce love.

I'd hate to believe my gluttony for Golden Grahams or all my tactics of distraction from writing and prayer hurt God. But I know they hurt me. They keep me from the life I want; they separate me from God. In that sense, they are sins. And Flannery is helping me take those sins seriously and honestly: "I am afraid of pain and I suppose that is what we have to have to get grace. Give me the courage to stand the pain to get the grace, Oh Lord. Help me with this life that seems so treacherous, so disappointing."

Life seemed so treacherous, so disappointing the day you gave me that illuminated Flannery manuscript. I'd fallen three times trying to walk on icy sidewalks. Blisters were forming on the bottoms of my feet—chemo catching up with me. I'd missed another writing deadline for no good reason. It pained me to look at the pink-orange sky because I failed to write it. I felt like an old lady, a hoarder holed up in a dim room looking through the blinds at the menace of daylight. But I didn't give in to her. I told you I was having a bad day.

You invited me over. You gave me that gift. You opened a window. Light shined on the table laid bare for writing, trying again.

Ash

∾

Dearest Ash,

I just read the whole prayer journal in the bath, in the facsimile version (checking confusing scribbles against the transcription from time to time). Flannery's young handwriting on wide-ruled pages seems so much closer than the printed and corrected text. In the quiet and warmth I somehow felt the aura of the archive; I knew the book was just a book, but it felt precious, and instinctively I clutched it tight so the historic manuscript wouldn't fall into the suds.

There's so much to tell you, but what I wanted to say first, almost to warn you, is that she prays for desire like a deadly cancer, desire as consuming and overwhelming as your cancer wants to be. She prays for suffering and for grace. Her friend who edited the book seems to see her lupus, which arrived a few years later, as an answer to prayer. I think about this young woman of appetites and ambition and I hate to think that God read her earnest scribbling and sent her death; but if you must suffer, it is of course better if the suffering helps your writing and your faith. I am using the generic second person here, but I mean you, dear Ash. I love you, and I leave this practical theology to you.

I don't know much about suffering, but I know about writing stress and night-eating and erotic thought. ("Today I have proved myself a glutton—for Scotch oatmeal cookies and erotic thought. There is nothing left to say of me": the most irresistibly quotable lines in the journal, and some of the best concluding lines in literature.) I'm almost fifteen years older than Flannery was then, and Lord knows I have filled up several shelves of blank books with similar confessions, though I prefer ice cream and erotic thought to oatmeal cookies.

Somewhere I have the old journals I wrote to God when I was Flannery's age. I was fighting through some of the same things she was, the conflict between self and faith, the battle for attentiveness and gratitude, the desires for experience, publication, grace, and God, though I lacked her genius and her Catholic clarity. It's not that these conflicting desires have gone away, it's just that I gave up on serious striving so long ago, and I am still not sure how to be ambitious without what Flannery calls "nervousness." I have made a truce with life that I don't want to trouble, and it's not clear to me where the urgency and tenacity would come from to write something good, even if I had the talent.

I rarely write private prayers to God anymore: I avoid unguarded introspection in general, the kind that is open to the future and full of desire.

Bri

~

Dear God,

Why am I such a dull lump? You give us leaven and salt and the moon shoaling blue, even as new daylight glades into morning. I want to wake early to write by that imperceptible changing of light when you can't tell if it's dark still or day yet. Sometimes you give me, on the cusp of waking from sleep, words, arranging themselves as if in the corners of the ceiling, lines fine and fragile as gossamer, the unseen seam between death and life. And I press snooze. Ten more minutes and ten more and so on, until those strands of You are lost to me. Next thing I know, I'm shuffling up to make coffee.

Lord, help me to sit here and tolerate this mangle of words. The belabored metaphors that mar the page, the lame turns of phrase I cross out and then try to salvage. Help me stand the pain to get the grace.

Help me sit here and work every day. I'll mess up most of the time and blunder, sometimes, back to the blue glow of daybreak.

Ash

~

Dear Bri,

Thank you! For naming how I want to pray—open and full of desire. If only my drive to write were as voracious as my cancer. And yet I don't want anything so consuming anymore. I worry I'm too scared and tired to strive like I used to.

Flannery was going on 22 when she wrote God from Iowa: "Oh Lord please make this dead desire living, living in life, living as it will probably have to live in suffering. I feel too mediocre now to suffer." I was around that age when I wrote this prayer from New York:

> to write You, Lord
> to write You
> to Write.

And here I am, thirteen years later, a cancer patient, terrified of writing. My body is slowly unraveling, and I can hardly sit still. I dart from thing to thing, like a squirrel, frantic to get all my living in before I get sick. Dividing and dividing my attention. What happened to my dire desire to write God?

"It is hard to want to suffer," young Flannery writes. "I presume Grace is necessary for the want. I am a mediocre of the spirit but there is hope. I am at least of the spirit and that means alive."

Three years later, her body started dying, on her train ride home for Christmas. Her friend W. A. Sessions writes that she left Connecticut a vibrant young woman and arrived in Georgia "drawn and bent, 'like an old man.'" She'd had her first flare of lupus on the train. I wonder what she prayed. (I bet it was about writing.)

Most days I don't know what to say to God. I don't want to suffer. I want the grace to stand the pain.

Ash

∼

Hello again dear Ash,

It's December now and you're here at my house for a day of writing and pumpkin chili in the glow of the Christmas lights. I love our writing days together. I love how almost every time I see you we light a candle and pray. When we're out together we even pray in restaurants, like a Norman Rockwell painting.

I found my old journals.

July 24, 2001

Writing is hard. Writing is different from more routine forms of work, writers tend to be more fluky and various in the ways they work . . . I am usually fairly miserable, very tense, quite caffeinated, tired (buzzing!), and late. Sometimes there are brief thrills or moments of satisfaction. Most of the time I am frustrated and scared and just want to read mysteries and eat comfort food, my idea of heaven.

July 31, 2001

There is a desire to escape work, to use God to let you off the hook, seeking for a guarantee of spiritual purity attainable by passivity, withdrawal, inaction. But God requires us to give, to serve, to think . . . he doesn't make it easier.

September 1, 2001

Re work, grad school apps—I can wholly apply myself to the present tasks, straining and rejoicing and exhausting myself. Remembering what the stakes are! No, professional life can't be separated from "real" life, it is a part of "real" life, but God's standards are different. He looks at the heart; and the state of a heart that is right with God is never inert. My heart rejoices to do God's will. Faith is necessary. All my instincts will be panic and self-preservation. I must resist them.

I panicked that day you fell on the ice. When you texted to tell me about your blistering feet, I let my tears take me over for an hour. I thought: There is nothing to be done. Then: Writing is what you do when there is nothing to be done.

In the absence of adequate words of my own, I found Flannery's, and I found comfort in the practice of writing as a physical act, as if the pressure of my pen against the paper could push away the forces of death and decay. As if the gold ink could become a healing balm.

Bri

∾

Dear Flannery,

You write, "I do not mean to deny the traditional prayers I have said all my life; but I have been saying them and not feeling them."

My own prayers have gotten more traditional since the days I wrote them out and I admit I mostly feel them less, but I mean them just as much. I am a believer in rationing feelings these days. I wonder if you rationed yours any in your thirties? As another famous Southern lady once said, "Honey, you know as well as I do that a single girl, a girl alone in the world, has got to keep a firm hold on her emotions or she'll be lost!"

As it happens, it was two days before September 11, 2001 when I wrote this urgent prayer: "Now I am immeasurably blessed. At any moment this could all be taken. I need to love you now so I can love you always. All the people who harm the body but cannot harm the soul: make them completely unable to harm." My prayer was not answered. I didn't expect it to be, but I didn't expect it to be so spectacularly ignored. Still, I have never stopped praying.

September 14, 2001

In lives, this is where Jesus lives in the world; my body can be part of his body. I'm not a naturally religious person but that doesn't matter. I'm taken into his body.

For a long time in the mornings I've lit a candle in the pewter holder that says "All shall be well and all shall be well and all manner of thing shall be well," and I name all the people and places that I want so much to be well. On my teaching days I pray for my students (ha!). On my writing days I hesitate to pray for my writing, because I worry it won't go well and I don't want my faith in prayer to dissipate, and my prayers for writing feel optional in a way that my prayers for other people and the world do not.

I pray with the red cloth-bound *Book of Common Prayer* my grandma Bette received when she was confirmed at age 32, in the midst of her losing battle with lethal mental illness. She was born within a year of Flannery, and she died at 35, five years before her. Sometimes I read the psalms of the day, and sometimes I skim for one that will say what is in my heart, looking at the Latin titles and guessing what they mean: *Hear me. Lean toward me. Judge me. Be merciful. God is light. Wonderment. Out of the depths. Rejoice.*

And I pray with the small dun *Prayer Book for Soldiers and Sailors* my grandpa got for Christmas in 1943, a battered book literally designed to be used in foxholes. It has prayers for help, for protection, for aid against perils, for world peace, for grace to forgive, for prisoners, for the lonely, for those who mourn, for the wounded, for the dying, for one departed.

In the evenings I light a candle in the pewter holder that says "At night I give my troubles to God. She's going to be up all night anyway." This summer Ash and I lit candles for you at your church in Milledgeville, in front of the brightly painted Virgin. I didn't write a prayer for you, or say one. I just let a prayer float up to you where you were sitting up all night with God, waiting for your body to rise and share forever in the glory of your soul.

Bri

≈

Dear Flan,

I'm on the train from New Haven to Boston. I feel as if I'm looking out the window into a snow globe. Except the snow isn't flakes, suspended in a circle of glass. It looks more like sand, storming side to side. I can all but feel the grains on my eyes.

I suppose with all these qualifiers snow globe isn't the right image for the view out my window. You would sit with it, suffer with it, until the words came. But I look away, take another sip of coffee, another bite of clementine. I watch the gulls scuttle up a rusty pole in the river—a remnant of a pier a storm tore up?

Even though I've divided my attention, another image is given. Light sears, silver vermillion, over the broken trees. A shock of radiation, bone lightning. Ezekiel raving God raising the dead.

A startle of sun blares white. I close one eye and see the stark circle it is. A center that holds. And yet a yolk I know could burst and seep like a bleed in the brain. Grandmother after the stroke—her body, half paralyzed. The little slanting cross. The sign of the body, glorified.

Ash

TENDING MY OVEN

Now a man is born to go a-lovin'
A woman's born to weep and fret
To stay at home and tend her oven
And drown her past regrets
In coffee and cigarettes . . .

— *PAUL FRANCIS WEBSTER*, "BLACK COFFEE"

THERE WAS A time when I couldn't stop listening to "Black Coffee," a rich and bitter torch song based on a melody by Mary Lou Williams, the First Lady of Piano, and sung down to the last drop by Ella Fitzgerald, Peggy Lee, Rosemary Clooney, and Sarah Vaughan. (In Vaughan's late live version she calls it "cawfee," in a Jersey-girl accent, and adds a little brandy to it.)

I like my torch songs like I like my men—with a penchant for wordplay and wry remarks—so I was primed to lean into lyrics like "moonin' all the mornin' and mournin' all the night" and "a man is born to go a-lovin', a woman's born to . . . tend her oven." For a long time the song was just a sardonic self-indulgent sulk, which is what I needed it to be—at least at first. It was #1 on my insomnia playlist. But after the hundredth listen, I started to think more about what it means to "tend your oven," beyond domestic drudgery. What do women do in between weeping and fretting to keep their pilot light lit? How do they generate their own warmth? This is a question about auto-eroticism, maybe. Certainly it is about baking.

There are many reasons to bake, and Nigella Lawson, a self-proclaimed domestic goddess, articulates some of the most primal. Baking, for her, is about "feeling good, wafting along in the warm, sweet-smelling air, unwinding, no longer being entirely an office creature." Nigella doesn't write or speak much about all the coldness and bitterness she's had to endure during her decades of baking: about losing her mother, her sister, and her first husband to cancer when they were young and their children were small, and then leaving her abusive second marriage in the wake of what she characterized in court as "intimate terrorism." But this undercurrent of loss and terror adds an urgency to her descriptions of oven warmth and "nutmeggy fumes," and gives weight to her claim that baking is "a way of reclaiming our lost Eden." Making something warm and sweet allows her to be warm and sweet in a world that so often isn't.

My Facebook friend Rhiana explains why this sense of baking as refuge is so sustaining to her:

Baking allows me to be my softest, most vulnerable self. My daily life requires so much armor and energy—just to get people to treat my black lady self with the respect and care I deserve. But deep down, I just want to show love and be loved and feel warm and safe. For me, baking is a physical manifestation of those feelings. When I bake, I get to put the soft, gooey parts of myself into the stuff I create and then give those things to other people.

For Rhiana, baking is a space of authenticity and generosity and much-needed relief. When she's communing with a cake-in-progress, she gets to lay down her armor for a while and revel in unguarded self-expression.

For some bakers, though, the relationship to their soft-and-sweet baking selves is more vexed. My friend Angharad is one of the most accomplished bakers I know—she infuses delicate petit fours with shades of lavender and Earl Grey, and makes frosting roses that really look like roses—and she sums up her entire ethical creed in terms of baking: "My aim in life is never to do anything so bad that it can't be fixed with baked goods. Some people might call that manipulative, but they'll change their minds when they taste my miniature coffee éclairs." Still, when I asked her how she felt about baking, she said,

> Honestly, I have So Many Feelings about baking, but the one that makes its presence most keenly felt—cutting through the sweetness, if you will—is guilt. Not just standard Calvinist self-indulgence why-are-you-spending-money-on-good-butter-when-you-could-give-it-to-those-who-need-it guilt, but also feminist guilt.

For Angharad, baking forces her to confront two incompatible visions of feminism:

In a world where traditionally feminine attributes (warmth, gentleness, hospitality, care for others, the beauty of the everyday) have been and continue to be undervalued, are you staking your claim that Every Way of Being Should Be Respected by providing room and nourishment for a way of being that is naturally femme to flourish (and implying, but never explicitly stating, that those who value you less on account of it can go and jump in the lake), or are you falling into the claws of restrictive gender norms and unconsciously enacting the politically/religiously conservative mode of womanhood that you are, in theory, in rebellion against?

Is tending your oven a way to fight the patriarchy, in other words, or is it a capitulation to it? Practically speaking, it's clear what side of the debate Angharad has come down on—she enthusiastically bakes for every occasion, and recommends rousing articles on why baking is a feminist act—but her guilt still remains.

Cathy's way of dealing with this quandary is to embrace the stigma and to practice what she calls "fierce baking." When she started her job at Yale, an older female mentor told her, "Whatever you do, don't bake for your students. You'll never be taken seriously." For Cathy, unapologetically bringing her students cookies is a way of resisting the system that says that brains matter and bodies don't; that men matter and women don't. It's a symbol of what she isn't willing to let go of in order to be taken seriously.

I love thinking about the politics of cupcakes, and my friends' feelings all resonate with me, to varying degrees. I am moved by their experiences of baking as a space of refuge, of ambivalence, of defiance. These are some of baking's most essential functions in a harsh and gendered world. For me, though, tending my oven often involves a somewhat different set of feelings: less sweet, guilty, or rebellious; more driven, fretful, and absorbed.

~

I first learned how to bake from my mom, who started me off as soon as I could reach the counter by standing on a chair, and taught me satisfying skills like leveling cups of flour to perfect smoothness with the back of a table knife and separating eggs by sliding the yolk back and forth from one half-shell to the other while the white glopped down into a bowl below.

My mom is an excellent baker, but unlike me she believes baking should be wholesome. Her bread was always perfect, but her cookies featured raisins and oats more often than I liked, and she taught me to halve the sweetener in every recipe and always mix white flour with whole wheat. (I still do this sometimes, but only if it tastes better that way—a hint of whole wheat is perfect in peach cake.) My own baking proclivities are closer to my great-grandmothers', one of whom liked to make scandalously excessive "dump cookies" full of marsh-mallows, coconut, chocolate, and butterscotch, and the other of whom had a recipe for blueberry muffins that consisted of adding blueberries to Bisquick. Their desserts were either deadly or lazy. During my youthful years of involuntary sugar rationing, I couldn't wait to grow up and make something similarly indefensible.

For my mom, baking is primarily about nourishing others, but for me, it is both more personal and more fraught. Though I first learned to bake from my mom, I learned how to bake *compulsively* from a friend I made in my twenties who taught me to obsess about cake, to bake into the night, to bake until you got it right, to bake when others might throw in the towel or take an Ambien. This friend was the kind of baker who would attempt ambitious multipage recipes and follow them to the letter, to the sixteenth of a teaspoon, to the exact degree of Fahrenheit; who would trawl multiple grocery stores for the right kind of caster sugar; who refused to settle for semi-sweet chocolate when what she needed was bittersweet. For her, baking was not necessarily about relaxing into her own deep authentic sweetness. Nor was it primarily about nourishing others, rebelliously or otherwise—she lived alone, and a proliferation of baked goods presented a new problem to be solved. Instead, baking seemed to be a way to channel her ever-present background-noise obsessiveness; to fill an empty house with blasts of heat and waves of aroma; to counter overwhelming longing with absurd excess, stacking the layers until they were too high to fit under the cake stand cover, until they threatened to lean perilously into nothingness like the tower of Pisa.

Baking is so addictive partly because of how prescriptive it is, and how precise: When your life is chaos, you need the strict structure of a recipe that must be followed more or less exactly. Unlike cooking, which often demands and rewards improvisation, baking is an obsessive's friend. But baking is also addictive because it's magic: You slide something shapeless and inedible into the oven, and an hour later out comes something soaring and fragrant that belongs in your mouth. For my friend, the alchemy of baking was not just turning flour and sugar into cake, but turning anxiety into cake; turning loneliness into cake; turning thwarted necessity into cake. At her house we ate Seven-Layer Insomnia Cake with Bitterness Buttercream Frosting. It was delicious.

It was around this time that I began to experience baking as something that I couldn't do without; that I couldn't seem to stop.

∼

For the past many years I've baked the same things over and over, to keep the world turning steadily and the stars moving across the sky. I bake from scratch, like a real baker, but like an amateur I make the same simple things over and over. Fall and winter are *Joy of Cooking* gingerbread, but with twice the spices and a handful of crystallized ginger—sometimes served with homemade applesauce and homemade sticky toffee sauce and homemade molasses whipped cream. For Thanksgiving I make apple cake in a Bundt pan from my friend Rebecca. For Christmas I make a tiny chocolate cake village for my goddaughter—small brown houses and a little brown church on a white plate sprinkled with sifted powdered-sugar snow. She and her sister like to make the snow fall. I use the same recipe to make my students cupcakes at the end of every semester. The cupcakes happen to be vegan, which they like, though they have the option to ruin the vegan-ness with the peanut butter cream cheese frosting I provide on the side. On Galentine's Day I make tomato soup cake with a can of Campbell's using Sylvia Plath's recipe. Spring and summer are shortcake—strawberry or bumbleberry (which just means a combination of three or more berries), or fruit torte made with whatever fruit came in the CSA.

And that is it. I suppose I could try a new recipe, but I rarely do. I don't seek out new adventures. I crave repetition, the chance to zone out and rely on muscle memory, the escape from my thoughts, the blurring of time. It's not unusual for me to bake late at night, or at dawn. It's not unusual for me to triple the recipe and cover every counter with cake, and then get anxious and bake some more. After a long night of baking I rest my hand on the neck of my hot red KitchenAid like a jockey caressing a horse after a race.

Baking is a habit of care, a kind of self-tending that shows the limits of solitude. I do it for myself, but I need others to consume it.

For years I lived with roommates who were unsatisfying from a baker's perspective. One of them was a rower who was supposedly strictly paleo and never bought himself honey or sugar; though once in the morning I discovered that he'd clawed handfuls out of a pristine cake in the middle of the night, unable to deny his hunger for sweetness. Another roommate was a runner who measured out her quinoa carefully, never cheating. When I'd offer her cake she would silently, soberly shake her head. When I finally got roommates who happily ate the cake I offered and eagerly asked for more, I was almost scared by how euphoric it made me.

Sometimes baking seems like the only available expression of love. In times of uncertainty, I have sometimes turned to baking as a code for conveying care safely without the dangerous ambiguity of words. For a while, when some friends and I seemed mired in a mutual misunderstanding that was partly of my making, I kept baking them shortcake as a way to express what I couldn't figure out how to say any other way: that I meant well, and wished them well, and wanted their lives to be sweet. Communicating in carbohydrates was a way to demonstrate affection without risking further hurt. I hoped that berry-drenched biscuits could tide us over until a space for words returned, and I think perhaps they did.

During the tempestuous fall when Yale students were protesting racism in crowds across campus and I didn't know what to do or say, I baked for them. When editors asked me to opine in print, I told them to ask the students instead, and mixed up another batch of chocolate batter. I baked because I didn't see a way for me to pronounce in public on the students' behalf without co-opting or self-aggrandizing or turning their protest into a personal byline, but I wanted them to know that they had their teachers' support. The more that clickbait articles accused student protesters of being "coddled" and "snowflakes" because they dared to demand justice and respect, the more I felt compelled to coddle them with cupcakes. I made dozen after dozen to fuel their March of Resilience.

Later, when the storm of protest had passed, I invited students over and we baked together.

March of Resilience Cupcakes

This simple vegan chocolate cake supposedly dates back to World War II and the days of rationing. In her 1960 culinary classic *The I Hate to Cook Book*, Peg Bracken calls her version "Cockeyed Cake." It is also known as Wacky Cake and Crazy Cake. I got the recipe from Cathy years ago, and by leaving out some or all of the cocoa and adding other flavors I have turned it into mocha cake, red velvet cake, funfetti cake, and pink lemonade cake. It is fast and almost effortless, and you can make it even when you've run out of eggs.

In a big bowl, mix:

3 cups flour

2 cups sugar

1 cup cocoa (feel free to substitute other flavorings)

2 teaspoons baking soda

1 teaspoon salt

In a smaller bowl, mix:

2 cups water (or leftover coffee for a more complicated flavor)

⅔ cup oil

2 tablespoons vinegar

2 teaspoons vanilla

Pour the wet ingredients into the dry and stir it all together. The batter tastes like chocolate pudding, and since there are no raw eggs it's safe to lick the spoon. There is enough for two dozen cupcakes or two layers of a layer cake. Bake at 350 degrees, about 15 to 25 minutes for cupcakes and longer for cake. You'll know it's done when you stick a fork in it and it comes out clean.

For the frosting:
1 stick butter
8 ounces cream cheese (i.e., one whole silver-foil rectangle of Philly)
1 teaspoon vanilla
peanut butter to taste (optional)
3 cups powdered sugar

Beat the butter and cream cheese together for several minutes till creamy (a hot red KitchenAid is quite useful for this). Add the vanilla and peanut butter. Then sift in the powdered sugar a bit at a time. Wait for the cupcakes to cool before frosting them.

Love Is Hard but Shortcake Is Easy

There is a hard way to make shortcake that involves painstakingly cutting small pea-sized pieces of chilled butter into triple-sifted flour, rolling out the dough until it is perfectly smooth and even, and cutting out each piece of shortcake with a biscuit cutter or an upside down glass tumbler. This is not that way. This is the easy way.

Begin by washing the fruit you're using, slicing it if necessary, sprinkling it with brown sugar to coax out the juices, and putting it in the fridge in a covered bowl.

My favorite flavor combinations are strawberry and blackberry or peach and blueberry. You will also need cream. Whipped cream in a can is a magical food. If you make homemade whipped cream, drizzle a little molasses into it.

In a big bowl, mix:
4 cups flour
4 teaspoons baking powder
½ teaspoon baking soda
½ cup sugar (leave out the sugar if you want delicious drop biscuits)
1½ teaspoons salt
between 3 and 4 cups heavy cream (enough that the dough is malleable but not impossibly sticky)

It's thick dough, so you will end up mixing it with your hands. Form it into sixteen shortcake-shaped lumps and drop them on cookie sheets and bake at 400 degrees till done to taste. (I start checking on them after about ten minutes.) Some of my friends like their shortcake medium-well and toasted on top; others like it rare and tender. I like to make one sheet of each.

YOUNG ADULT CANCER STORY

O N T H E M O N D A Y when *The Fault in Our Stars* was the #1 movie in America, I spent the morning at Smilow Cancer Hospital at Yale New Haven learning about the intricate physics of intersecting radiation beams and marveling at an animated scan of the inside of my friend Ash's body: a Rorschach image of irregular black-and-white shapes that each emerged and grew and shrank and vanished as we moved down from her shoulders through her healthy heart, spotted lungs, scarred gastro-esophageal junction, stabilized liver, and newly enlarged lymph node.

It was the lymph node's fault that Ash and I couldn't go see *The Fault in Our Stars* together that week as we'd planned. The node wasn't responding to treatment, which meant that Ash was headed to the city for a second opinion at Weill Cornell Medical College plus some quality time with her friend Ritu in Brooklyn.

Ritu and I, along with Ash's friends Annette and Sarah, had read *The Fault in Our Stars* that spring at Ash's insistence. During a rough bout of chemo when she could barely eat or drink, Ash read it ravenously, immersing herself in the story of Hazel Grace Lancaster, a teenager who has incurable Stage IV cancer, a hot boyfriend, and a distinctively wise and nerdy voice combining perceptiveness and snark. Afterward Ash bought extra copies to give away. "You have to read it!" she kept telling us.

Ash, Annette, Ri, and I once had a conversation about what makes writers different from other people. We concluded that nonwriters worry that writing about their lives will get in the way of actually experiencing their lives, whereas writers worry that if they don't write about something then they'll fail to fully live it. By this definition and many others, Ash is a born writer, and thousands of people have been moved by her ability to write about her cancer through images of lit-up leaves, sunsets streaked and broken like egg yolks, and the swift-moving shadows of birds in flight. Like Hazel's, Ash's illness has always been text as well as flesh; ever since her first chemo spring when she would write at the infusion center with the toxins flowing in and the words flowing out as she sat and scribbled by a sunny window that overlooked a graveyard.

Most of Ash's experiences with cancer can't be shared: Even when we are with her, her cells and side effects remain hers alone. But we try to share what we can, and so we've all been reading and watching *The Fault in Our Stars*. Ritu read it on her Kindle in New York while she was visiting another loved one with cancer and went to see the movie with her husband a few weeks later. Sarah listened to the audiobook at home in Minnesota while nursing her new son and then saw the movie with a friend. Annette eagerly borrowed my copy when she came to visit and afterward we saw the movie "virtually together": She went to an afternoon matinee in Illinois the same day I went to one in Connecticut.

Personally, I read *The Fault in Our Stars* the way its protagonist Hazel Grace Lancaster falls in love with Augustus Waters: slowly, and then all at once. I started out reading it a chapter at a time in between the papers I was grading, and then I gave up on grading and read straight through till dawn.

I have no idea how I would feel about *The Fault in Our Stars* if I were one of the millions of teenagers who filled the theaters for months and kept the book on the bestseller list for years and flooded the internet with *TFIOS* memes, fan-fiction, selfies, and hashtags. I also have no idea how I would feel about the story if I were actually sick. I only know what it's like to read it as a woman in my mid-thirties who is friends with a woman in her mid-thirties who, like Hazel Grace Lancaster, has incurable Stage IV cancer.

Lately there's been a debate about why adults read YA novels. It's impossible to generalize, but I suspect that we read them for many of the same reasons we read any other kind of literature: We are looking for new or familiar aesthetic experiences; for intellectual challenges, or escape, or equipment for living. And when we are reading fiction about an affliction that is rewriting the story of our own lives, we read both for the simple consolations of identification with the characters and for the more complicated consolations of a perspective on our experience that is not already ours.

For Ash and many of her friends, *The Fault in Our Stars* has served all these purposes and more. Though we are unalike and far apart, *TFIOS* has become a common text that connects us across the miles. As we've read it, we all have felt our own experiences with cancer being expressed, confirmed, challenged, and given back to us in different words.

For Ash, it has provided a cultural shorthand for explaining what she is dealing with—a situation that refuses to fit the common cancer tropes of combat or triumph. She is constantly asked unanswerable questions like "You're beating it, right?" or "When are you done with treatment?" Ash will never be done with treatment, and she does not experience her life as a battle. Now that *TFIOS* is everywhere, she can explain, "I have a diagnosis kind of like Hazel's." But beyond that, *TFIOS* dramatizes an urgent truth she wants the world to know: that people with this diagnosis can have stories that are not just the story of their disease, and that their most ardent adventures can happen while they are sick.

Annette is in med school, and one of the things that stood out to her was the careful specificity of the book when it talked about different cancer experiences, and its unsparing descriptions of how illness and death look and feel. This descriptive specificity prompts a deeply uncomfortable kind of empathy. I also felt a particular shock of vicarious recognition, a flicker of illness, whenever Hazel described parts of her body as having a recalcitrant and alien volition of their own: "My lungs were acting desperate, gasping, pulling me out of the bed trying to find a position that could get them air, and I was embarrassed by their desperation, disgusted that they wouldn't just let go." Sickness is feeling that your body is not you, but still feeling everything it feels.

Sarah, a public health professor who researches the relationship between the media and health policy, was especially impressed by the book's take on social media and mourning. She loved Hazel's critical response to the endless overwrought, elegiac posts on a dead boy's Facebook wall, especially her evisceration of the cliché "you'll live forever in our hearts." As Hazel explains, "That particularly galled me, because it implied the immortality of those left behind: You will live forever in my memory, because I will live forever!" The novel helps us see how the virtual immortality of social media can obscure the fact of death, just as a healthy person's illusion of immortality can become yet another barrier between the sick and the well, the living and the dead.

Ritu works at an education nonprofit where she spends a lot of time thinking about teenagers, and she was struck by the novel's moving portrayal of the deep mutual love and annoyance that exists between Hazel and her parents, who share an intimacy that constantly comes up against the limits of their ability to understand what it is like to have or not have metastatic cancer. Hazel is both exasperated and deeply comforted by her mom's unflagging attempts to make things better: "She never stopped trying, my mom." And Ritu was haunted by the novel's depiction of grieving, and the idea of a lost person as a co-rememberer: "The pleasure of remembering had been taken from me, because there was no longer anyone to remember with. It felt like losing your co-rememberer meant losing the memory itself, as if the things we'd done were less real and important than they had been hours before."

I'm a writing teacher, so I especially appreciated all the different ways the novel shows the power and futility of the written word in the face of sickness and death—not just through the book-within-the-book, *An Imperial Affliction*, whose Amsterdam-based author gives the story its quest-based plot, but also through the cheerful mottoes Augustus's family hang on their walls ("My parents call them Encouragements," he explains), the texts Hazel and Augustus send each other, the emails, the eulogies, the Facebook posts, *The Diary of Anne Frank*. In the end no text and no kind of writing can completely satisfy, but none of them completely fail either, except maybe Facebook posts written entirely in cliché.

We were all affected by Hazel's explanation for why she avoids close relationships whenever possible: "I'm like a grenade, Mom. I'm a grenade and at some point I'm going to blow up and I would like to minimize the casualties, okay?" The book and movie resist Hazel's metaphor: A person is not a weapon, and minimizing casualties is not the point of love. Still, all of us felt her wariness in our bones. People who love in proximity to cancer are living in a state of vigilance, bracing themselves for what is coming. When Hazel compares herself to a grenade in the movie trailer, the cheerful pop soundtrack stops and the romantic scenes suddenly give way to dark slow-motion images of a medical emergency. It's quite dramatic, but I didn't require any cinematic cues to feel the ominous impact of her words.

The melodramatic trailer is a pretty good preview of the movie's spin on the story. In general the movie is, well, a movie: It turns the unpretentious midwestern narrative of the novel into a cinematic tale about glowingly beautiful cancer patients with gym-toned parents, upscale houses, and classy clothes, and simplifies the book's emotions with on-the-nose musical cues and a careful avoidance of the physical realities of death. The story of two kids falling in love is stretched into an extended golden fantasy montage, while the story of one kid dying and one kid grieving is shortened into little more than a postscript.

On the other hand, Shailene Woodley has one of the most expressive faces in Hollywood and one of the huskiest voice-over voices; Ansel Elgort is plenty charming; Willem Dafoe is suitably scabrous as the author of *An Imperial Affliction*; the script contains all the most important *Goodreads* quotes; and overall the film is excellent at capturing teen sarcasm and rapturous first love and the kind of irresistible grief that is a full ten on the pain scale. And I cried, as I'd wanted to. I melted gratefully into what A. O. Scott calls *TFIOS*'s "expertly built machine for the mass production of tears" the way a tired traveler sits down in an airport massage chair; the way a person with autism walks into the carefully calibrated embrace of a robot who doles out the calming pressure that the body craves when human comfort is either unavailable or too much to bear.

All this could be seen as damning with faint praise—an admission that the movie evinces all the faults cited in critical arguments against young adult fiction. But I left the theater thinking that maybe idealized wish-fulfillment and old-fashioned tear-jerking are necessary, in part because some tears must be forced, like flowers in winter, and in part because an adolescent's romantic partial view of life expresses a kind of truth that the more self-critical and philosophical parts of film and fiction can't.

I've read a lot about cancer in the past few years. I especially loved *Love's Work* by the late philosopher Gillian Rose, who brought an academic rigor to her reflections on love, labor, and her own early death. *The Emperor of All Maladies* is admittedly quite an impressive tome. Yet sometimes I think that YA is the perfect genre for cancer.

Supporting a friend who has cancer is simultaneously the most adult thing I've ever done and the most adolescent thing I've done since I grew up. There is nothing more adult than witnessing wills, learning the unexpected spellings and side effects of various chemo drugs, poring over lists of clinical trials, and comparing prescription plans on the Connecticut health care exchange. And these tasks are child's play next to the feats of maturity required to negotiate the roles and responsibilities of chosen family, or to simply keep showing up for the medical or emotional challenge of the day.

But in the midst of all this strenuous maturity, there is still something wantonly, brazenly young adult about what Ash has called "living as exuberantly as possible with metastatic cancer." As Ash and I sit in the waiting room with our laptops trying to find a good cancer novena online, we crack up at the exhibitionist tendencies of St. Peregrine, the patron saint of cancer patients, who is apparently fond of thrusting his diseased leg out of a slit in his long robe like Angelina Jolie at the Oscars. In the examination room, in between visits from doctors and nurses, we find ourselves falling into helpless giggle fits about the cute or awkward oncology fellows, or swooning over how badass Ash's middle-aged soccer-playing female oncologist is, like adoring high schoolers talking about our favorite teacher. Ash has been known to sing "My Xeloda" to the tune of "My Sharona," crazy in love with her favorite chemo drug—the one with the least side effects that leaves her free to go on a writing residency in the Adirondacks and pour herself into the refugee resettlement work she loves.

Ritu teasingly attributes Ash's frequent sky-high rushes of excitement to "cancer ecstasy." Our exuberant friend is so good at finding a way to turn her illness into enchantment that we've started hashtagging these feats of alchemy #AshMagic. She christened the first summer after her diagnosis "The Summer of Care and Delight," and we plunged into the season with willful joy. Thanks to the miracles of Xeloda, we are now on our third such summer of heightened delight: sipping vinho verde out on the deck, rewatching *Mystic Pizza*, celebrating Juneteenth with blueberry shortcake and strawberry soda, driving down an Alabama road in the rain with a bag of hot Atomic Fireballs open between us, writing meandering essays on obscure movies or saints, sprawling on a blanket on a hillside on the Fourth of July as the fireworks and fireflies light up the sky.

These summers are the stuff of adolescent fiction. They are urgently nostalgic. They are also a kind of escape. But they are no more narcissistic than pondering philosophical questions while cells mutate and multiply and hope wavers; no more self-absorbed than parsing someone else's suffering for ambiguities and existential truths. There will inevitably come a season for serious and adult contemplation—for piecing together a provisional pattern of meaning with the sharp shards of loss. There are plenty of literary works that offer this and only this. But a young adult novel also knows when to say: Whatever! Willful wish-fulfillment is what life is for. Now let's go on a romantic jaunt to Amsterdam!

Of course, most of us were never that kind of young adult: the kind who could seize the joy of the moment and hold on. And neither, often, are Augustus and Hazel. As the book-within-a-book *An Imperial Affliction* says, and as Hazel and Gus quote, "Pain demands to be felt."

When I was a teenager pain demanded to be felt, and I have the scars to show for it. Perhaps the biggest thing that has changed from my adolescence to my adulthood is that now pain sometimes demands not to be felt. Or: Pain makes demands, but being felt is not always one of them. I'm part of a care team and I have a job to do, which means in real life I have to keep it at least 70 percent together. These days I can cry for the length of a song, but not an album. I can rain down tears on the pages of a sentimental novel or in a movie theater full of strangers, but not in front of the friends I love. For Ash, the stakes of giving in to feeling are unimaginably higher, and the need to keep it together most of the time is nonnegotiable.

One morning as we were walking to the hospital again, Ash said, "One thing *The Fault in Our Stars* does is that it opens veins: the vein of dying early and the vein of wanting to fall in love with someone like Augustus Waters. And it neither leaves you bleeding nor Band-Aids you up. As you get older you get less willing to open veins."

This is what three-Kleenex films can do at their best, and what young adult fiction can do when it works: open your veins or your tear ducts, and then staunch the flow with something in between what you want and what you have—more drama but no answers; more love but no miracles.

I'd like to give Ash a version of what John Green gives Hazel: an age-appropriate Augustus Waters and a spot in a clinical trial that achieves unprecedentedly durable results.

("Durable"—what a beautiful word.) But the world is not a wish-granting factory, and so instead I will just share her stories with her—entering into the narratives she makes and loves from the world of real cancer, the world of *TFIOS*, and the space between.

EVERYTHING YOU'VE GOT

"ALL I KNEW was that it was a dark brown program on late at night."

That's how the actor Roger Rees described his first impression of *Cheers*, the sepia-tinted subterranean sitcom that dominated a decade of American television. It was my first impression too. As a kid I sometimes glimpsed it when I spent the night at my grandparents' house. My melancholic Czech grandpa would sit in the dark in his La-Z-Boy with his beer, *Cheers* glowing faintly on the screen in front of him like a fireplace of dying embers. I wasn't allowed to watch it; it was too adult, and I was supposed to be sleeping. But sometimes I would linger quietly on the edge of the screenlight on my way to bed and watch adulthood taking place in a basement bar.

Three thousand miles away, my future friend Xiao was catching glimpses of *Cheers* in her family's apartment in Queens. "Even when I was a kid and too young to watch the show," she remembers, "I stayed to watch the opening credits because the song and images gave me a feeling of nostalgia for something I hadn't even experienced, that is, bar life in the late 1800s/early 1900s as rendered in illustrations." She was drawn in by the atmospheric color scheme: "The set and costumes of every episode reproduce the colors of the opening credits sequence—browns, dark blues, ambers, reds." Xiao grew up to be a historian of nineteenth-century American art, though it's unclear whether her childhood fascination with *Cheers* was a cause or just an early symptom.

From the beginning, for both me and Xiao, *Cheers* meant the mystery of maturity and the melancholy of yearning. We weren't quite ready for it yet, but when we needed it, it was waiting for us.

~

Like many people of my generation, I began to watch *Cheers* because it was there. All eleven seasons of it, available on Netflix in bulk. As a nostalgic semi-known quantity available in convenient twenty-five-minute doses, *Cheers* is a natural choice for sleepy streamers and basic cable insomniacs looking for reliability and comfort. I wasn't the first or last of my friends to rediscover it. Dave was hooked from the pilot ("That show was 100 percent perfect right out of the gate"). Lisa always watches it on the Hallmark Channel when she's up at three A.M. Fadzilah watches it after long days of teaching in Singapore. Katie watches it after long days of teaching in Michigan. Xiao got through the entire series of 275 episodes in a single semester.

When I started to watch I couldn't stop either.

To begin with, there's that opening montage. An image of a modern Boston street blurs into an almost identical century-old version of itself, and pictures of long-ago beer drinkers and bartenders stand in seamlessly for their modern counterparts. The credits offer the impossible consolation of changelessness. They're a time-lapse record of a century, but without any lapse or loss.

And then there's the theme song, "Where Everybody Knows Your Name," which is a kind of love song. Heather, who watches *Cheers* with her boyfriend every night before bed, muses, "you could write a whole essay just on the song— it's so rousing and there is something about the chord progression that is just straight awesome." The music starts out intimate and gentle, just a voice and piano, before building to a percussive anthem of desire. And the lyrics are an empathetic invitation addressed directly to the listener, affirming our sense that sometimes just getting through the day takes everything we've got, and telling us to come in and take a load off. The song is like a synth-y, soft-rock setting of one of the most seductive verses in the Bible: "Come unto me, all ye who labor and are heavy-laden, and I will give you rest." I can't resist.

∼

I started watching *Cheers* because it was there, but I kept on watching because it kept on speaking to my deepest desires and discontents.

Cheers is, among other things, a riff on the friction between my two seemingly incompatible social classes, the working-class world I grew up in and the academic world I've made a life in as an adult. Of course, comedy has always played on the juxtaposition of high and low, going back forever—from *Frasier* and *The Fresh Prince of Bel-Air* to Shakespeare to the Greeks—but unlike most sitcoms that are structured on class difference, *Cheers* (at least for the first several seasons) features laughable elites who are not millionaires or celebrities but grad students, professors, aspiring writers, translators of Russian poetry, visual artists, and psychotherapists. *Cheers* is a class comedy created by English majors from a blue-collar background: in other words, my people.

The pilot is like a perfect play that puts characters from these contrasting classes together and watches the sparks fly. Diane Chambers, a preppy and WASPy comp lit grad student at BU, and her smug fiancé and mentor, Professor Sumner Sloane, who (as Diane likes to inform people) has an article in the current *Harper's*, stop by the underground bar on their way to get married, but their engagement quickly disintegrates under the cynical and sympathetic eye of the bartender/bar owner, Sam Malone. Sam is a divorced ex-relief-pitcher for the Red Sox who killed his baseball career with alcohol but has been sober for three years, and now presides over an informal bar-based society of friends. He knows within minutes what Diane's intellectual snobbery has prevented her from seeing for years: that her fiancé is not a good guy. At the end of the pilot, when Diane realizes she can't return to her job as Sumner's teaching assistant now that he has abandoned her for his ex-wife, Sam hires her to be a waitress, and thus begin five seasons of Sam vs. Diane drama, with Diane intermittently dismissing Sam as a dumb jock and Sam intermittently criticizing her as a snob as they fall in and out of love and friendship.

Sam was originally conceived of as a "Stanley Kowalski type," a brutal and musclebound embodiment of fetishized white working-class masculinity, but what makes *Cheers* work is that he obviously isn't. Though hints of this early characterization survive—Ted Danson seems to have slightly more facial skeleton than most people, which lends a bit of a Cro-Magnon quality to his forehead, and within the first few minutes of the pilot a woman refers to Sam as a "magnificent pagan beast"—Sam is in fact a stable and steadying force, a patient listener with a perceptiveness he describes as "bartender's intuition." Even Sam's compulsive flirting has a kind of dependable steadiness to it, at least in the first several seasons: His unmenacing and straightforward seduction routine relies on pickup lines with the simple and sunny premise, "I'm hot, and you're hot, so why not?" Sam's seemingly effortless sexual success, fading local celebrity, and day-at-a-time sobriety are a source of pride and existential support for his employees, Carla (a fiery Italian American single mother of many) and Coach (a permanently concussed veteran of a long and non-illustrious baseball career), as well as for the bar regulars, Norm (a wisecracking and self-deprecating alcoholic accountant) and Cliff (a know-it-all postal carrier).

Diane, who was voted "most likely to marry old money" in high school and at one point semi-seriously pronounces that she was "bred and educated to walk with kings," is from another world entirely, a world where people care about opera and John Donne. She dresses for the job she wants, not the one she has: Underneath her barmaid's apron, she is usually styled to attend a neo-Victorian Laura Ashley literary garden party. At first she ostentatiously reads poetry in public as a kind of shield and holds herself aloof from the denizens of Cheers, but over time she settles in to her place there. My poet friend Brandon sees her as "the show's ionic spark, serving as the necessary, cultured counter-charge to the narratival nucleus of Sam and his blue-collar clientele." Played by Shelley Long with what Brandon describes as "vulnerable charm," Diane is perhaps unique on television as a believable humanities grad student, eccentric, neurotic, and brimful of verbiage. As Xiao says, "I really identify with Diane. The things she says, her intellectual pretensions, her cultured manners . . . and sometimes the veneer comes off and she is just a softie at heart."

Diane is far too fond of flaunting her intellectual interests, and she often leaves herself open to deflating double-entendre teasing when she talks about going to bed with *The Brothers Karamazov* or "finishing off Kierkegaard." But thanks to her commitments to gay liberation and feminist sisterhood, she is also often the heart and conscience of the show—coaching Sam to rise to the occasion and publicly support his old baseball friend who has just come out of the closet, despite the homophobic disapproval of Norm, Cliff, and Carla; or organizing a bar-wide collection to provide for Carla's next impending fatherless baby. (In characteristically cloying-yet-endearing fashion, Diane leads the bar in a rousing serenade of "You'll Never Walk Alone" as the hugely pregnant Carla proudly holds her beer pitcher of money aloft.) As Sam bitterly half-jokes to Diane in the midst of one of their frequent fights, "Listen, before you came to work at this bar I never thought that much about morality and integrity . . . That's why I'm firing you." (He doesn't fire her.)

But even though Sam doesn't think that much about morality and integrity, he is very good at fostering friendship, which is part of what makes *Cheers*—both the place and the show—so sustaining. As Ted Danson says, "My job playing Sam Malone was to let the audience in, to love my bar full of people." Sam is the show's heart and conscience just as much as Diane, and he serves and observes his miscellaneous crew of employees and regulars with amused attention, listening to their endless bar-talk alongside us. Much of the show's verbal vibrancy depends on the classed contrasts between the characters' speech, and their constant sparring makes the show function almost like radio, a soothing soundtrack to fall asleep to. The pompous psychobabble of yuppie therapists Frasier and Lilith clashes pleasurably with Norm and Carla's borscht belt one-liners (a typical Carla insult: "The only notches on your bedpost come from banging your head in frustration!"), while Cliff supplies an endless stream of surreal and self-important musings. "How would the Civil War have changed," he wonders at one point, "if Abraham Lincoln had octopus tentacles instead of a beard?"

There's something rare and consoling about the fact that in the class-conscious microcosm of *Cheers*, both working-class people and professional intellectuals are shown to be insular and absurd, just as both are seen to have their own forms of intelligence and insight. *Cheers* is not a show that exists at anyone's expense. There are no Archie Bunkers. As my 1987 first edition of *The Official Cheers Scrapbook* puts it: "*Cheers* is that rare breed of show that appeals to the broadest audience—young urban professionals and blue-collar workers alike. Conversation runs the gamut from the Red Sox to

Rembrandt, to arguments on the 'sweatiest movie ever made.' There's something for everyone at Cheers." In its heyday, *Cheers* became an imaginary gathering place for an extraordinarily capacious crowd of viewers that included my high school dropout grandpa, Prince, Kurt Vonnegut, and 93.5 million other people. It created a unified American public that no longer exists, and maybe never existed anywhere else.

Of course, *Cheers* is a wishful fiction. Historically, *Cheers*-era Boston was just a few years removed from the vicious busing riots of the seventies, in which white Bostonians resisted school desegregation with the same unhinged rage as the mobs who threatened the Little Rock Nine in 1957. The show originally aired during the fiercest years of the 1980s culture wars, and in the depths of the pre-Clinton recession. But in its imaginary underground utopia, Boston is an indivisible city united by the Red Sox, the Bruins, and the Pats, and the bitterly fought life-and-death battles over sexuality that raged at the nadir of the AIDS epidemic are restaged as a space of comedy and ethical growth.

Brandon especially loves the gentle ending of the homophobia episode. When Norm ignorantly insists that Cheers is and ought to be a queer-free zone, Diane tells him he's making an idiot of himself and that there are in fact two gay guys in the bar now. Then the two customers standing on either side of Norm proceed to out themselves by sweetly kissing him on each cheek. In a real bar, this kind of move might lead to violence; in Cheers, it prompts Norm to consider the error of his ways, and he calmly quips that they are better kissers than his wife. In a similar fashion, the regular incursions of severe economic trouble—Carla's chronically precarious single motherhood, Norm's long bout of unemployment—can somehow be solved by passing a pitcher around the bar for donations, or extending Norm's bar tab indefinitely.

I've spent most of the past decade in a segregated and stratified New England city that's starkly divided between ACADEMIC and NOT, and while I am mostly acclimatized to existing in a strange subculture in which most people I meet are writing a book, I feel an aching sense of exile from a world in which people do other things. During my decade in New Haven, two old "dark brown" dive bars that blended town and gown, Rudy's and the Anchor, each closed after seventy years in business. Both bars have since reopened as new and unrecognizable versions of themselves—in some ways maybe even as better versions—but they still seem somehow of a piece with the luxury parka shopping destination that much of downtown New Haven has become, with its Patagonia, Barbour, Gant, and L.L.Bean stores all in a row, corporate monuments to exclusive education and its attendant expensive outerwear in the midst of a city of spectacular and seemingly intractable inequality.

I am aware that academia is in fact my home now, as much as any place is. And I know it's a mistake to overidealize the motley world of *Cheers*, which has its own obvious exclusions. I know that inequality is not a joke, and I know it won't be solved through dive bars or TV. But I still can't help craving a less class-riven existence, for myself and for everyone else. And though I can't always find it in my own daily life, I can always find it at Cheers.

∾

Cheers is not just a consoling fiction for people caught between classes. It is also a surprisingly nuanced guide to the plot puzzle of one's thirties and forties: Have you already peaked? Are you still on your way to wherever it is you are headed? Or perhaps there's no longer any plot at all?

It has meant a lot to me to watch characters my own age navigate this at once belated and premature period between youth and midlife, in which you are supposed to have checked off some or all the boxes of adulthood, or at least figured out the thing that you were put on earth to do. In different ways I find myself unwillingly identifying with all the denizens of Cheers, including Norm, who says he's never had ambition because "dreams just give you heartache," and Cliff, who finds a grandiose glory in his work as a mail carrier, reveling in the honor of his uniform. But mostly I'm torn between Sam and Diane.

Sam became a professional baseball player before finishing high school and spent his youth performing extraordinary athletic feats for a national audience, but then he turned to drinking to deal with the pressure and threw away his shot at lasting fame. He now exists in the endless day-at-a-time stasis of sobriety, his equilibrium and self-respect mostly keeping restlessness at bay. Still, there is a painful discrepancy between his life then and his life now, and the show won't let it go. Over and over, Sam is made to reckon with how far he's fallen, in recurrent episodes designed for maximum punishment. He is booked for an interview on a sports show, but then ditched mid-interview when they get someone more famous; he donates an old jersey to a charity auction, and no one bids on it; he is offered the chance to star in commercials as a former sports celebrity, but he has to keep sleeping with his agent to get bookings; a literary celebrity encourages him to think about writing a memoir, but then tells him his proposal is not interesting enough to publish. It's funny and awful, in the manner of a Looney Tunes Acme anvil that keeps falling on the fragile hopes of someone you like.

After nine seasons of variations on this pattern, the show escalates to the ultimate potential humiliation: Sam attempts to return to professional baseball by trying out for the Red Sox farm team. Cliff contemplates the terrifying midlife crisis that might ensue if Sam fails to get chosen: "A thing like that can really hit a guy hard. He'll probably storm back in here, go in the office, lock himself in, and maybe start taking inventory of his life. Peruse over the setbacks, the humiliations, the wrong turns, all the while fashioning his belt into a makeshift noose. I mean we've all done it a hundred times." In the end, what happens is more anticlimactic: Sam makes the team, but now that he's sober, tired, and middle-aged, he discovers he hates both baseball and life on the road. Exhausted by the physical work of pitching and the excessive energy of his youthful teammates, he quits almost immediately. He returns to his job at the bar with no dreams left.

Though I'm neither a sports star nor an alcoholic, I spent my twenties training for the academic big leagues and then failed to get a tenure-track job. I subsequently spent most of my thirties teaching introductory writing classes at Yale, feeling simultaneously lucky, restless, and resigned. Yale's traditional term for my type of non-tenure-track teacher was "non-ladder faculty": My job was defined as one in which I could not make progress or climb. I spent seven years living in the same apartment and teaching the same classes; I taught "Reading and Writing the Modern Essay" seventeen times and graded approximately 3,668 papers. (Over the course of *Cheers* Sam must have cut up approximately 3,668 lemons.) It was a meaningful job and I was very glad to have it, but sometimes I was overwhelmed by the thought that I'd be living the same day over and over again forever, assuming I was lucky enough not to lose what I had. Like Sam, I hadn't fully reconciled myself to the end of interesting plot developments, but I wasn't entirely sure whether I wanted deep feelings or hopes to rattle my steady rhythm.

Meanwhile Diane, the perpetual grad student/teaching assistant/waitress, is either delusional or right to believe that one day she will become a writer. Decades before Lena Dunham's character Hannah Horvath on *Girls* would make a similar declaration, Diane proclaims grandiloquently to the entire bar: "My name is Diane Chambers, and I would like one day to be known as the voice of my generation!" Unfortunately, according to the inscrutable, immutable rules of the show, Diane can have either love or writing, but not both. She begins her job at Cheers telling herself she's collecting material for her novel, but five years later she still hasn't written it. Instead she's filled endless journals with her feelings about Sam, and sent him scores of love letters.

Diane's repeated thwarted attempts to achieve some kind of late-blooming literary or artistic success are a symmetrical accompaniment to Sam's painful reckonings. She is asked to read a poem on the local news, but thinks it's a practical joke, and instead does a humiliating imitation of a chicken laying an egg. She accepts an invitation to her professor's house for Thanksgiving dinner, thinking she will be schmoozing with famous writers like William Styron, but instead finds out she's expected to be unpaid catering staff. Channeling her ambition into dance, she decides to audition for the Boston Ballet as an untrained thirty-something amateur in lurid Lycra leggings, passionately psyching herself up by asking, "Isn't the real heartache knowing that you had the potential to do something but never tried? . . . I still have a fighting chance to make my dreams come true!" only to be humiliated in public by a painful truth she has never had to confront before: She is a truly terrible dancer.

In my friend Fadzilah's favorite episode, Diane has a full-on chain-smoking, daytime-pajama-wearing breakdown after she discovers that the seemingly encouraging rejection letter she received from a literary journal is actually nothing but a form letter, and that a poem Sam submitted on a bet has been accepted: "I've struggled so hard for so long to keep my dreams alive, and I haven't fooled anyone but myself . . . I'm never going to be Diane Chambers, the great poet, the world-famous novelist, the revered artist. I've gone as high as I'm going to go. I'm a waitress in a beer hall. And not a very good one. I'm a waitress. A waitress. A waitress."

"It's not easy to watch those people you scoffed at run past you while you remain stuck in the mud like a weighted-down elephant," Sam teases. But he can relate to Diane's despair. And he shares her elation when he confesses that the poem he submitted was actually hers, and she is finally a published writer. It's a rare moment of professional triumph in a show that doles them out very sparingly.

Sometimes Sam and Diane swap taunts (Diane: "Nothing's sadder than a man hanging on to a dead dream." Sam: "Unless it's a blonde struggling to keep her hopes up"), and sometimes they take turns giving each other pep talks, and sometimes they are in it together, facing decay and mortality side by side.

In one of my favorite episodes, Sam gets a hernia and is so mortified at having what he thinks of as an old man's health problem that he refuses to tell his friends that he's going in for surgery. Diane tracks him down at the hospital and attempts to encourage him to accept growing older and falling apart, but when she finds out that Sam's doctor is someone she used to tutor when he was a kid, she instantly plummets into her own parallel midlife crisis: "I'm old and alone in Boston." After she leaves, Sam is further humiliated when he crassly hits on a much younger woman who turns out to be the daughter of his roommate, a man his own age. She clearly thinks of him as ancient and calls him "sir." In the last shot, Sam is sitting alone in his hospital gown and staring out the window into the rain, trying to withstand a new surge of shame and fear.

≈

Given their clashing class status, stalled career trajectories, and dangerously post-youth time of life, it's no wonder Sam and Diane repeatedly come together and split apart with such searingly high-voltage energy. ("I was drawn into the show by Diane and Sam's magical chemistry," Xiao says. "Those are some huge sparks.") At various times, their arduous ardor pushes Sam off the wagon and plunges him into the moat of an Italian castle; sends Diane to a psych hospital and a nunnery and plunges her into a chilly New England harbor; and finally winds them both up in criminal court. Sam's exasperated courtroom speech toward the end of season 5 efficiently captures the drama: "You want me to propose to you; I propose to you. You say no; I say fine, I never want to see you again. You drive me nuts telling me you want me to propose again; I do, you turn me down. Next thing I know I'm in a court of law where I've gotta propose to you or I'll go to jail. It's the classic American love story." As Diane testifies to the judge, "I guess you could describe our relationship as a bit stormy. That's also part of its excitement."

For Sam, the storm is the point. When Diane first walks into the bar, his life is too easy. His friends idolize him, his job doesn't challenge him, and the women he dates don't either. What Diane offers, instantly, is difficulty, and lots of it. She criticizes him. She mocks his tastes. She doesn't care about sports. The first time he tries to kiss her, she flips him flat on his back with a martial arts move she learned in a class called "Practical Feminism." What's even more of a threat: She still has untarnished hopes and dreams, plus a maddening propensity to analyze everything to death. Nothing is ever enough for her. After just a few episodes, Sam summons her to the pool room to complain that she's ruined his reliable everyday pleasures: "Because of you, my life isn't *fun* anymore!" But Diane's brand of un-fun is his life's first new development in a long time. When he finally announces to the bar that they are officially an item, he further explains (to her chagrin) that he knows he may have to "work a little harder on this one," and indeed he does. Throughout their affair, he is navigating the waves of her tempestuous moodiness and ambition.

Meanwhile, for Diane, Sam offers an intermittent but real reprieve from the relentless hunger for artistic achievement that has driven her for years. If getting engaged to Sumner Sloane was Diane's attempt to achieve a literary life instantly and vicariously by partnering with an alleged genius, falling in love with Sam allows her to escape from these self-imposed pressures entirely for significant stretches of time and simply enjoy being a body, a besotted girlfriend, a woman utterly unfamiliar to herself. When Diane is slurping bouillabaisse with Sam at Melville's Restaurant, or lolling under the comforter with him at the Pequod Inn, or buying him over-priced scalped tickets for a brutal prizefight she refuses to go to and doesn't even approve of, or chasing him around the bar with a squirt gun, she gets to forget about trying to become the voice of her generation.

But the reprieve never lasts. Diane can't help wanting more, which means she can't help wanting Sam to be someone else. She has absurd sex dreams in which he is revealed to be a brilliant classical composer wearing a velvet smoking jacket. She drags him to concerts and galleries. She narrates their romance to him in purple prose ("Last week we were at passion's portal, standing on the threshold of a new and excitingly textured relationship") and she wants him to meet her words with words, but Sam's love language is not language. Sometimes this thrills Diane—like when she realizes Sam can say the words "I love you" to everyone but her, which means, perhaps, that he really loves her. And sometimes it maddens her—like when she asks him to take a week to find the words to express what their relationship means to him, and he comes up with nothing.

Diane's need to define their relationship is existential. If she's effectively giving up ambition for love, then the love has to mean a lot. But for a long time Sam is wary. At first he can't commit to more than an AA-style, day-at-a-time approach to dating. Several seasons later, on the brink of sex, he tells her: "I'm only going to agree to do this if we agree it doesn't mean anything." He holds back partly because he's a sex addict daunted by monogamy, but mostly because he doesn't want to be a consolation prize. Meanwhile Diane takes out her chronic frustration with him and with her life by constantly accusing him of stupidity. "Hey, I thought you said you weren't going to call me stupid now that we're being intimate," Sam protests at one point. "No," she clarifies, "I said I wouldn't call you stupid WHILE we're being intimate."

Sam and Diane are one of the all-time great TV couples: a classic Tracy-and-Hepburn pair that captured the imagination of a nation. But as much as I love them, it's impossible for me to simply sit back and enjoy the legendary will-they-or-won't-they sexual tension of the early seasons, or the will-they-or-won't-they-get-married of the later ones, because I know their getting together would not be just a pleasant plot resolution or setup for a new set of jokes. It would be—and to some extent is—an act of desperate resignation; a grasp at the impossible that becomes a bitter and resented sacrifice. They are both seeking a safe (if stormy) passage out of the midlife doldrums, and that's something they ultimately can't give each other. But they can't stop looking for it in each other.

It's a tough knot for the show to untangle, but the fifth season finale resolves it beautifully by borrowing a classic ending from *Casablanca* and giving it a feminist spin. In the middle of Sam and Diane's wedding ceremony at Cheers, after Sam's "I do" but before Diane's, the phone rings and we learn that her ex-fiancé, Sumner, has submitted one of Diane's old novels for publication, and she has been offered a book contract that would require her to get the messy manuscript ready in six months. Diane has never found a way to incorporate writing into her life with Sam; she knows that she has to choose between him and the book.

She tells him she is choosing him. But he won't let her.

Like his fellow middle-aged bar-owner Rick Blaine, Sam decides to sacrifice his romantic future for the greater good, which in this case is not fighting the Nazis but promoting one woman's artistic ambition. As he says in an impassioned speech to Diane, in front of the bar full of antsy guests who have all placed bets on whether the wedding is actually going to happen:

> Look. You gotta do this book. You *have* to . . . I don't want to be married to a woman who's going to be always asking "What if?" . . . You're good at writing! . . . This is important for you. I mean, I had my day in the sun. I may not have been the greatest relief pitcher in the world, but the point is, I took a shot. You gotta take your shot.

At first Diane protests, but some part of her clearly wants to believe him. And when he asks her, "Do you agree we shouldn't get married?" she fervently vows, "I do."

It's the best possible resolution, but it still hurts. *Cheers* softens the blow by having Diane promise to come back in six months (Sam knows she won't), and by concluding with a sweet and wistful counterfactual future: Sam's daydream of them happily growing old together. In the episode's last scene, a gray-haired Sam and Diane slowly dance a waltz together after decades of imaginary togetherness.

~

I used to wish that *Cheers* had stopped with Diane's departure. I wished this partly because of the deep narrative satisfaction of the first five seasons, and partly because of what *Cheers* does (and fails to do) with Diane's replacement, Rebecca Howe, played by Kirstie Alley. Rebecca arrives on the scene as Sam's glamorous and formidable new boss, rife with power and potential in a resplendent red leather jacket, but almost immediately she is turned into a misogynistic joke. The first time I watched season 6, I complained about my frustrations in my diary:

> So the reliable bleakness and drabness of *Cheers* is still working for me, but it has lost its heart-twisting magic post-Diane. The fact is that Rebecca is an anti-feminist cliché. The other women on the show are all so strong and weird (Diane, Carla, Lilith). Rebecca is just an uptight

embodiment of 1980s post-feminist backlash who bursts into tears because even though she's successful it doesn't matter since all she wants is marriage and kids, and who is hot but sexually insecure because she used to be fat in high school, etc. It is all so boring and cardboard.

Diane cares about art and politics; Rebecca cares about marrying money. Diane declares she wants to be the voice of her generation; Rebecca declares she wants to date Donald Trump. Rebecca is also a mess. *Cheers* co-creator James Burrows later unapologetically spelled out the infuriating political symbolism of Rebecca's extreme klutziness: "I remember us going, 'Oh, my God, this is what this character is: a woman of the '80s, during the feminist movement, who thinks she has control of everything, and she can't open a freaking door.'" As she bawls and stumbles her way through the last six seasons, Rebecca is less Sam's love interest than the object of his compulsive sexual nagging. (In a particularly nasty moment in season 8, Sam whines about Rebecca's decision not to date him: "I spent three years loosening the cap on that peanut butter jar, and right now she's sticking to the roof of someone else's mouth.")

Sam's increasing sleaziness is perhaps the most painful part of post-Diane *Cheers*. The sometimes sexist Sam of seasons 1 through 5 would definitely ask a woman to smile. The sordid Sam of season 6 first asks Rebecca to smile, and then insults her smile. In the space between seasons, he has gone from being Humphrey Bogart in *Casablanca* to a negging pickup artist. It's a development that makes a kind of psychological sense (he is bitter, if unsurprised, that Diane never came back, which lends his sexual persona a new undercurrent of sadness and cynicism), but we can't be expected to approve, or to enjoy it.

In the later seasons, as the stakes get ever lower and the characters become more like caricatures, the show is increasingly cheerless. As I lamented to my diary: "I don't especially need any of these people to be happy, but this particular version of unhappiness is not funny. I miss all the laughing out loud I used to do in that stale-cigarette-smelling basement."

Still, there are always friendships, and there's still the same familiar place to gather. For eleven long years, the friends at *Cheers* continue to age alongside their audience, which gives their relationship with one another and with us the weight of duration, and the irreplaceable intimacy that comes with low-quality, high-quantity time. Their faces weather; their bodies settle; they lose their sparkle and their edge; their jokes and habits stay the same. It's depressing and it's comforting.

I think this is why I'm grateful for the existence of the last six seasons of *Cheers*, even though they are nowhere near as good as the first five and I rarely choose to re-watch them. Life doesn't end with youth and hope, and neither should TV.

~

The critic Jeff Jensen once condemned the flash-in-the-pan TV series *Weird Loners* for being "one more show that presents community as a balm to existential angst and pain . . . but makes it look so easy to come by. Television in general needs to get wiser and tougher with this theme." At its best, *Cheers* is both wise and tough, and it is never wiser or tougher

than in its final episodes, which dare to dramatize the difficulty of community, and the existential angst and pain that
community can't cure.

Cheers ends, appropriately enough, with a massive midlife
crisis. The crisis is Sam's, and it is precipitated by seeing Diane
for the first time in six years when he glimpses her on a cable-
TV awards show after he gets back from yet another grim
evening at his sex compulsion therapy group. She is accepting
her award for Best Writing of a Movie or Mini-series for her
work on *The Heart Held Hostage*, and before being played off
the stage, she manages to thank each of the Greek muses by
name, as well as the Amazon rain forest and Sylvia Plath. Sam
impulsively sends her a telegram in L.A. to congratulate her,
and they end up talking on the phone, each of them bragging about their imaginary spouse and children to prove that
their lives are rich and full. Next thing he knows, Diane shows
up at Cheers, and their pretend marriages quickly fall apart.
They proceed to compare notes on their midlife malaise over
lunch before heading off to have some hot mid-afternoon
consolation sex. Sexual ecstasy reawakens their dormant
desires for an escape from the status quo, and the following
morning they appear at Cheers and announce that they are
getting married after all. Sam will be moving to L.A. to work
in a juice bar.

This plan is met with a universal lack of enthusiasm. No
one is happy for them, and no one thinks it's a good idea.

Sam, desperate for his friends' blessing, tries to explain why
he needs to leave them: "I just want to get my life going here.
I mean, look at me. What have I got? No family, no future,

nothing to look forward to . . . I want to get off the bench! I want to get in the game!"

But his friends don't care. They need him, and they need the gathering place he has made for them. "Sammy, what's going to happen to us?" Norm asks, and Carla wails, "Are you going to desert us? Like a traitor?"

Sam loses it. "I NEED MORE THAN THIS!" he yells at his friends. "YOU SHOULD NEED MORE THAN THIS! I AM NOT YOUR MOTHER! THIS IS NOT YOUR HOME!" His tirade is a betrayal of the show's foundational belief, which is that Cheers is indeed both family and home, and maybe there isn't anything more important in life than what it has to offer.

Sam's treachery is devastating, but it turns out to be temporary. After he and Diane head to the airport ("I gave that man the best years of my life," laments Norm), they board the plane to L.A. only to each hear personalized cautionary messages over the PA system, warnings from the parts of their self they're trying to repress: "Are you really in love with this woman, or are you trying to love her because you're afraid of ending up alone?" the pilot asks Sam, while the flight attendant asks Diane, "Will this man stimulate your gift, or be an anchor pulling you to the bottom of the sea of mediocrity?" When the flight is canceled, Sam and Diane take it as a sign that it's time to say their last good-byes to each other.

When Sam returns alone to Cheers, he decides to break out the Cuban cigars that he's been saving for a special occasion— for the wedding or baby that will never come. He asks his friends to stay and smoke with him after closing time. For a few minutes they punish him for his previous disloyalty by pretending to leave, but of course they all return to keep him company.

In a long, slow, seven-minute scene—an eternity in sitcom time—they settle in with their cigars for one more talk. Sam leans back in an armchair, Frasier sits on a table and uses a chair as a footrest, Woody sprawls on the floor, Carla perches cross-legged on the bar, and Norm and Cliff are ensconced on their usual stools, resting against the brass bar rail. Their bodies are clearly at home.

Sam, who for so many years has been supplying meaning for all of them, admits that he can't find enough meaning for himself. "One by one I seem to be losing my thrills and tingles, you know? I keep asking myself: What is the point to life?"

Quietly, one by one, they try to reply. Cliff says it's comfortable shoes. Carla and Frasier start to answer—children, friendship—and then their voices fade away. For the first time in all their years together, they fall into silence.

This scene is why *Cheers* had to last for eleven seasons: to earn this exhaustion, this quietude, this sense of restful spentness.

After everyone else leaves, Norm lingers because he has something to say to Sam alone: "I knew you'd come back. You could never be unfaithful to your one true love. You always come back to her."

"Who is that?" Sam asks, mentally running through the names in his little black book.

"Think about it, Sammy."

When Norm leaves, Sam thinks about it, alone in Cheers. He laughs to himself when he figures it out, and relaxes, and exhales. He says to himself with a kind of wonder: "I'm the luckiest son of a bitch on earth." There is relief in his voice, as well as an unsettling echo of Lou Gehrig (because if this is luck, who wants it?). For a second he rests his hand on the bar possessively, almost euphorically. His one true love.

~

Maybe we return to *Cheers* because we could never be unfaithful to it. Or maybe we just need to come in from the cold for a while.

In a typically bleak late-season episode, Frasier takes the regulars' emotional temperature: "I sense the mood of the bar. You're all suffering from the winter blues, the shortened daylight hours, the cold, numbing weather, the bleak sense of isolation. It's what we in the psychiatric professions call the jackpot." There's certainly no better weather for gathering at *Cheers* than a long dark winter of the soul. *Cheers* is like a quiet hearth—not a crackling fire, but raked-over coals that still cast a glow and thaw cold hearts at a glacial rate.

Frasier finally left Cheers behind for warmer climes, and others have as well. After her semester of fathoms-deep *Cheers* immersion, Xiao felt ready to progress beyond its drab, dingy, claustrophobic hibernation cave. Seamlessly segueing from one streaming Kelsey Grammer vehicle to another, she emerged into *Frasier*'s sparkle and brightness, its sprightly dialogue and spectacularly unreal Seattle view. "*Cheers* actually gets me quite depressed," she confessed to me. "I feel safer with *Frasier*."

I'm glad for Xiao, and I hear her. I do. But *Frasier* is far too bright and airy for me. I feel much safer with *Cheers*. Or maybe I crave it because it's less safe: because it's still so close to the bone. If so, I'm not alone. As Katie wrote me when I asked her why she loved it, "It's funny and warm, but also really about . . . What do you have when the illusions are gone? When your dreams are over? When you just have to figure out a way to make do and find some joy and possibility in that because what else is there? That speaks to my early-middle-aged soul."

It speaks to mine as well. And I agree with Katie: "We need more shows about middle-aged disappointments."

The comforting bleakness of *Cheers* is what I keep coming back to. I find myself descending yet again into this static stagnant basement place that somehow knows my name and has my number. *Cheers* lets me dwell for a while in the half-believed hope that romance is possible and striving's worth a try, and then it helps me settle once more for friendship and resignation. Like Persephone in thrall to the underworld, I may spend some time away, but I always return.

COASTING

ASH CALLED the ups and downs of her illness "the Cancercoaster," and the friends on her care team rode it with her, holding on tight through the fast escalations and faster plummets, then catching our breaths and bracing ourselves during the slow deceptive lulls.

Escalations were group text threads full of cancer pictures: a still life of a plastic cup full of bitter pre-scan contrast dye mixed with Crystal Light; a selfie of Ash and Lisa posing with a throw pillow from the hospital gift shop that proclaimed "Too Blessed to be Stressed!"; a close-up portrait of the least photogenic tropical fish in the waiting room aquarium who looked like a sad potato. They were the long email chains of the notes we took at doctors' appointments, each of us taking turns as scribe, with the subject line "Ash's Esophageal Adventures." They were the regular slumber parties with out-of-town members of the care team: Sarah from Minneapolis, Lisa from Houston, Ritu from Brooklyn. They were Ash's plans for the copper beech she wanted us to plant in her memory.

Plummets were serious new side effects and bad scan results and midnights in hospitals and morphine as needed.

When Ash first got her thunderbolt diagnosis—heading to the health center because she felt like she might be a little anemic, and subsequently being told she had an incurable illness—it was utterly unclear what her life would look like. It wasn't just that the course of the disease was uncertain; it was the unknown logistics of her day-to-day care. She didn't have a partner to help her, and both of her parents were ill and far away.

"At first I didn't understand what was going to happen," Ritu recalls. "And then I remember watching her community shift and form and figure out a way to come together and hold her. And she let herself be held. There's so much to say for being held. For knowing how to be held." Over the years, Ash had made so many friends who were ready to hold her—some I knew, and many I didn't. And one of the ways she knew how to be held was by welcoming us into her experience.

Ash invited me to write with her at the chemo infusion center as if she were giving me an entrée into a secret writing retreat or a cool hidden-away café. There was the most amazing natural light! she enthused. The most comfortable chairs! Hours-long stretches of time to spend communing with your thoughts! When she asked me to come with her to the hospital, she wasn't asking me for a favor; she was giving me a gift. And she was right: It really was a gift. But she was equally generous about inviting us into her most difficult experiences—the ones that couldn't be spun as delight. It would have been easy and understandable for Ash to accept the care she needed from us while keeping us at a distance. But somehow she seemed to believe that our attempts at empathy were a kind of real connection—that despite the unbridgeable gaps between our experiences, our lives were truly shared.

Though countless people were part of Ash's many overlapping circles of care, over the long haul four of us tended to function as a care-team core, stitched together by text and email threads. Ritu and Sarah had known Ash since college; Lisa and I had met her in divinity school. We were strangers, acquaintances, and friends who were united by Ash's illness and our shared grief over it, by our collective desire for her well-being, and by a love that came to blur the edges between us. It was her life, but we really were along for the ride. And for years the ride just didn't let up.

Until, unexpectedly, it did.

~

A few months after Ash's long-term chemo drug started to fail, a space opened up for her in a clinical trial at Yale New Haven Hospital. Ash was among a small group of patients who experienced unprecedented and dramatic results. The experimental immunotherapy treatment she received trained her own immune system to combat the cancer, and her once aggressive disease gradually slowed to a halt.

It was a miracle. Not an overnight miracle, or an effortless one. It was a grueling miracle, one that initially pushed Ash's body to its limit, revving up her immune system so much that her healthy systems were forced on the defensive as well as her cancer. For a while she was sicker than she'd ever been. But then, over time, she started to be well.

Ash has been out of treatment for several years now, and her scans keep coming back stable. Her life has returned to something that's a lot like normal, and she is beginning to feel like she can imagine a future. In the meantime, she writes essays, goes to work, goes to yoga, hangs out with friends. The first summer after immunotherapy, she found a good man on OKCupid and they've since moved in together. Lisa and I joke that Ash is the luckiest unlucky girl in the world.

~

In the years since Ash's miracle, the care team has mostly dispersed—or perhaps it's just that we already live so far apart, and now we no longer have an urgent reason to keep coming back together. We still participate in occasional text flurries, but in a lot of ways we've reverted from our temporary single circle into a symmetrical Venn diagram: Ash and Sarah and Ritu in one circle, and Ash and Lisa and me in the other, each small circle with its own history and rituals and traditions and reunions and jokes. Meanwhile our individual friendships with Ash have found old or new forms.

In the midst of Ash's crisis I improvised friendship in the moment, but in these welcome doldrum years I've had more time to reflect. I've been thinking a lot about love and illness, about the ways that crisis shapes us even when it has passed, about the afterlife of care and the ways it persists. For a long time I kept wanting to talk to the care team again—to ask how they remembered it all, and to learn how friendship had changed for them since. I talk or text with Lisa most days, but I hadn't checked in with Sarah and Ritu in a while. When we finally scheduled times to talk, more than a year had gone by since I'd seen them.

~

Sarah told me she remembers the Cancercoaster as a time when she always had multiple used Minneapolis-to-Hartford boarding passes at the bottom of her bag; when she was always looking at her calendar to find the next weekend she could leave her job and her husband and kids (or could bring her family, or at least the baby) and come see Ash, even just for a couple of days. Sarah's regular visits were immersive and intense: two- or three-day trips in which her regular life would recede and she would give herself over to the needs of the moment. She remembers the anxiety she felt before her visits, but what I remember is the reassurance I always felt when she was here. Sarah emanates peace and good humor even when she might not be feeling it, and she knows how to break down immense medical or bureaucratic challenges into a list of concrete manageable tasks. Her angel baby Mattan provided smile therapy for everyone.

Sarah has saved and filed all the care team emails, though she hesitates to open them. They sit unread in a scary folder in the depths of her laptop. (While we were on the phone she did briefly open the folder to find out when the idea of the "care team" first appeared. It turned out Ri called the team into being within a month of Ash's diagnosis.) The emails might be too hard to revisit, but they remind Sarah of the one thing she misses: the strong structures of friendship that arose in response to the crisis. These days she feels the absence of the constant communication, the consistent visits, the clear expectations and shared purpose and unquestioned belonging that we created with one another. "If you have to stop to think 'Does it make sense to travel right now? Do I really have the time for this?' then you'll almost never do it," she says. The intensity of Ash's crisis took these everyday practical calculations out of the equation, and made prioritizing friendship nonnegotiable in the same way that caring for her family was nonnegotiable. "In some ways life is lonelier without the care team," Sarah says. "It's more like what regular adult life is like."

I was surprised to learn after all these years that before Ash's diagnosis, Sarah and Ritu weren't especially close: They were just college acquaintances with a mutual friend. "Learning to love and lean on Ritu was a very important part of the story," Sarah told me, and I was struck by the symmetry: Lisa and I were also acquaintances from school who learned to love and lean on each other during those years when our friend was in crisis.

When I asked Sarah about her friendship with Ash before and after cancer, she remembered "the bliss of meeting one another as freshmen." She and Ash became friends when they were teenagers living in the same dorm, and they established a loving and sturdy intimacy that has lasted ever since. I was surprised, and awed, when Sarah said that her friendship with Ash had not been altered by Ash's illness. "I don't know why, but the emotional register of our friendship hasn't changed. It's like after all that acceleration and deceleration, we just got back to the baseline. We went back to that familiar feeling—the same way we've had of being friends for twenty years." Sarah's friendship with Ash, like Ash herself, is a marvel of resilience.

~

Lisa, who spent the first year and a half of the Cancercoaster as Ash's roommate and the next few years almost two thousand miles away, remembers how hard it was to be so close, and how hard it was to be so far. Before I joined the care team about seven months in, Lisa was the only member of the team who was local, so she was present for almost everything, from the diagnosis onward.

Lisa is one of the best caregivers I have ever met: tactful, insightful, warm, wise. She has been working as a chaplain for years now, and it is work she was born to do. But caring for someone you live with and love is not like caring for a patient and then going home at the end of a day. It is all-encompassing. And the intensity of that time was magnified for Lisa because Ash was also her closest friend, which meant that the very person Lisa would have wanted to turn to for emotional support was the one person she couldn't.

When I first met Lisa a few years before Ash's diagnosis I thought she and Ash might be a couple. (Ash asked if she could bring Lisa to my holiday party. Ash was dating someone at the time, but Lisa was still the person she wanted to bring.) They weren't actually romantically involved, but they were soul mates. Neither of them was raised especially religious, but they were pilgrims on parallel spiritual journeys.

They both chose to be baptized as adults in the faith of a parent (Lisa as a Catholic like her mother, Ash as a Coptic Christian like her father), and their friendship was rooted in their faith. They were prayer partners as well as domestic partners.

Lisa is the only child of a widowed father, so more than most, her family requires supplementation. Long before Ash's diagnosis, she had come to feel that Ash was her family, but she didn't know if their closeness would continue after they graduated and moved away. More than anything, Lisa wanted their bond to last. When Ash got sick a few months before graduation and had to stay in New Haven indefinitely for treatment, Lisa had the horrible feeling of having gotten what she wished for, in a nightmarish devil's bargain way. The fate that was keeping her friend close was also threatening to kill her.

Ash and Lisa are fully family now. Though it's possible they might have stayed connected even if Ash had never gotten sick, there is no doubt that the years of illness deepened their bond. Before cancer, they often fit their friendship into the corners of their overscheduled lives, but in the midst of cancer, their relationship became central and essential. "There were times when Ash's illness forced her to slow down," Lisa remembers, "which was awful for her, but it was transformative for our friendship." During the Cancercoaster years, they regularly spent hours and days of enforced downtime, waiting and enduring.

Several years ago, Lisa moved to Houston to be closer to her dad, and now Ash flies down to see her for birthdays and holidays. For the past several years, Lisa and Ash have celebrated Holy Week together. Neither of them cares for the happy-ending, flowers-and-trumpets service on Easter Sunday. Instead, they love the slowness and quiet of the Easter vigil. Each year on Holy Saturday they spend hours waiting together in the darkness, hoping and praying for resurrection.

~

Ash and I have an intimacy that was precipitated by illness. It's awful to admit that we owe our current closeness to cancer, but it is almost certainly true. And one of the things I remember most clearly from the blurred Cancercoaster years was Ash's very literal sense of deadlines. I used to feel the frantic energy in her as we wrote together and she faced down her last words. When she was told she only had a short time left on the planet, Ash often prioritized a poem over every- thing else. I admired her formidable sense of purpose, and it has forever changed the way I think about writing, but I am so grateful every day that those days are gone. I'm glad her writing can bloom more slowly if it likes; I'm glad it has room to grow at its own pace.

These days we can revel in the gift of lower stakes. Now Ash and I have the luxury of rescheduling a lunch or flaking out on a gym date, knowing that there will always be others. The urgency has dispersed. What remains, what has always remained, is writing. I've written most of this essay, as I've written so many, with Ash sitting next to me, the glow of her laptop illuminating her face, her pages of scribbles spread out next to mine. Ash and I know each other's hand- writing and grammatical cadences, the rising rhythm of the other's voice. We each admire what the other can do, and we know enough to help each other figure out how to do it. I love how freely we hand each other our work in progress, trusting each other with any stage of scrawl and mess. We are shameless.

We have co-written essays before, sharing a byline, and we will again. In the meantime, in all our separate essays about love and survival, I feel like we are still writing together. Our essays are chapters in the serial story of our shared lives. I believe that one day, in the fullness of time, our books will sit next to each other on a shelf, just as they have grown next to each other in our notebooks and conversations for so many fast and slow years.

∾

During the Cancercoaster, Ritu was usually the one who brought us all together. "That was often my role," she remembers, "corralling the community around a common purpose." Since then, Ritu has become a therapist, and she sees the work we did in the care team as a kind of family therapy: "We prepared as a group and individually so much for the loss, and it feels like we did that work, and now we have the good stuff, the best stuff. We have this history of intensity, and we'll always have that feeling of support."

For decades, Ash and Ri shared the kind of familial intimacy in which they defined themselves in relation to the other, with clear-cut, contrasting, complementary roles. Ri is generous, emotionally available, and deeply attuned to the social dynamics around her. Ash tends to be more inwardly attuned, self-contained, and independent. Ri is a planner; Ash lives in the present. Ri is resourceful and practical—the kind of person you want to help you bring order out of chaos or solve a problem. Ash has an uncanny ability to tolerate ambiguity and thrive in uncertainty; she's well practiced at drowning out everyday distractions to prioritize ritual, creativity, and a spiritual sense of beauty and meaning.

Crisis was the catalyst for what Ritu calls "the co-mingling of middle-aged friendship," in which each of them took on some of the strengths of the other. Ash credits Ritu with pushing her to devote much more time and attention to the tedious and bureaucratic parts of being a cancer patient than she wanted to—a difficult adjustment that Ash believes has helped to prolong her life. Meanwhile Ritu's practical perspective is now suffused with a sense of magical possibility that she always admired in Ash but never experienced before. "I sincerely feel more hopeful," she told me, with a kind of delight. "And that is Ashley. Because even in the absolute worst times, Ash knew that life is random and not random at the same time, and when it is random, you might as well hope."

$\approx$

I initially wanted to write about friendship after the Cancercoaster as a story about anticlimax and happy endings—as if we were all slowly coasting to safety at the end of an amusement park ride before shakily returning to solid ground. I wanted to narrate a kind of resolution; a kind of relief. This was a story with a miracle in it, after all.

But when I suggested this narrative to Ritu, she pushed back. "I don't feel that the weight of crisis has lifted," she said.

"Instead, my relationship to crisis has shifted. Crisis has become family instead of being a stranger."

Ritu was talking about Ash, who is still living a life shadowed by cancer, but I know that is not all she meant. Ash is not Ri's only close friend to receive a life-altering diagnosis, and friends are not the only people Ri is caring for and mourning.

Among the care team, I was exceptional and lucky in that for years Ash's illness was my only substantial caregiving responsibility, and my sole source of mortal grief and dread. When Lisa got the news of Ash's diagnosis, she was still reeling from the sudden death of her mother just a few months before, and during the first year of the Cancercoaster, she was also working as a chaplain at a trauma center hospital, on call to death every day. Meanwhile Sarah and Ritu combined their immersive, whole-souled care for Ash with, as Ritu puts it, "losing people and creating people": with caring for and then mourning their fathers-in-law, and giving birth to and caring for their sons. And Ash lost her father within a year of her diagnosis, bearing the heavy weight of his grief about her deadly illness even as she carried her grief about his. Throughout her illness, she continued to work with refugees: a category of people defined by disaster.

I have wanted to believe that crisis, once known, could become a stranger again: that it could arrive without warning, turn our friendships into family, comingle our souls, teach us to hope, spare us the worst, and then leave us in peace. But I know that's too simple; I know Ritu is right. Crisis is always there, whether I remember it or not, and it has become family for me too.

In the years since Ash got a miracle, two more of my closest friends have been diagnosed with cancer. During the week I was writing this essay, Ash got the best scan results of her life, and another friend called to tell me that the results of her latest scan were unexpectedly ominous. No illness is ever the same as another; no friendship is ever the same as another. But the intimacy of illness and friendship has become as familiar as déjà vu. Even as I have basked in these miraculous years of calm with Ash, I have returned with other friends to those tumultuous times when love and dread carry us along with their own momentum. In sickness and in health, I have spent so many days lying next to the women I love and talking with them for hours, as if being together is all that matters, because sometimes, during the sickening plunges and long lulls between miracles, it is all that does.

ON SISTERS

Nancy Mitford: Sisters are a shield against life's cruel adversity.
Decca Mitford: But sisters ARE life's cruel adversity!

—QUOTED IN MARY S. LOVELL, THE SISTERS:
THE SAGA OF THE MITFORD FAMILY

L IKE ELIZABETH BENNET,[1] Hilton Als,[2] Charles D'Ambrosio,[3] and Jazmine Hughes,[4] I have four sisters. My original plan for this essay was to see the Tina Fey–Amy Poehler comedy *Sisters* with my sisters over the holidays and write a kind of conversational film review—a transcription of all of our during-the-movie snarky whispers and post-movie summary judgments. On *Sisters*, by sisters!

---

1. See Jane Austen, *Pride and Prejudice* (1813), or the endlessly rewatchable 1995 BBC adaptation.

2. See Hilton Als, *The Women* (1996).

3. But he saves his best sentences for his brothers. See "Salinger and Sobs," reprinted in *Loitering* (2014).

4. See Jazmine Hughes, "Sisters, Ranked," *Hairpin*, December 15, 2014.

I texted them all about it before my trip home in December, and they were open to the idea—especially since I was paying—though they were not exactly enthusiastic.

Second Sister: I was just thinking how awful that movie looked! But if it's free, heck, why not.

First Sister (Me): Say snarky things I can quote!

Second Sister: They'll be copyrighted.

When I arrived home, it turned out that my sisters didn't actually need to see the movie in order to start getting snarky about it.

Fourth Sister: Tina and Amy are like, "We're strong women writers and actors in Hollywood blah blah blah." No you're not. You're racist as fuck and you're kinda boring.

First Sister: Yay, that's great! Let me write that down.

Though they were far more interested in seeing *Creed* (*Fifth Sister: Yes plz all I want for Christmas is biceps*), we made vague plans to see *Sisters* the day after Christmas. But then, being real-life sisters—not cooperative figments of my writerly imagination—they rebelled. Or, to be more accurate, they fell into the kind of mildly resistant inertia that is one of our primary sister stances when we all get together: immobile, immovable, not really interested in anything that would require putting on a bra and going out into the world.

Third Sister: If I were to sum up the last 20 years of my relation-ships with any of my four sisters, it would not be a highlights reel.

I love all my sisters and have fond memories with each, but the relationships—in their various states—have been shattered and restored and hewn by tragedies and births and deaths and near-deaths and hospitalizations and marriage and years of absence and thousands of miles of distance. The highlights for me are the times when we are all in the same place, which happens less than once a year, and we spend like an hour together—hanging out in sweat-pants and drinking coffee—that is totally devoid of conflict.

The five of us live in four states on two coasts, and over the decades we have done devastating and unforgettable things to each other. We've professed our dislike for each other; we've unfriended and blocked each other; we've abandoned the family to move far away; we've dropped out; we've blacked out; we've had to be bailed out; we've decided not to invite each other to our weddings; we've used that gentle patron-izing tone that grates like a shredder; we've gone straight for the jugular; we've broken each other's codependent hearts.

Second Sister: We've been pretty bad, but we've never stolen each other's boyfriends or burned each other's manuscripts.

But when we find ourselves back in the falling-apart house we grew up in, we revert to a kind of timeless tableau of togetherness, as if some malevolent (or benevolent?) fairy had stopped the clocks, surrounded our house with insur-mountable brambles, and frozen us in place with our mugs in our hands.

Second Sister: Our love has life-choking roots that are tangled underground.

At times like these, we become almost interchangeable, finishing each other's phrases, cuddling each other's children, wearing our hair in matching messy blonde topknots, and taking our coffee the exact same way (2 percent milk; no sugar). We are sisters beneath the skin: We have matching tattoos, five anchors to moor us in harbor. And of course I am one of us, even though I moved far away over a decade ago and sometimes suffer from sister imposter syndrome. So there I was after Christmas in my sweats with my coffee, glad to sit around hour after hour and snark about nothing and take turns holding the adorable six-month-old baby that one of my sisters had made.

Part of me wanted to get out of the house and watch a movie and write, but mostly I didn't want to break the spell, and I knew I couldn't even if I tried.

So stuck, so static, so trapped in a pattern.

So familiar, so effortless, so intimate.

~

In the end I saw *Sisters* with my friend Leslie when I got back to New Haven, and it turns out that a friend was the perfect person to see it with, since at its best it's really a movie about friends.

As they do in their 2008 film *Baby Mama*, Amy Poehler and Tina Fey play an odd couple: a financially precarious, fertile party girl and a financially stable, childless, uptight career woman. But in *Sisters*, the roles are flipped, with Amy as the tightly wound neurotic and Tina as the wild child. In both movies, the plot, such as it is, pushes both women toward the middle, with the party girl learning to embrace maternal responsibility and the prim woman learning to get drunk and get laid. Problems solved!

Baby Mama is a pretty joyless variation on the theme. Tina's character is constrained by the role of a conventional rom-com heroine, with none of Liz Lemon's (or Tina's) abrasive eccentricity, and Amy's character is a flat, white-trash stereotype. Their chemistry is nonexistent. *Sisters*, on the other hand, mainly consists of a mellow succession of montages showcasing Tina and Amy's comfy, bouncy pleasure in each other's company: a road-trip montage, a trying-on-slutty-clothes montage, a playing-with-1980s-toys-in-their-childhood-bedroom montage, a shopping-for-party-supplies montage, a getting-crazy-at-the-last-party-they-throw-in-their-childhood-home-with-their-high-school-friends montage.

They bump bellies. They give each other pep talks. They read their diaries to each other in the bathtub. They are each other's best wing-women. It's an *SNL* sketch mixed with a Golden Globes spiel. It's not really going anywhere in particular, but it's kind of a hoot.

This low-stakes celebration of playfulness is what the film does best. And on a very basic level, it is nice to see female friends in their forties taking up so much screen time and having so much ridiculous fun: not just Tina and Amy but Samantha Bee and Rachel Dratch as well, who play drunken revelers, and an especially glorious Maya Rudolph as Brinda, the ultimate party crasher. The sisters' romantic interests—a warm, unusually understated Ike Barinholtz and a deadpan John Cena—are a delight.

But incredibly, during all this happy, loopy time, we're expected to believe that the sisters are reeling from a major unresolved loss. Tina's teenage daughter has recently run away because of Tina's chronic irresponsibility, homelessness, and substance abuse, and Tina has no idea where she is. Eventually we learn (spoiler alert) that Amy has been taking care of her homeless niece and keeping it a secret from Tina. This is a complex family drama that might be expected to plunge us into the depths of thwarted maternal feeling and ancient sisterly rivalry. But for most of the movie, this intimate history of loss and betrayal casts little to no shadow on the sisters' easy, breezy, montage-y relationship.

The chasms of difference separating the sisters—chasms of class, educational achievement, sexual experience, solvency, sobriety, closeness with their parents, closeness with their niece or daughter—are basically a nonissue. Even in the midst of a crisis, these strangely friendly sisters can access nostalgia without navigating the minefields of memory. They can give each other advice without crushing eggshells underfoot. There's some mud wrestling tacked on toward the end for belated conflict, but it's too little, too late.

It is obvious throughout that Tina and Amy, who are best friends in real life, have zero actual sisters.

Third Sister: I saw promotional interviews they did about the movie and they said they'd been friends for 20 years so they were basically sisters. *The interviewer asked if they'd ever fought, and they said no. ROFL. Sisters, my ass.*

First Sister: Sisters are like the OPPOSITE of friends!!!

Tina and Amy's friendship—founded on writing and work, ticking steadily and undramatically into its third decade—resembles many of the friendships I've loved the most. "Tina reminds me of how far I have come," Amy writes in *Yes Please*. "She knew me when. When we are together I feel strong and powerful." And later: "Tina shows her love for you by writing for you. I can't tell you how many times she wrote something special and wonderful for me." Meanwhile, in a chapter of *Bossypants* subtitled "One in a series of love letters to Amy Poehler," Tina remembers her delight when Amy shut down a male *SNL* performer who was criticizing her comedy on the grounds that it wasn't cute. Tina recalls, "I was so happy. . . . I remember thinking, 'My friend is here! My friend is here!' . . . With Amy there, I felt less alone."

This is friendship as I know it now: an alliance that sustains ambition and endeavor, a mutual appreciation society, a balm for loneliness. It's what Leslie Knope and Ann Perkins celebrate on Galentine's Day with waffles, and what my friends and I celebrate on Galentine's Day with tomato soup cake. It's a far cry from the enervating, self-dissolving fun-house mirror of sisterhood.

Friendships can be fraught, of course, and sisterhood can be fun.

Third Sister: Not all sister relationships resemble Hopper sister relationships.

And not all friendships resemble Fey-Poehler friendships. I've lost close female friends twice since I grew up. Neither of my lost friends had sisters, and each of them found in our friendship a scope for sister-style ardor, recrimination, and fury that I ultimately couldn't share. Our intimacy couldn't bear its own weight. There are estranged sisters, but there are no former sisters. Even a dead sister is always a sister. But these two women are not my estranged friends; they are no longer my friends at all. When they cut ties, there was no root system to keep us connected or grow us back together.

Sisterhood often has to sustain itself through things that can end or prevent intimate friendships: distance, betrayal, unkindness, dislike, or a backbreakingly heavy backstory. And the miraculous and absurd thing is that it often does.

≈

Sisterhood cinema is a twisted and heart-twisting tradition, encompassing *Sense and Sensibility, Little Women, A Stolen Life, The Parent Trap,* and *What Ever Happened to Baby Jane?,* with the sisters movies I love the most combining laughter with panic. I'm thinking of *The Miracle of Morgan's Creek,* a raunchy screwball farce about sisters supporting each other through a catastrophic unplanned pregnancy; the wry melodramedy *Holiday,* in which an agoraphobic Katharine Hepburn is forced to choose whether or not to steal her sister's fiancé, Cary Grant; and the unsettling and intense *Your Sister's Sister,* an independent film with a telenovela plot, in which the prospect of pregnancy pulls sisters together and pushes them apart. Then there are the movies I watch over and over with my sisters: *Three Smart Girls*, which is about sisterhood as an embattled conspiracy, and *White Christmas*, which features a sister-act song about sisterly loyalty, ruthlessness, and betrayal.

Family comedies thrive on love-hate relationships, with their tension and ambivalence and creatively worded insults, and I couldn't help hoping that Tina and Amy would bring some of the bite of *Mean Girls* to their contribution to the genre. But *Sisters* is emotionally simple and slack. Stories about substance abuse and codependence require deeper wounds and darker humor in order to earn their overdetermined happy endings. *Sisters* is a substance abuse story, whether it wants to admit it or not, and its premise that partying problems can be solved by a party is an unfunny joke.

Despite its superficial take on family relationships, *Sisters* was a more or less fine way to kill time in a theater. What it really needed—besides a better part for the talented Greta Lee, scandalously consigned to a series of troubling Asian stereotypes (heavily accented manicurist, exoticized sex object, white guy's trophy wife)—was more textured subtext and substantive conflict. If only it had chosen to do more with the classic Jane Austen potential of odd-couple sisters and the deep complexity of its ostensible story. But it mostly squandered both. Like Amy Poehler's Smart Girls, an "online community" featuring an upbeat meme stream of pep talks and self-esteem, *Sisters* celebrates a friendly kind of sisterhood that is all girl power and no grief. It's a feminist fantasy that depends on denying the difficulty of intimacy and the combustibility of women together.

Amy and Tina are friends who love each other and who have never fought once in twenty years, and that is great. But when I think about my numerous sisters and the number we have done on one another, I am conscious of a different kind of bond. We are tied together by our boundary-blurring identification, our unwilled oceanic empathy, our mutually defining dependence (*Why do you get to be the smart one and I have to be the pretty one?*), our intimate observations shot like perfectly aimed arrows, our whispered conspiracies, our rapturous reunions, our fracked bedrock connections, and our resentful and mostly unspoken mutual respect. We have not been friends, but, as one sister says about another in Miriam Toews's *All My Puny Sorrows*, we have been "enemies who loved each other."

THE STARS

THERE ARE many ways to be starstruck. Some people are content to bask in the glow of polished perfection. Others are seeking a fiercer light.

James Baldwin stargazed at Bette Davis because she embodied women who were blazingly ugly and angry. In *The Devil Finds Work*, his long essay on film, he writes about how when he was a child he was taught to think of himself as hideous because of his enormous eyes. It wasn't until he went to the movies and saw his eyes in her face that the meaning of his alleged ugliness changed, its possibilities opening up: "So here, now, was Bette Davis, on that Saturday afternoon, in close-up, over a champagne glass, pop-eyes popping. I was astounded." Baldwin found intelligence and disaster in her face, and unhinged freedom in her moods and speech.

In his autobiographical novel *Go Tell It on the Mountain*, he describes the effect of one of her on-screen rages on the novel's movie-loving protagonist, John:

The woman was most evil. She was blonde and pasty white . . . Nothing tamed or broke her, nothing touched her, neither kindness, nor scorn, nor hatred, nor love. She had never thought of prayer . . . John could not have found in his heart, had he dared to search it, any wish for her redemption. He wanted to be like her, only more powerful, more thorough, more cruel; to make those around him, all who hurt him, suffer . . . Go on girl, he whispered . . . Go on girl. One day he would talk like that.

Bette's wild white womanhood and silver-screen stardom gave her the enviable license to rail against a white man at the top of her lungs, and to express repudiation and disgust with every expression and gesture. Somewhere in her untamed words was the cadence Baldwin craved.

The needs I bring to Bette are different from Baldwin's, but my identification with her has been almost as urgent and ardent. For me as well, she is an embodiment of astounding ugliness and dubious desires; of scintillating passions I've been taught not to voice or claim. Bette embodies an extreme, exhilarating, incandescent version of her audience, offering a sparkling new take on old sadness and shame.

Baldwin's formative ugly Bette is the screaming syphilitic sex worker Mildred in *Of Human Bondage*. Mine is Charlotte Vale in *Now, Voyager*, a hideous and awkward spinster aunt. Charlotte may be milder in manner than Mildred, but she is equally passionate, and equally resistant to the conventions of love.

∾

I have loved *Now, Voyager* for so long now, and it is always such solace to be enveloped by it. I'll never forget seeing it on the big screen twelve years ago in London. The red velvet curtains swept aside, the music swelled, the prow of an ocean liner cut through a frothy sea, and hundreds of women and gay men reached for their Kleenex in unison. Thanks in part to the seductive string-section stylings of Max Steiner and Peter Ilyich Tchaikovsky, *Now, Voyager* is a perfect melodrama. It is also a dieter's and drag queen's dream—a film in which you can lose your eyebrows and some weight, don a pompadour and a corsage, and find yourself.

As befits a tale with a title from Walt Whitman, self-transformation in *Now, Voyager* is fully embodied. Salvation requires sex, altered flesh, and literal voyages, while freedom in this film is defined through food and fat, not least through women controlling their own fat and one another's. Our heroine is a sheltered thirty-something spinster who still lives with her mother in her childhood home, unable to find a way to flee. She is given a new lease on life when she has a nervous breakdown and follows a stay at a mental institution with a restorative cruise to Brazil. She breaks free from her domineering mother, who "doesn't believe in diets," by dieting; she triumphantly quells her bullying niece by calling her "Roly-Poly"; and she proves her own suitability for motherhood by persuading her anorexic future foster daughter to eat ice cream. The film's conflation of weight and well-being is both resonant and troubling.

But despite its status as the quintessential melodrama and makeover/eating-disorder movie, *Now, Voyager* exceeds

definitions. It is not so much the story of a single makeover as
it is a series of metamorphoses, and it defies melodramatic
convention by allowing its heroine, in two short hours, to play
nearly every mythic women's role, from the tragic to the
comic, the grotesque to the mundane. Bette Davis as Charlotte
Vale embodies the classic heroines Galatea, Cordelia, Cinder-
ella, and Camille; the clichés of the Impatient Virgin, the
Woman in Love with Her Analyst, and the Other Woman;
the primal archetypes of Daughter, Sister, Aunt, and Mother
(this is a highly matriarchal cinematic world); and the glowing
advertising images of the Outdoorswoman, the Hostess with
the Mostest, and the Most Popular Woman on Board. And she
manages all this while at all times being (at least technically)
that other cliché, the Old Maid.

Though it was no doubt made for unhappily married
middle-aged housewives (as all Hollywood melodramas
supposedly were), *Now, Voyager* is not about them, at least not
in the way that classic "women's pictures" like *Stella Dallas*
or *Mildred Pierce* or *Magnificent Obsession* or *Imitation of Life* or
All That Heaven Allows are about them. In those films, restless married mothers are forced to redefine the meaning of
their lives when they lose their children or their partners or
both. Unlike these movies, *Now, Voyager* is not a fantasy
fulfillment of a thirty- or fortyish woman's need for a second
act after marriage and children have somehow failed to satisfy.
Instead it is a fantasy about what can happen when that first
act never materializes.

What can happen, in brief, is that you can steam up some
parked cars on a ship à la Kate Winslet in *Titanic*; meet a
charming shrink with whom you have great chemistry

(Claude Rains, most famous for playing Captain Renault in *Casablanca*); check yourself back into his delightful mental hospital; go on a diet; borrow some hot clothes; go on a vacay to Brazil and hook up with a sexy and inexplicably Austrian-accented, married architect named Jerry (Paul Henreid, most famous for playing Victor Laszlo in *Casablanca*); feel *alive* for the first time; nobly and passionately renounce Jerry because he can never get a divorce because he doesn't want to lose custody of his children; feel *unafraid* for the first time; get engaged to a boring Bostonian WASP just because; get bored and break it off; inherit a million dollars from the mother you hated; check yourself back in to the mental hospital for a minute and banter with your shrink some more; make friends with a young patient at the mental hospital who happens to be your architect ex's adorable anorexic daughter, Tina; unofficially adopt your architect ex's adorable anorexic daughter, Tina (it turns out she hates her bio-mom, and conveniently the feeling is mutual); and spend the rest of your life bouncing energetically around your mansion with your friends and your kid, parenting, partying, playing loud music, roasting hot dogs in the fire-places, flirting with your former shrink, and using your money and know-how to help shape mental health care policy.

Very occasionally, say in the final minutes of your film, you may find yourself floating into a delicious moment of sky-high melodrama with your architect ex, who likes to light two cigarettes in his mouth at once and then soulfully pass one to you. By the transitive property, it will be like your lips are touching his—a thrill you will live on for years.

In that last scene, Jerry, oblivious straight man that he is, tries to tell Charlotte that she should want "some man who'll make you happy," but Charlotte, a self-described "sentimental fool," ridicules this notion as "the most conventional, pretentious, pious speech I've ever heard in my life!" What she really wants is not the closure of a marriage plot—something Jerry can never give her—but an end to the emotional exclusion she experienced as an odd and ugly spinster. She wants no longer "to be shut out, barred out, to be always an outsider or an extra!" She wants full participation in her passions, even if that means settling for what she calls "that little strip of territory that's ours": a sexless emotional affair with a married man and shared custody of his daughter. When he asks her, "But are you happy, Charlotte?" she melodramatically and magnificently pushes the question aside: "Oh, Jerry, don't let's ask for the moon; we have the stars." Her face is lit with a celestial glow.

Charlotte's last words—"we have the stars"—are just a fancier version of "Nobody's perfect," the famous last lines of *Some Like It Hot*, delivered by Jack Lemmon's new husband at the climactic moment when Jack tears off his drag wig and confesses he's a man (turns out it's not a deal-breaker). Resigned and defiant one-liners like these are a gay man's or spinster's classic response to the straight happy ending. They are strong statements about the irrelevance of a clichéd straight happiness, or straight sadness—an alternative to the impulse that prompts Donna Reed in *It's a Wonderful Life* to ask Jimmy Stewart for the moon, and get it.

∾

Over the decades, Charlotte's star-crossed story has served a dazzling array of purposes for viewers who find themselves invisible or caught between categories. Nadia Ellis, a scholar of African diasporic, Caribbean, and postcolonial literature, has written with perceptiveness and pleasure about Charlotte's unlikely fascination for the West Indian historian, activist, and Melville scholar C. L. R. James, who watched *Now, Voyager* six times in the theater after moving to the United States from England in the 1940s. Ellis argues that his identification with Charlotte helped James to work out "the conditions of belonging in a place of uncertain belonging"—a kind of "territory of the soul." More recently, Charlotte's status as simultaneously sick and strong provided the critic and essayist Angelica Jade Bastién with a hopeful, humane way of thinking about mental illness when she needed an alternative to despair and shame. "Charlotte Vale and I are separated by race and class, culture and access," Bastien writes. "But in my late teens, shuffling between mental hospitals and new medications, *Now, Voyager* gave me what I couldn't find in reality . . . the ability to be seen and even understood."

Now, Voyager has made me feel seen and understood as well. As a spinster with a passionate past, I appreciate the way Charlotte illuminates possibilities for a romantic and familial future even as she insists on the ways that love is limited by convention. Because no matter how privileged Charlotte may be, her deepest desires must remain invisible and unfulfilled. "Charlotte doesn't escape marginalization entirely," my friend Ivan observes. "She merely makes it a more enchanting space."

Now, Voyager does not end happily ever after. But it does not end tragically either. It rewrites the *Stella Dallas* or *Mildred Pierce* melodramas of doomed self-sacrificing single motherhood, and takes out the self-sacrifice and the doom. In the end, Stella and Mildred lose their daughters and their dreams of romantic love. By settling for the stars, Charlotte manages to keep both. Her choice to devote herself to a foster daughter rather than marrying a man she doesn't love allows her to feel continuing currents of romantic emotion; it even swells and floods them. For Charlotte, taking care of Tina will never be a fully satisfying substitute for a sex life or a secure social status, but it is better than trying to force herself to be content with a happiness she doesn't want. Instead, Charlotte improvises a new family form while remaining dazzled by desire for the man she can never have.

Marriage and happy ending be damned, she gets to revel shameless in her starry, moonless night.

THE FOUNDLING MUSEUM

L AST SUMMER I spent a day in London at the Foundling
Museum, a place I'd first visited years before and have
been haunted by ever since. The museum commemorates the
Foundling Hospital, a children's home established in the eigh-
teenth century as a response to "the inhumane Custom of
exposing New born children to Perish in the Streets." Before
birth control, abortion, and formalized systems of adoption,
during a time when the stigma of extramarital sex could doom
a woman's hopes of maintaining a job or a place in society,
mothers often felt they had no choice but to abandon their
children to the elements. This practice contributed to already
grim rates of child mortality: 75 percent of children in London
died before they were five years old. The Foundling Hospital
offered some women another option. Infants left there would
be fostered in families for a few years until they were returned
to the Hospital to be trained for service or trades. Between
1741 and 1954, the Hospital was home to about twenty-five
thousand foundlings.

Many of the women who surrendered their children
hoped to reclaim them. If they were literate, they might

write a note affirming their relationship with the child. Others left everyday objects to attach to their child's file, so they could return one day and say: *Mine was the baby with the hazelnut shell.* These tokens have been displayed to the public since the nineteenth century, arranged in neat rows in large glass cases, and I have spent hours gazing at them: buttons, thimbles, hairpins, medals, keys without padlocks, padlocks without keys, scraps of fabric, splinters of bone. Each token represents a child who was likely never reclaimed, and a mother who never reclaimed them. The objects are sacred and ordinary and opaque, each one holding a story that may never be told: an unwieldy narrative of sex, shame, labor, pain, hope, love, and loss compressed in a piece of metal, cloth, or clay.

The foundling tokens haunt me because they are a reckoning with the place between maternity and childlessness; between choosing to be a mother and choosing not to be. They are placeholders for an absence, souvenirs of an unlived life. They are a way of holding on and letting go at the same time.

"To us, a small scrap of fabric linking mother and child seems ineffably fragile," writes the textile historian John Styles; "surely the thread will snap." In most cases the thread wasn't strong enough. For the first decades of the Hospital's existence, fewer than one in a hundred babies was reclaimed. But sometimes, against all odds, the thread held. Styles writes about a piece of patchwork with a heart embroidered on it in red, one of the very few tokens representing a baby who was redeemed: "One half of the heart was left with the Hospital.

The other was, presumably, kept by the mother until the reunion, when the heart was made whole."

~

When I am able to tear myself away from the tokens—even for an onlooker, leaving them behind feels like a kind of abandonment—I walk to the quiet upstairs room, where I can be alone with the large eighteenth-century painting of Hagar and Ishmael in the wilderness.

According to the book of Genesis, Hagar was an Egyptian woman enslaved by Sarah, Abraham's infertile wife. In an attempt to have children by indirect means, Sarah told Abraham to use Hagar as a sexual surrogate to conceive a child on her behalf. As a person considered property, Hagar had no choice. Even though Hagar's rape was originally Sarah's idea, when Hagar got pregnant Sarah was eaten up with envy and complained to Abraham about her. Abraham told Sarah, "Your slave-girl is in your power; do to her as you please." Sarah was cruel to Hagar and so she ran away, but an angel told her to return, promising her that she would have a son named Ishmael—meaning "God hears"—because God had heard her affliction. Later, Sarah had a son of her own—a legitimate son, Isaac—and now that she and Abraham had a real family, their improvised family involving Ishmael and Hagar was no longer necessary. Sarah couldn't bear to look at them. She told Abraham to cast them out, and he did, sending them off with bread and water to wander in the wilderness.

Before long they ran out of water. Hagar found some bushes and placed Ishmael underneath them, hoping the shade might protect him for a while. Then she walked away, because she didn't want to watch him die. She said aloud, maybe to God, "Do not make me watch the death of my child." Then she wept. An angel called to her and told her, "Don't be afraid; God has heard your son's voice. Go to him and hold him. I will make a great nation of him." And then she saw that God had made a well of water, and she gave her son the water, and they lived.

In 1746, the English artist Joseph Highmore painted Hagar and Ishmael and the angel in the desert and presented the painting to the Foundling Hospital, and it has been there ever since. Perhaps some mothers saw it when they came to relinquish their children. "A tale about a female servant being mistreated by a master who fathers her child would have spoken strongly to those who argued that foundling mothers were the agents of their fate," suggests the author of a booklet about the museum. The image certainly seems to emphasize Hagar's powerlessness. Ishmael is dying, and Hagar is praying, and the angel is interrupting her with words of hope. The angel must be telling Hagar, "Don't be afraid! Your child will live!" In the Bible, the angel also commands Hagar to hold on to her son, but if the painting is an allegory of the Foundling Hospital, that can't be what he is saying. Instead of telling Hagar to hold on to her child, he must be telling her to let him go.

≈

When my mother was my age, she had been pregnant and given birth eight times. Six of her children lived, one was stillborn, and one died of birth trauma on the day he was born. My mother is in her sixties now, and she has had children living with her since she was twenty-two. She loves all of her children, but they have never been easy. When I told her I hoped to become a mother, she said, "Are you *sure*? It would be so much more convenient if you didn't."

Of course she is right. Even when you have a husband and a home, motherhood is a highly inconvenient desire.

My mother did not intend to have so many children. When I was small I used to pray every night for a brand-new baby sister, and she would shake her head at me and refuse to say Amen. Still, once they arrived she was glad to see them.

~

To say I have always wanted to be a mother doesn't feel adequate. It would be more accurate to say I always thought of myself as a mother—just one who didn't happen to have children yet.

I was balancing babies on my hips before I had hips. In elementary school, I learned to stand a-kilter to keep my sisters from sliding off the place my hip would one day be. In pictures of me playing the piano as a child, I usually have an infant sister sitting on my lap, or a toddler sister next to me on the bench, leaning against me as we play a duet. Pianos are still triangulated objects for me—when I play one alone, I feel an absence.

In a formal photo of me and my siblings when I was sixteen, I look like a harried parent surrounded by my progeny, holding on tight to the baby on my lap. Often I would try to ignore my siblings or hide from them in a book, but at night I was haunted by maternal anxiety dreams: I had to drive them to safety, but I didn't yet know how to drive. I had to keep them safe inside the house from the danger lurking outside, but they kept climbing out the windows.

I never had an idealized notion of motherhood. I witnessed six of my mother's pregnancies, and I saw the toll they took on her. I was twelve when she came home from the hospital after delivering my stillborn sister, her teeth chattering uncontrollably in reaction to the labor-inducing hormones. I was terrified. And of course my mother's living children were much harder on her than her dead ones. By the time I was in my twenties I had put her through the wringer, and my siblings were starting to as well.

Still, I was certain I wanted children, for reasons I couldn't explain. If pressed, I might have said that a child can turn a love story into an origin story; a personal ritual into a shared tradition; a pointless job into an urgent purpose. Children are what hips and pianos are for.

In high school and college, I was already collecting books for my future children to read and babysitting for free to keep in practice. When I began grad school, my sense of my professional future was hazy, but I was certain I wanted at least three kids. I decided to start having them in my twenties: I'd read a book about aging and infertility, and I didn't want to be one of those women who put off motherhood until it was too late.

~

The years since then have sometimes seemed designed to teach me about reproductive powerlessness. Despite my decision to have children as soon as possible, I spent the most fertile years of my life craving kids while doubling up on birth control. For a long time I dated men who weren't yet ready to have children (though I hoped they would be someday), and then I was single for a decade. I was in grad school until my early thirties, often making less than $25,000 a year, and when I finally got a job, my student loan payments cost about as much as childcare. At one point a friend with two kids teasingly referred to my student debt as my "loan baby." I began to imagine my loan baby as a malevolent ghost, a changeling who had pushed my real baby out of the nest before it could be born.

~

I know there is all the difference in the world between the agony of losing a child and the ache of never having one. I hesitate even to compare these pains, for fear that my words might clumsily brush up against someone's bruise or wound. Neither of these sorrows is yet mine to represent. I have never lost a child, and as someone who hasn't yet given up hope of having one, I can't even speak authoritatively about the ache.

I also know that in a way I am blessed not to have a child to lose. Even as I write this, there are women crossing the Sonoran Desert, looking for shade, looking for water, afraid to watch their children die. There are women divided from their children by bureaucracy—the official forms of ICE or CPS that tear families in two. These women are Hagar's sisters, and the sisters of the women whose tokens fill the glass cases. I know the angels are on their side, and I want to be on their side as well. But as a woman with food and water and freedom and protection, I know I have more in common with Sarah. If I'm not careful, I could fall into her feelings: resentment; bitterness; obliviousness to my relative power.

∼

When I first visited the Foundling Museum in my twenties, I was overcome by the helplessness of Hagar and the found-ling mothers. They moved me because they represented maternal powerlessness in the face of fate. I projected onto their stories a kind of romance of resignation, a sublime submission to suffering. Their desperation became bearable and beautiful when mediated through the aesthetics of a curi-osity cabinet or swirls of oil on canvas, mellowed with the patina of time.

I'm still overcome when I contemplate their hardships, but now my sense of their suffering is tempered by a respect for their resourcefulness when they were faced with hardships I can barely imagine.

In her book on the Foundling Hospital in the Victo-rian age, the historian Jessica Sheetz-Nguyen cautions against viewing the foundling mothers as "hapless victims." She is interested not just in the "dire choices" these women faced, but in their hard work to find a way through them. She documents how the mothers persistently sought out help in the midst of their crisis: writing or dictating petitions, crafting their own stories into compelling narratives, and braving difficult interviews with the administrators of the Foundling Hospital in order to argue that their babies deserved a place there. In a world where single women could not keep their children without losing their livelihoods, these women were fighting fiercely for their own future as well as their children's.

Meanwhile Hagar is not nearly as helpless as she seemed. In the white American Christian tradition I was raised in, Hagar is seen as a castaway woman on the edge of the story, but as an enslaved African woman who survived exploitation and was blessed by God to raise up a nation, Hagar has long been an iconic figure in African American theology. "The African-American community has taken Hagar's story unto itself," Delores S. Williams writes in her classic of womanist theology, *Sisters in the Wilderness*, which takes Hagar's story as its central theme:

> She and Ishmael together, as family, model many black American families in which a lone woman/mother struggles to hold the family together in spite of the poverty to which ruling class economics consign it. Hagar, like many black women, goes into the wide world to make a living for herself and her child, with only God by her side.

Despite the terror and desperation of the desert, Williams and other womanist theologians write Hagar's story as one of defiant tenacity. Not powerlessness, but power. Not letting go, but holding on.

∾

I am not a mother, and maybe I never will be. For a long time I have been trying to understand and manage that anticipated maternal ache—to see my childlessness as an effect of my privilege as well as of my powerlessness; as a gift from affordable birth control as much as it is as a curse from the men who didn't love me enough. The Foundling Museum has been a site of pilgrimage that has put my own ambivalent experience in the perspective of thousands of years of suffering and strength. I've kept returning there, in body and in spirit, because I feel compelled to mourn the ways that maternity is thwarted by circumstance, and to honor the ways women have found to survive nonetheless.

WAVEFORMS AND THE
WOMEN'S MARCH

I ARRIVED IN D.C. on Friday morning as the inauguration was taking place. My friend Samira met me outside Union Station wearing a pussy hat she'd knitted, and handed an identical one to me. When I put it on, I felt none of the minor embarrassment I'd expected to feel, just warmth against the cold. At first we weren't sure whether we wanted to go home to Samira's place and hunker down until the Women's March or walk around and, as I said, "look at history." She's a scholar of American religion; I'm a writer. We realized we couldn't look away.

We walked into a sea of Inauguration Day protesters—Black Lives Matter, #NoDAPL, Obama-nostalgic, antifa. There was a man in a polar bear suit protesting climate change. There was an elephant-sized, elephant-shaped balloon with a giant sign on its side saying RACISM. We bought an assortment of Shepard Fairey "We the People" posters for a dollar each, and later gave the poster with a picture of an old water protector to a young Native woman who asked us where she could get one. Meanwhile the street vendors were trying in vain to move their Trump/Pence merchandise, and right-wing propaganda vehicles were driving slowly by: an antiabortion van plastered with pictures of fetal body parts; a violent transmisogyny truck covered with all-caps endorsements of the bathroom bill and injunctions to BE A MAN and DEFEND THE CHILDREN, plus many pictures of guns.

I heard Trump's twenty-one-gun salute without knowing at first what it was. It sounded ominous, like thunder.

For hours that day we marched with the crowd. If there was a route or a plan, no one seemed to know it. Along the way, we saw riot police, at least thirty of them, watching and waiting from the side of the road. Even on a gray day there was a glare on their glassy exoskeletons. A few hours later, they were tear-gassing protesters in McPherson Square. Samira and I ended up following the crowd up an on-ramp and onto the beltway and shutting it down.

For a while, we stood together in the parted sea of traffic. On one side of us were stranded cabs and motionless stretch limos full of angry men in MAGA hats, and on the other side, a post-apocalyptically deserted highway. Above us, helicopters swooped and surveilled. We thought about staying and maybe getting arrested, but decided not to. We had to march again the next day.

≈

Published the month after the 2016 election, the anthology *Waveform: Twenty-First-Century Essays by Women* arrived as an anachronism, like a birthday cake at a wake. "Women's essays today are exuberant in all senses of the word—plentiful, energetic, lively, and unrestrained," effuses its editor, Marcia Aldrich, in her introduction. "The essays are coming in waves." In accounting for this oceanic exuberance, Aldrich mentions several defining aspects of contemporary culture that had already taken on sinister new meanings by the time the book reached print:

> Social media have made everyone a potential author—all it takes is a few keystrokes and a post . . . Boundaries between fiction and nonfiction . . . have melted . . . Reality television makes the claim that anyone's life is worth documentation. And so on.

As an essayist who owes much of my writing career to the kind of confessional, click-friendly cultural populism that Aldrich celebrates here, I'm swept up by her enthusiasm. But I also can't help recognizing that the factors that produced an outpouring of new writerly forms and voices—social media, blurred genres, reality TV—are the same factors that produced fake news, alternative facts, and Donald Trump.

They are also some of the factors that produced the Women's March—a surging viral protest that was impulsively conceived by amateurs on social media, and within a few tumultuous months had changed forms and platforms multiple times, falling into ideological infighting and verging on failure before being salvaged by seasoned organizers and ultimately swelling into the biggest global protest in the history of the world, a tsunami that swept over seven continents.

≈

Samira and I took the Metro into the city together the morning of the march, and then we parted ways: She and her friends planned to meet up with a progressive Jewish group, while I was marching with my old friend Amelia, my new friend Shirley, and Shirley's boyfriend, Colin.

Like the half million people who surrounded us, my friends and I did not all share the same gender, race, citizenship status, or national origin. We were gathered under the word "women," but our concerns were varied and cosmic. We wanted to be together; we wanted to wield power; we wanted to sing, chant, get in formation, and become the body electric.

Amelia marched with a beautiful Shepard Fairey portrait of a woman with a flower in her hair who, as we later learned, was San Antonio middle school teacher Maribel Valdez Gonzalez. Shirley wore a Beyoncé T-shirt and held a sign that said ANOTHER FUTURE IS POSSIBLE. One side of my sign was a naked expression of my existential dread (DEMANDS FOR DONALD: 1. DON'T BLOW UP THE WORLD 2. DON'T BOIL THE WORLD 3. DON'T GET RE-ELECTED). The other side was a list of the platform planks from the Women's March website (ENDING VIOLENCE, REPRODUCTIVE RIGHTS, LGBTQIA RIGHTS, WORKERS' RIGHTS, CIVIL RIGHTS, DISABILITY RIGHTS, IMMIGRANT RIGHTS, ENVIRONMENTAL JUSTICE).

Over the course of the day, we chanted about black lives, health care, tax returns, equal pay, abortion, immigration, and what-do-we-do-when-we're-under-attack. Some of the best chants were the simplest, like "SCI-*ENCE*, SCI-*ENCE*!" When we marched past the Trump hotel, we yelled: "SHAME!"

Like *Waveform*, the Women's March was an attempt to use "women" as an organizing term without either defining it or presuming that it could or should be defined. As Aldrich writes of *Waveform*, the march "was not wed to a fixed theme, or even women's experience per se," and it offered "the appeal of the miscellany."

An anthology of women's writing unbounded by a set definition of women's themes and experiences allows for a new emphasis on formal exploration and innovation. In *Waveform*, essays come in the guise of alphabets, notes, letters, lists, annotated images, rewritings, readings, and wounds. The subjects include cowboys, volcanoes, disco, show tunes, cats, butterflies, mealworms, and wolves. As Aldrich promises, when one is reading *Waveform*, "the pleasures of surprise come to the fore."

Similarly, the Women's March, with its sudden floods of miscellaneous multitudes, made room for surprising new forms of collective decision-making and new uses of gendered public space. My former student Micah, who has researched the role of women in the civil rights movement, wrote to me about what happened when her bus stopped at a rest stop in Delaware on the way to the march:

Of course, the line for the women's restroom was insane, per usual. However, when I got toward the front, I looked over at the line for the men's restroom and I saw that the line for the men's restroom was full of women as well. It was this great moment all around, because it was this simple practical form of pushback. That day women refused to wait. Or rather, decided that we would all wait together as equal. And it made me think of this concept Myles Horton talks about in the book *The Long Haul*. Which is that we should stop talking about doing the right thing and just start doing it. If I believe that gender is a social construct, why do I let these arbitrary categories affect me? Not that I'm going to go on a one-woman patriarchy smashing spree after that. But it was nice to see how little power social categories have when we choose to lay them aside and live out different convictions.

A march, like an anthology, is a complex collection of motives and voices. But in the midst of the mixture, unanticipated moments of meaning can arise: surprising pleasures that will remain resonant for years.

Given the wild miscellany of the protesters, it's not surprising that one of the most popular memes from the Women's Marches was "Woke Baby": a small toddler at the march in Charlotte, North Carolina, sitting on her father's shoulders and holding high a corrugated cardboard sign covered in multicolored marker scribbles. The scribbles were a kind of Rorschach blot that contained as many visions of the march as it had viewers—the infinite list of reasons to protest—as well as the inscrutable promise of formal and political innovation pointing the way forward.

The meaning of the march was in the eye of the beholder. It seems fitting that, like Woke Baby's sign, the march's most iconic symbol was unofficial and open to endless interpretation.

≈

It was second wave and seventies: crafty, fiber artsy, fuzzy, essentialist. It was retro women's handwork and normative cisgender female anatomy.

It was post-third-wave: cute, consumerist, corporate, Komenesque. It was a wearable Snapchat filter. It was *Mean Girls* conformity and the pinkification of a movement.

The pussy hat, like women's essays, like women's bodies, is a site of ambivalence.

Though it was never an officially authorized uniform (as the FAQ page of the Women's March website pointedly explained: "Q: Is there a single color we can wear to unite us? A: We are not planning to wear anything in particular except VERY WARM CLOTHING. Please do the same and have fun planning ways to connect visually with your friends, groups and family members"), the pussy hat ended up as the ubiquitous symbol for the march, vying with the red MAGA baseball cap for the *TIME* Headwear of the Year cover.

The Women's March and *Waveform* explicitly or implicitly refused to define women based on particular bodily forms and experiences, but individual marchers and writers felt free to identify with them nevertheless. In *Waveform*, traditional tropes of female embodiment appear on the very first page and practically in the very first sentence, with Cheryl Strayed, in her persona of the advice columnist Sugar, telling us, "Stop worrying about whether you're fat. You're not fat. Or rather, you're sometimes a little bit fat, but who gives a shit?" Later, Adriana Paramo recites an alphabet of her body beginning with her Ass, Breasts, and Clitoris, continuing through her Ovaries and Uterus, and concluding with her missing Y Chromosome. On the last page of the anthology, Marcia

Aldrich is in labor, and her baby is crowning. In between, there are at least six essays dealing with sexual assault—more rapes than I can bear to go back and recount. Misogynistic violence might actually be the most common theme of the essays in *Waveform*, as well as the link that connects women across gender categories and spectrums. Trans people are primarily represented in *Waveform* in a found essay by Torrey Peters compiled from a list of 226 reported murders—a relentless litany of victims.

At the Women's March, normative women's bodies came back in the form of the pussy hat—kitschy, winky, and blandly obscene.

My friend Greta wrote about the pussy hat controversy on Facebook:

> I did not wear a pussy hat (I'm on the trans spectrum, do not have breasts, do not believe that biology provides a useful uniting term for people working against patriarchy, and furthermore just don't love "cute" as an aesthetic), but I have read a lot of what feels like kneejerk rejection of vagina-speak with some ambivalence. I don't think that specific bodily configurations (vaginas, for example) should be the sign under which anyone who identifies as "women" organizes, but neither do I think that vaginas—understood here as a specific bodily configuration shared by people of many different genders that require different kinds of care that have historically been deprioritized, especially if you're a POC—are irrelevant to feminist organizing.

In Wyoming, my friend Erin and her five-year-old daughter Lena and thousands of others marched behind a bison-antlered banner proclaiming WILD WOMBS OF THE WEST, and Lena carried a sparkly uterus poster she'd made at a sign-making party. Erin told me that, "while I was somewhat uncomfortable with what seemed to be an essentialist confla-tion of uteri with 'women,' Lena, while she was making and carrying her sign, found many opportunities to talk about how not all women have uteruses, while some men do."

I was acutely aware of my own particular woman's body and its wild womb on the day of the march. I'd chosen that godforsaken year to try to get pregnant, and on the last night of the Obama era I'd gotten some potentially encouraging news on that front: I'd asked a close friend to be a sperm donor, and he'd texted to tell me that he was inclined to say yes. Then, on the morning of the march, he'd emailed to say no. On a day when my fertility felt far removed from any choice that I could make, it felt especially good to yell "MY BODY, MY CHOICE" over and over at the top of my lungs.

My own take on the pussy hat: I wore one partly because my friend made it for me, and my politics often take the form of friendship. Marching with and for people I love is more important to me than political purity. But mainly I wore it because pussy was what Trump said he liked to grab. Pussy didn't actually grab back on Election Day, despite all the memes and T-shirts promising it would, but on Inauguration Weekend it grabbed back with a vengeance. As my friend Robin pointed out, maybe the real purpose of the pussy hats was to prevent the president from pretending that pictures of the marchers filling and overflowing the Mall were actually pictures of his own followers and fans.

In the end, the pussy hat was a plague against Pharaoh, like the time the Nile ran red.

≈

I will never forget the cheers that greeted every Metro train as they arrived in the station: the platforms and balconies full of marchers of all ages lifting their voices in welcome. Amelia said at her station they were singing the Black National Anthem. Later in the day we sang "This Land Is Your Land," which always makes me feel patriotic, and "The Star-Spangled Banner," which never does; but singing it in that crowd almost made me want to put my hand on my heart.

My friend Kim said the march was the first time she'd felt hopeful since the election. Cathy, who went to the rally in Hartford with her family, felt like her daughters' pleasure in political participation gave her permission to feel good about it too, instead of just anxious. This wave of good feeling swept across the Atlantic. From Barcelona, Rebecca wrote to me about "the humor, wit, and creativity of the march. It was a gathering of women from different generations, different backgrounds. As I walked with my daughters, my mother-in-law, sister-in-law, we saw signs in Catalan, Spanish, and English proclaiming 'Now, grandma is angry!' and 'Women's Rights are Human Rights.'"

The exhilaration we all felt in these moments was mixed with an almost painful sense of release. We hadn't been sure we would feel political pleasure again, and the Women's

March gave it back to us for a day. It gave us permission to feel pleasure the way Leslie Jamison's epic crowd-sourced *Waveform* essay "A Grand Unified Theory of Female Pain" gives us permission to feel pain. In the guarded, paranoid time of Trump, the unguarded desire expressed in the essay's last lines is particularly poignant: "I want our hearts to be open. I just wrote that. I want our hearts to be open. I mean it."

The night before the march, I listened to "Bread and Roses" on YouTube with an open heart. I keep returning to the version of the song from the movie *Pride*, which is based on a true story from the 1980s when gay and lesbian activists in London forged an unlikely alliance with Welsh miners on strike. At a moment of political despair, a woman begins to sing "As we go marching, marching . . ." and then everyone joins in, women and men, gay and straight, English and Irish and Welsh, and an orchestral accompaniment swells in the background, and I start to cry. The story and the song offer me a wave of feeling based on the hope that entrenched divisions can be overcome by people marching and lifting their voices. And I cry partly because I don't actually believe in this hope, even as I can't help coming back to it.

We've heard again and again that the 2016 election pitted urban queer people and their friends against the rural religious white working class. This story isn't all wrong. And yet it fails to address the even deeper chasms that divide us.

While some of my friends and I were energized by the march, my friend Katherine felt emptiness. Katherine has been organizing for civil rights and against systemic racism for years, and after the march she felt frustrated, wanting "an action that actually centers folks of color and their issues instead of merely paying lip service to them." She posted a link to a viral Facebook post by D.C. marcher Lakeshia Robinson, which narrates how a white woman Robinson calls #BeckyinthePinkHat rudely informed her there was no room for her in a Metro car, grabbed her arm, and tried to physically prevent her from entering the train while other pussy-hatted white women looked on in silence. Robinson writes that what happened to her demonstrates

> exactly why being black around lots of white people is dangerous for black flesh. . . . I have never felt free enough to touch a white woman. I am scared of white women, if I'm being honest. And for good reason. White women's tears get people who look like me killed.

In the week after the march, a white woman whose tears once got a black boy killed was in the news again. Carolyn Bryant, the woman whose false testimony incited the murder of Emmett Till in 1955, had belatedly confessed, over half a century too late, that her allegations had been a lie. But Bryant did not express any guilt or responsibility for having caused Till's lynching. Instead, as she told the Civil Rights Movement historian Timothy Tyson, she consoled herself by emotionally identifying with the black woman whose son she had stolen, whose life she had devastated:

> [Bryant] admitted she "felt tender sorrow . . . for Mamie Till-Mobley"—Emmett Till's mother, who died in 2003 after a lifetime spent crusading for civil rights. (She had

bravely insisted that her son's casket remain open at his funeral in order to show America what had been done to him.) "When Carolyn herself [later] lost one of her sons, she thought about the grief that Mamie must have felt and grieved all the more."[5]

What kind of real shared wave of feeling can possibly survive the history of violence and violation that divides our lives?

I read the pieces about Bryant and Till-Mobley alongside various black and Native women's critiques of the march, and alongside the many essays in *Waveform* that map and critique the outsized social force of white women's feelings, both its vast scope and its appalling limits. In "Gun Shy," Jocelyn Bartkevicius writes about showing up at a shooting range that had

> a life-size cardboard figure of then presidential candidate Barack Obama . . . near a sign that read, This man will take away your right to own a gun. Walk into that range with a target in the shape of man, and Obama's is the last face you see.

Bartkevicius is shocked that the range incites anger at a black presidential candidate in order to prime people to open

---

5. Sheila Weller, "How Author Timothy Tyson Found the Woman at the Center of the Emmett Till Case," *Vanity Fair,* January 26, 2017.

fire on human-shaped targets, but she stays and shoots anyway. In an unsparing and self-reflective essay wryly titled "Difference Maker," Meghan Daum talks about how she mentors and advocates for kids of color as a way of dealing with what she calls the "Central Sadness" of her childless marriage. At one point, she attempts to correct a teenager's understanding of racism, and "tried to explain that President Bush most likely did not, as she put it . . . 'hate black people' but, rather, had policies that were unfavorable toward all but the wealthiest Americans." And Alexandria Marzano-Lesnevich probes the racial failures of empathy at the Angola Prison Rodeo, a troubling Louisiana tradition in which prisoners are conscripted to be bucked by broncos and charged by bulls as part of a money-making entertainment scheme for the prison. Why is the audience of unincarcerated and predominantly white paying customers so ready to believe that the prisoners don't and won't get hurt when they are thrown off horses and tossed by bulls? And why, she wonders, is it so hard for her to admit to herself what's happening, and to ask follow-up questions about what it means? Could it be because over three-quarters of the prisoners are black?

These essays and histories and questions matter because they help to put the march's euphoric wave of feeling in a broader and longer perspective. They remind us of the terrorizing tradition of armed resistance to black equality; of white people's habitual inclination to deny or defend racism when it is pointed out by people of color; of what Michelle Alexander calls the "New Jim Crow" of mass incarceration. They belong alongside the viral photo of Angela Peoples, the blasé black woman at the D.C. march sucking on a lollipop and holding a sign saying DON'T FORGET: WHITE WOMEN VOTED FOR TRUMP while three happy #BeckysinPinkHats stand obliviously behind her, focusing on their phones. Trump is terrible, but our divisions predate Trump, and will outlast him. This is a very long fight, and many of us are still trying to find our place in it.

A wave of feeling can carry some of us along for a while, and God knows some of us needed it. I definitely did. But it won't carry all of us, and it won't carry us far enough.

What we need, what I crave: not just a wave, but a turning of the tides.

≈

I grew up within walking distance of salt water, and in times of trouble I would escape to a bluff overlooking Puget Sound and stare at the expanse of water and sky. I used to lose myself in the vastness of the view: a panorama of bright blue or implacable gray. The ocean gave me a reprieve from the crisis of the moment. It reminded me of currents that were stronger than emotions.

These days the ocean is too far for me to walk to, but on the door of my office I've taped a postcard with words that evoke oceanic time:

To stand at the edge of the sea, to sense the ebb and flow of the tides, to feel the breath of a mist moving over a great salt marsh, to watch the flight of shore birds that have swept

up and down the sun lines of the continents for untold
thousands of year . . . is to have knowledge of things that
are as nearly eternal as any earthly life can be.

The quote is from the environmentalist Rachel Carson,
and the postcard is based on a broadside made by the illustrator Chandler O'Leary and the letterpress artist Jessica
Spring. For eleven years, O'Leary and Spring have responded
to a series of crises (ICE raids, gun violence, anti-LGBT laws)
by making broadsides honoring relevant figures in women's
history—hence the title of their book, *Dead Feminists*. After
the Deepwater Horizon oil spill, they began reading and
researching Carson, poring over pictures of shorebirds, maps
of oil slicks, and old ads for DDT. They chose and lettered
the quote; illustrated it with dolphins, walruses, pelicans,
otters, and roseate spoonbills; printed it in colors evoking
sand, water, feathers, and oil; and donated the proceeds to the
environmental organization Oceana.

So far O'Leary and Spring have created broadsides honoring
women from Sappho to Fatima al-Fihri to Harriet Tubman
to Lili'uokalani to Emma Goldman to Shirley Chisholm.
Each woman is included in their book, which is simultaneously a finished work of art, a lavish visual representation of
an ongoing creative process, and a practical model of how to
sustain friendship, creativity, and purpose through a deep
sense of history and a commitment to the future. The book
arrived in my mailbox on the eve of the 2016 election,
and it has continued to give me courage in the months and
years since.

Like *Waveform* and the Women's March, *Dead Feminists* is a collection of women and their words that aspires to be collaborative, intersectional, and attentive to form. What it adds is a broad and expansive horizon of historical perspective—there's even a two-page timeline spanning from 630 B.C.E. to 2015—that sees women's role today not as a single cresting wave of creativity or crisis, but as part of a long ebb and flow of political struggle and meaningful work.

This tidal sense of ebb and flow reminds me of the woman Samira and I met on the Metro before the march, who told us that the last time she'd come to D.C. was for the May Day protests in 1971. In her four and a half decades in between world-historic protests, she raised two kids as a single parent and became a lawyer and midwife, representing thousands of clients and witnessing thousands of births. I thought of her again last Sunday when I ran into my friend Heather at church. Heather arrived in New Haven during the decade of the Black Panther trials, when the city was rocked by protests and bombs, and she has been a midwife and teacher of midwifery ever since. "I've never lived through a time when the world wasn't ending," she told me, after our grim conversation about the week's worst news. "But at every birth, I've seen the world begin again."

≈

The night before the march, Samira hosted a Shabbat dinner for her friends who had traveled to D.C. to protest. Emily blessed the candles, Rachel blessed the wine, and Samira blessed the bread. My role as the token Christian was just to eat and drink and bask in the light. We were descendants of immigrants or refugees or resentful nativists; continuing long-standing practices of protest, or beginning new ones; marching for the children we'd left back at home, or the children we hoped to have, or would never have. In the candlelight, we talked together about what the future might bring.

Like the March on Washington for Jobs and Freedom, the Women's March gave people the occasion to dream. A few weeks later, Emily was still seeing visions:

> Last night I dreamed that all the women and men who participated in marches were invited to a huge banquet. A long table was set with flowers and elegant dishes, stretching for longer than the eye could see. A buffet of delicacies awaited the hungry stomachs of pink-hatted thousands. Children eyed the dessert table with cakes and ice creams, and everyone looked with longing at the sky-blue ocean waters of the nearby beaches and swimming pools. No one shouted angry words or tried to cut in line, but when I awoke, it vanished like a mirage.

Despite our desires, the utopian moment of the march couldn't last. These days, dining by placid swimming pools is a pastime for presidents. The rest of us know that the sky-blue ocean waters are more tempestuous than they seem.

We are looking out to sea, where the waves are converging from every direction. Currents are meeting and forming maelstroms. Cracks are appearing along the foundations of the dams and across the continent of ice. The waters are rising and warming. The seawall has been breached.

I remember the story of how once, long ago, the waters of the Red Sea were parted, and the people marched to freedom on dry land. But we can't afford to hope for such miraculous waveforms now. A march will not deliver us. Instead we must learn to navigate this ancient ocean.

We stay awake to see what form the waves will take.

MOBY-DICK

L AST YEAR I discovered DICK, and for a while I couldn't get enough. I was instantly addicted to its pleasures, its absurdities, its uncanny ability to make me feel connected to very different kinds of people for a few hours and to infuse instant life into an otherwise dull evening, and its intriguing tendency to suddenly become surprisingly hard.

DICK is a card game closely modeled on (or plagiarized from) Cards Against Humanity. Each player holds a handful of white cards printed with random phrases, and everyone must respond to a random prompt from a green card as best they can with one of their white cards (sample prompts: "I tend to be an anxious person, but the one thing that always puts me at ease is _____"; "Many women feel that they have to choose between having a career and _____"). The person with the best answer wins the hand. The only substantial difference between Cards Against Humanity and DICK is that all the answers in DICK are lifted from the best book ever written about monomaniacally hunting sperm whales, aka the Great American Extended

Double Entendre, Melville's *Moby-Dick*. This means that while you are playing you are liable to find your hands full of *white curdling cream, perilous fluid, tons of tumultuous white curds, creamy foam, the milk of queens, tubs of sperm, hogsheads of sperm, spermy heaps,* and *the very whitest and daintiest of fragrant spermaceti.*

It's probably not a coincidence that I became obsessed with DICK around the same time I decided to try to get pregnant via a sperm donor.

I played a lot of DICK with my roommates and friends, and I spent a lot of time thinking about sperm, this ubiquitous substance that is all around us, quietly and continuously being whipped up in small batches behind half the zip and button flies that walk by, constantly wadded up in heaps of Kleenexes, swirled down thousands of shower drains, caught in countless condoms, spurting across myriads of legs and faces and backs and butts and bellies, dribbling down chins, sliding down throats, and, about half a million times a day, successfully flagellating its way to a freshly dropped egg.

Sperm is everywhere. It is practically dripping from the trees. It costs virtually nothing to make. It has a significant yuck factor. And yet it retails for hundreds of dollars per flash-frozen vial at your local sperm bank or, as Melville might term it, at your local *ice palace made of frozen sighs.* It's nothing, it's disgusting, it's a warm and enthusiastic effusion, it's a cold and sterile neatly packaged product, and it's the mysterious perpetuation of all human life. Part of the pleasure of *Moby-Dick* and, by extension, of DICK, is that it gives lavish language to the strange mixture of nonchalance, revulsion,

sentimentality, commerce, and existential philosophizing
that is prompted by prolonged pondering of *that inexpressible sperm.*

As my late-thirties biological-clock deadline loomed larger
and larger on the horizon and I started the slow process of
forcing myself to finally abandon my youthful hopes of having
children with a man I loved, I got a kind of comfort from
the bracing and ridiculous language of *Moby-Dick.* I wasn't
sure I could ever make peace with the impersonality, the
randomness, the unsettling consumerism of becoming a
single parent "by choice" (a turn of events that often felt less
like choice and more like fate), but I thought maybe I might
be able to handle heading down to the *ice palace* and springing
for *a jar of spermaceti* with *cash—aye, cash!* If I was going to
make myself do this, I needed to cultivate some heavy-duty
ironic detachment—possibly whale-based. I needed to lean
into the absurdity.

≈

It wasn't just DICK's stylized, sea-salted words and phrases
that helped me. It was the structure of the game itself. Because
DICK depends on a long series of decisions between set after
set of multiple choices, and there are no clear right answers
or clear wrong ones. The person who is designated as that
hand's Dick Judge (heh heh) selects one white card as "best"
based on arbitrary criteria of their own choosing, but no
choice can ever be proven to be the best. It simply happens
to be chosen. Hence the hardness: You are tasked not just with

making a choice but with coming up with a logic for that choice, among infinite possible rationales.

More and more, the process of trying to become a mother has felt like being faced with a series of multiple-choice challenges and constantly having to improvise some haphazard and possibly indefensible decision-making criteria that will enable me to move forward. Because once you give up on having kids "the old-fashioned way" (i.e., being a person who drops viable eggs and has unprotected sex with a life partner who shoots viable sperm, or vice versa), how on earth do you decide how to have a baby? Do you choose on the basis of cost, conventionality, convenience, sentiment, eugenics, efficiency, a feeling in your gut?

A gay friend once told me that he'd always wanted kids, but his partner was on the fence. "If we were straight," my friend explained, "we'd probably already have a couple kids by now, but since we're gay it might never happen. If you're straight, sometimes all it takes is a missed pill or a broken condom or a night of getting a little drunk and deciding to just go for it. But if you're gay, there are all these conversations and lawyers, and it all has to happen sober, and it's just so much paperwork."

I knew what he meant. For a lot of people, most of the difficult decisions that go into conceiving children are submerged by inertia or carried along by tidal currents of convention or swept away in the heat of the moment. The line between planned and unplanned parenthood can get a bit blurred, and many choices are made by default. But for the rest of us—the paperwork people—all the ambiguities rise to the surface. And you have no choice but to keep on

choosing and choosing, as Fate keeps posing question after
question and dealing out hand after hand.

Have you ever thought about adopting _____?

a three days' old Congo baby
an Indian infant
anonymous babies
orphans whose unwedded mothers die in bearing them[6]

By the time I decided to embark on my hunt for sperm, I'd
already spent years looking into adoption. But private adoption
(whether domestic or international) cost more money than
I had. And fostering-to-adopt, which I kept going to info
sessions about and trying to talk myself into, required emotional
and ethical acrobatics I didn't feel I could perform. The primary
goal of foster care is usually to reunify the child with their family
of origin, but since what I really wanted was to adopt I would
be entering the program secretly hoping and praying that
struggling mothers would have their parental rights severed so
I could claim their children as my own. It didn't seem right.

I still wanted to adopt, and I still may. But when I was
thirty-seven I saw my nephew enter the world and watched
him take his first breath, and during the month after his birth,
as my sisters and I held him for hours every day and felt his
heart beat next to ours, I thought: Even though it might be
too late for me to grow my own baby, I at least have to try.
But where am I going to get the sperm?

---

6. All the multiple choice answers in this chapter are from *Moby-Dick*.

Maybe you should make a baby the semi-old-fashioned way! Also known as _____.

one dexterous fling
infernal orgies
the seven hundred and seventy-seventh lay

I know someone who met her baby's dad on Tinder around the same time she decided to start looking for an anonymous sperm donor. Even though she had been seeing this guy for only a short while, she decided to take him at his word when he said, "I'm interested in having kids too. Don't rule me out." She got pregnant within a few months, and a few years later they are still living together and co-parenting. One of her friends joked, "I've seen you spend longer picking out paint colors than you spent picking out the father of your child." But for her the choice made sense. She wasn't sure what the future held for her and her Tinder man, but she knew he was a good person, and she believed it would be better for her child to have a good dad than no dad.

I have nothing but respect for her choice. And I also know a few pretty perfect people who are the result of *dexterous flings* that were over long before they were born. But it's been years since I met a man who I wanted to be in my life in some form forever, or (the only acceptable alternative) who seemed guaranteed to disappear completely. In the end, a workable "semi-old-fashioned way" possibility never arose, so I began to think about who I might want to ask for sperm.

Perhaps your sperm donor will be _____.

a bosom friend
a mature man who uses hair-oil
something queer

Even after I'd reconciled myself to being a single parent, I still strongly preferred the idea of getting pregnant with sperm from someone I knew. My preference for non-stranger sperm seems natural enough to me (most people do, after all, know the person whose sperm got them pregnant), but it's clearly not obvious to everyone. My friends and therapist foresaw lots of potential complications with the known-donor scenario: legal, logistical, emotional. Even my friend who conceived her child with a known donor told me, "*Definitely* go to a sperm bank." The whole time she was pregnant she'd had intolerably vivid dreams about her donor, who, awkwardly, was her wife's brother. Everything worked out fine—she has a great kid, and the dreams went away—but her donor's repeated invasion of her subconscious added a preventable layer of weirdness to the experience.

I think a lot of my preference for friend sperm came down to my basic preference for the known over the unknown. I hate unsolved mysteries, and I especially hate unsolvable ones. I wanted to spare my child and myself unnecessary uncertainty, so mystery sperm seemed about as appealing to me as mystery meat. But there was more to it than that. After growing up in a house teeming with people, I couldn't help thinking of a two-person family as absurdly inadequate. I was willing to risk some avoidable complications in order to give my child a slightly branchier family tree.

I didn't expect my sperm donor to be a co-parent—that seemed like far too much to ask of the universe or anyone in it—but I was attached to the idea of him being a godparent, or similar: distantly avuncular and vaguely interested, maybe someone who lived in another state but would visit us every year or two and intermittently remember to send well-intentioned but slightly age-inappropriate birthday presents. It was a sentimental fantasy, but it seemed like a relatively modest one—a daydream that I could afford to let myself indulge.

There were a couple of friends I wanted to ask, both queer-identified men who I thought might enjoy vague avuncular-hood for different reasons, but I kept putting off asking them. I was worried not just about rejection but also about the possibility that merely mentioning their sperm would create a weirdness from which our friendship would never recover. It didn't help that a couple other friends had recently confided in me about times they'd turned down sperm requests—in each case because they didn't want entanglement. And entanglement, however limited and tenuous, was what I was looking for.

In the end I made my first request—my first throw of the harpoon, as it were—on the night before Trump's inaugura-tion. A sudden overwhelming sense of "fuck it" gave me the courage to impulse-text a brief sperm plea to one of my potential donors (who, as it happens, is a *mature man who uses hair-oil,* or at any rate a significant amount of "product").

His immediate, ambivalently encouraging reply ("My first instinct is 'of course' . . . But let me think about this further") buoyed me up a bit during the awful Inauguration Day that followed. But an unambiguous rejection arrived by email promptly the next morning. For a variety of reasons—ecological, existential, inexpressible—he had decided to hold on to his sperm.

I couldn't help feeling helpless and hopeless, and even though our friendship seemed certain to survive the weirdness, I realized I simply didn't have it in me to ask anyone else. I spent the rest of the day at the Women's March surrounded by giant pink posters of uteri, an unsubtle reproductive reminder that could have been painful but instead was oddly consoling. In the midst of the sea of anatomical imagery, I thought: Well, I may not have sperm, but I still have a womb! And I knew that even in the absence of a known donor I had to continue my quest.

Your initial feelings about choosing an anonymous donor can best be described as _____.

a deep helpless sadness
a certain nameless terror
intellectual and spiritual exasperations
ordinary irrational horrors of the world

At first the prospect of using an unknown donor almost overwhelmed me. Even though I knew it was the logical next step, I had a visceral resistance to it that I didn't know how to overcome.

Part of this resistance was pure squeamishness. For months, even thinking about stranger sperm caused a mild vasovagal response of nausea and light writhing. The problem seemed incurable, but it had a simple if difficult fix: I just needed to move forward with my pursuit of sperm and try not to think about it. If I fainted from disgust on the insemination table, that would eventually become yet another maternal war story, one of the thousands I would doubtless accrue on my circuitous quest for a kid.

The more intractable obstacle, which was probably related to the bouts of nausea, was one that I resisted admitting to myself, though I finally had to face it. The truth was that the prospect of having to buy sperm made me feel like a failure. Not a sexual failure: Like most women who have spent time on dating apps, I'm aware that if I wanted to I could find some free sperm on the internet any night of the week. Rather, having to pay for sperm felt like a damning referendum on the depth of my friendships. In self-pitying moments, I thought to myself: You've devoted decades to loving the people you love, and you've spent endless hours and immense emotional energy getting to know them and taking care of them, but you've apparently reached the age of almost-forty without having a single solitary person in your life who is willing to jack off into a cup for you.

Of course I knew this take on the situation was irrational. Sperm is not actually a currency of friendship, or at least it isn't in my circles. It would be different if I were with Ishmael on the *Pequod*, accidentally-on-purpose squeezing my ship-mates' submerged hands as we sat side by side processing fresh spermaceti, elbow-deep in *the very milk and sperm of kindness*; but for better and worse, my friendships have always involved more mutual admiration than mutual masturbation.

Deep down I was aware that the absence of sperm is not the absence of affection, and that knowingly causing a pregnancy is a much bigger deal than having a casual wank. At the same time, the process of trying to get pregnant, which I'd hoped could be kept in the family of my preexisting friendships, was forcing me to venture outside them. Instead of validating their sufficiency, it demonstrated their limits. Even my most familial friendships were not as intimate as I needed them to be. If I were going to become a parent, I would have to sail into uncharted waters.

There's a moment early in *Moby-Dick* when Ishmael explains the paradoxical dangers of sailing too close to the port in a storm:

> in the port is safety, comfort, hearthstone, supper, warm blankets, friends, all that's kind to our mortalities. But in that gale, the port, the land, is that ship's direst jeopardy; she must fly all hospitality; one touch of land, though it but graze the keel, would make her shudder through and through.

I didn't want to leave the safe and cozy harbor of friendship. But asking more friends for sperm felt too close for comfort, and the prospect of being rejected again made me shudder through and through. I had to venture out into the unknown, or risk the shipwreck of my maternal hopes.

You must now proceed to search for your donor among _____.

thousands upon thousands of mortal men
every robust healthy boy
eight or ten lazy fellows
a mob of young collegians

Overnight, my number of possible sperm donors went from two to what seemed like infinity. I found myself awash in the terrifying tumult of Big Sperm, the lightly regulated billion-dollar sex cell industrial complex that lures fertile young men with "free movie tickets, a massage chair, and free snacks," not to mention *cash—aye, cash!* to the tune of up to $1,500 a month.

Commercial donors are typically tall, college-educated men between the ages of eighteen and thirty-nine. They must be U.S. citizens. They can't be autodidacts. They can't be sick or fat. They are not allowed to have sex with men, for the same dubious reasons that gay men aren't allowed to give blood. Their sperm must be tough enough to withstand freezing and thawing. Beyond that, assuming they sail through a family medical history interview and pass a battery of STI and genetic tests, they can be anything.

Sperm-seeking customers can scroll through thousands of profiles illustrated with donors' baby pictures and filled with evocative information including their favorite animal (dolphin, duck, Yorkshire terrier), favorite food (pizza, papaya, pulled pork), sense of humor (quirky, British, Kevin Hart), dream destinations (Croatia, Patagonia, American Samoa), and fantasy lunch companion (Jesus, Vince Vaughn, Fidel Castro). As with online dating, sites offer multiple levels of data. A low-level membership gets you access to a donor's basic profile and personal essay; higher subscription fees get you access to more extensive information, including recordings of his voice and examples of his original poetry or favorite recipes. You can also pay extra to view a range of "a la carte items" including a handwriting analysis or a "facial features report" ($25 each).

Each donor is identified by a tagline that can be flirty ("BONJOUR!," "HELLO SUNSHINE," "HEY GOOD LOOKIN'!," "WHAT'S COOKIN'?"), cutesy ("JAZZ HANDS," "COOL KAT," "MR. NICE GUY," "MR. HAPPY PANTS"), cryptic ("MAN VS. COBRA," "WHO NEEDS SHARK TANK?," "THE LAW'S LONG LASHES," "I'LL HAVE A LARGE MOUNTAIN WITH CHEESE"), punning ("LAUGHLETE," "ZENDLESS POSSIBILITIES," "IF IT'S NOT BAROQUE, DON'T FIX IT"), sentimental ("LOVES HIS MOM," "MOM'S BEST FRIEND," "EVERYONE'S FRIEND," "MAKES A HOUSE A HOME"), topical ("BUILDING SAND-CASTLES" [Beyoncé?], "THE MARTIAL ART OF THE DEAL" [Trump!]), and/or grandiose ("SUCCESS," "SAVING THE WORLD," "BUILDING AN EMPIRE," "THE HUMAN CONDITION").

I don't think I will ever be ready to be injected with sperm called THE HUMAN CONDITION.

It's hard to adequately represent the scale of Big Sperm. There are thousands upon thousands of donors; each donor can donate sperm multiple times a week; each of their donations can fill multiple vials; each vial can result in multiple fertilized eggs; and the leftover sperm can be stored indefinitely. A single donor can be the biological father of hundreds of children over multiple decades. The number of children conceived from California Cryobank sperm alone could fill Madison Square Garden twice over.

I was predestined to be appalled by Big Sperm. My family of origin has a small business. I like to shop local. A nearby farm delivers groceries to my front porch each week in a reusable box, because sometimes even going to the grocery store feels too impersonal. I was never going to be on board with corporate sperm culture, with its In-House Donor Selection Consultation service that costs $19 a minute, and its celebrity Donor Look-a-Likes™ matching option, as seen on CNN, NBC, *Perez Hilton*, and *The Colbert Report*, which allows you to pick your sperm based on its squirter's resemblance to Common, Keanu Reeves, or Benedict Cumberbatch.

Nor was I sure I could afford it. Commercial sperm sells for about $900 a vial, plus a $300 shipping and handling fee, and my doctor had recommended that I start trying to get pregnant using IUI, a slightly more sophisticated turkey baster method, which requires two to four vials a month. The insemination procedure was covered by my insurance, but the sperm wasn't, and at my age I knew it might take a while (or forever) to get pregnant and have it stick. I wasn't sure how long I could afford to go spending more than twice my monthly rent on sperm.

I was also paralyzed by the complexity of the massive multiple-choice question that a commercial sperm bank represented. Any possible rubric for choosing seemed hard to defend and/or impossible to apply. Should I decide based on height? Hair texture? Vocal timbre? Recipe quality? Deciding on the basis of stats alone felt like a cold neo-fascist experiment in eugenics, but choosing based on more intangible factors seemed like it would require endless hours of pro-and-con listing and second-guessing and reading between the lines.

My only friends who have conceived with anonymous sperm—a caring and thoughtful lesbian couple whose wedding I'd officiated—said that their main criteria were: Would we be friends with this person? Does he seem like a good guy? This standard made a lot of sense to me, but I didn't think I could adopt it for myself. As a writing teacher who grades about three hundred assignments in a typical semester, I was exhausted by the prospect of evaluating thousands of donor essays for friend potential and moral merit. And as a single person who was feeling more alone than I liked, I didn't think I had the emotional and ethical wherewithal to make these judgments on my own.

For a while I felt utterly stuck. But eventually, thanks to a mixture of love and luck, I found a way out.

First, I enlisted the help of my shipmates, aka my roommates, Mira and Daniel, an engaged couple who had been listening to my almost-daily sperm laments with almost-saintly patience. When I asked them if they were willing to provide an amateur version of an In-House Donor Selection Consultation service, they immediately said yes, generously waiving the standard $19-a-minute fee. I told them I was delegating the entire task of choosing sperm to them, carte blanche. They were responsible for coming up with both the criteria for selecting and the sperm selection itself, though I retained veto power.

Delegating the decision to my roommates felt liberating almost to the point of exhilaration. This was partly because I trusted them and had faith in their collective judgment. I believed that together they would bring to bear a balanced combination of reason, sentiment, ethical considerations, and irrational prejudices, and somehow, through their preference for polyglots and disdain for blue eyes, an excellent choice would emerge. I also hoped that their relative detachment from the insemination process (while they genuinely cared about me and any kid I might have, they didn't have to worry about a stranger shooting their bodies full of alien fluid) would allow them to come to a decision relatively painlessly, so that in shifting the burden of decision-making to them I would also be making it lighter. More than all of that, I loved them, and I correctly suspected that our affection for one another would help to assuage some of the brutal grimness of the impending sperm transaction that had been weighing so heavily on my mind.

I'm deeply dependent on narratives, sometimes far too much for my own and others' good, and I'd been vainly struggling to figure out how to turn choosing and using anonymous sperm into a story I could live with. My beloved roommates' presence in the plot made it bearable, and perhaps even pleasant. The help they provided made me feel that even if the voyage to pregnancy was taking me into unknown oceans, I didn't have to navigate them on my own. And I couldn't help thinking that "Your wonderful godparents Aunt Mira and Uncle Daniel helped to pick out your donor!" would make a much better origin story to tell a child than "Mama spent a million hours sitting alone in the dark with her laptop and her credit card trying not to think like a Nazi, and then she finally gave up and flipped a coin."

My roommates' assistance helped me move past my anonymous donor problem, but they couldn't help me with my money problem. As a non-tenure-track writing instructor, I couldn't really afford to blow what might end up being a year's worth of daycare money on sperm. I kept crunching the numbers, but no matter how I crunched them, buying commercial sperm would require me to max out my credit card if I were unable to get pregnant within the first few months. Part of me was like: I can't really afford to have a kid anyway, so why not max out my credit card on sperm? But the more sensible part of me was like: I can't really afford to have a kid anyway, so I definitely shouldn't max out my credit card on sperm!

As luck would have it, I did have one other option. It was a possibility I'd known about from the beginning: a dramatically more affordable and straightforward sperm source that offered the same quantity of vials for just a fraction of the price. I'd resisted this option as long as I could, since in some ways it seemed even more bizarre and unthinkable than Big Sperm. In fact, it struck me as elitist, incestuous, and a total mindfuck.

Ultimately, unable to argue with the price and the convenience, I gave in, and committed myself on a course of action that at first had seemed utterly beyond the pale. To wit:

I made the decision to give up on corporate sperm entirely, and reduce my number of sperm donor options from infinity to seventeen in one fell swoop.

I opted to shop very, very local.

I decided to buy my sperm from the official Yale University sperm bank.

Describe your experience with the Yale Fertility Center Sperm Physiology Laboratory.

Science!
some remarkable documents that may be consulted
the best cruising grounds
a thing barely tolerable
"Don't ye love sperm?"

When I first heard that Yale had a sperm bank, I was shocked. But I should have known. Yale has an urban farm, four dinosaur skeletons, a 43-ton 54-bell carillon, several archival boxes of famous writers' teeth and pubic hair that you can peruse in the rare books library, and a complete Yale-brand liberal arts college in Singapore. Of course it has a sperm bank. And of course it's a small, nonprofit, research-focused, boutique sperm bank that sells its wares only to patients at the Yale Fertility Center, sourcing sperm only from the highest-quality local undergrads. You can guess where most of them go to school.

I learned about the Yale sperm bank a few years ago from a lesbian grad student whose wife was trying to get pregnant. I was gobsmacked, and not just because of the inherent absurdity of Yale-brand sperm (the ultimate Ivy League souvenir). I was stunned because the grad student and I both taught Yale undergrads. We've spent years of our lives planning lessons for them, coaching and comforting them in office hours, bragging about them when they are brilliant, complaining about them when they are cantankerous, and eye-rolling about them when they are exhausting. They are our job and our responsibility. Yes, they are legally adults, and sometimes they are also awe-inspiring and formidable, but they are also teenagers, or barely out of their teens.

My own relation to my students has always been somewhat maternal, especially now that I am actually old enough to be their mother, and trying to imagine a classroom full of students as potential SPERM DONORS almost did my head in. Their sweet, young, eager-to-learn faces floated before me . . . attached to fast-whipping flagellant tails, like horrifying homunculi. I didn't know which was worse: imagining the sperm of the patience-straining problem-child students whose sloppy, typo-ridden essay drafts sometimes drove me nuts, or the sperm of the many endlessly endearing students whom I lovingly mentored and counseled and cared for over the years.

I wanted to be supportive of my grad student friend's fertility journey, but I couldn't help saying something like, "Wow. Yale undergrads. Doesn't that feel a little weird?"

"You *Just. Can't. Think. about it*," she said with determination.

Unwittingly, she was echoing the words of Yale sperm donor Alex Munns, Class of 2007, who, when asked by the *Yale Daily News* how he felt about the existence of unknown children with his DNA living somewhere in the world, responded, "To tell you the truth, I don't think about it. The only way you can deal with it is if you don't think about it."

Or, as *Pequod* second mate Stubb would say: "Think not, is my eleventh commandment." And with the Yale sperm bank, there was an awful lot not to think about.

For one thing, there was the incestuousness. Yale is a small school, and I'd taught and advised hundreds of undergrads. Odds were good that I would be at most two and maybe merely one degree removed from my donor. I could try to mitigate the potential weirdness by choosing a donor whose vital statistics did not seem to resemble any of my current or former students, but at any moment a student matching my donor's description might show up in one of my classes, and I would need to be able to handle that situation with appropriate levels of detachment and calm.

For another thing, there were my own mixed feelings about Yale itself. After spending most of two decades at Yale and Princeton, I'm aware of the strange social aura that surrounds these names. They have a Midas-like magic, adding glitter to everything they touch—even eggs and sperm. Many prospective parents are prepared to pay thousands of dollars extra for certified Ivy League sex cells. But as a westerner who grew up working class, I'm wary of the Yale allure, and skeptical of the dubious eugenics that justifies a preference for Yale genes. Three of my siblings don't have a degree; three of us do. One of my parents went to college, and the other one dropped out of school in ninth grade. There is absolutely no correlation in my family between intelligence and academic credentials: What divides the PhDs from the GEDs is simply temperament and luck.

I remember reading *Moby-Dick* for the first time when I was a student at Tacoma Community College, working for minimum wage. I thrilled to Ishmael's declaration that "a whale-ship was my Yale College and my Harvard," because it was such a defiant rebuttal to the dominant American assumption that credentials are the measure of one's worth. I have good reason to know that a fancy degree says more about someone's class status than about their abilities, and I believed, and still believe, that a whale ship or a barbershop or a community college or a prison can be someone's Yale College and their Harvard. I grew up buying generic groceries at the dented can store, and I like to tell myself that if I could buy a case of discount generic sperm from the dented can store, I would.

As it happens, one of the unexpected and welcome ironies of my experience with the Yale sperm bank is that, despite its undeniable exclusivity, in some ways it offers the closest available approximation of the generic discount store experience. Yale's sperm selection is not just limited and inexpensive; it is also as plainly and minimally labeled as possible. In contrast to the colorful and playful websites of California Cryo and its ilk, the Yale Sperm Physiology Lab offers a plain blue folder containing a two-page photocopied Excel spreadsheet that sums up the entire bank's worth of sperm in a scant handful of statistics. The available donor information is limited to Race (on the list I received, there was one Hispanic donor, fourteen Caucasians, and two African Americans—people seeking an Asian donor are apparently shit out of luck); Age (always between nineteen and twenty-two); Blood Type/Rh; Eye Color; Hair Color; "Ht."; "Maternal Ethn.

Origin"; "Paternal Ethn. Origin" (several donors just had "USA" listed as their ethnic origin—I'm sorry, but USA is not an ethnicity!); "Edu" (a pointless category since the answer is always "College"); and Hobbies.

When I brought the list home from the fertility clinic, it didn't take Mira and Daniel too long to settle on some sperm. They selected a 6'2" donor ("The height thing is fairly arbitrary but why not, if we don't have other information, make as large a person as possible?") with brown hair and brown eyes ("We don't want you to look like you are trying to populate the world with blond Aryans!"). He had listed rowing and running as hobbies, which indicated he was at least somewhat healthy, and his interests in chess and Chinese didn't seem to count against him. They also chose a couple of backup donor options. It was all extremely anticlimactic.

I was happy and grateful and relieved. I didn't know what the future held, but it seemed settled that if I were going to have a baby, it would probably be large and brown-eyed, which seemed fine. I thought my sperm-picking days were finally done.

Of course, it was never going to be that easy.

Thank you for using Counsyl genetic testing. We have discovered you are a carrier for a rare genetic disease. If your donor is also a carrier, your child could be born with _____.

sprained wrists and ankles
too many heads

a globular brain
a mildewed skull

When I signed the stack of paperwork committing to the brown-eyed sperm, I'd almost forgotten about the saliva sample I'd dropped in the mail several weeks earlier. Despite all the worrying I'd been doing at every stage, I'd never thought to fret about my genetic test results. Perhaps this was because my genes are utterly beyond my control, and my anxiety was focused on my choices. But then a message appeared in my inbox, ominous and impossible to ignore: an official warning that if I chose the wrong donor, my child would be at high risk for a rare genetic condition that causes porous bones, scoliosis, knock knees, pigeon chest, myopia, glaucoma, cataracts, detached retinas, seizures, psychosis, intellectual disability, and a one in four chance of dying of a heart attack before age thirty.

This seemed like way too much for a baby to have to deal with.

I wrote to the Yale sperm bank to see if my donor had been tested for the mutation. It turned out he hadn't. None of them had. The test for my mutation was so new that none of their donors had taken it.

The timing of my sperm search was both unfortunate and lucky. If I'd spit in the test tube six months earlier, my genes would have gotten a clean bill of health, and I might have gotten pregnant with my original sperm, and odds are that everything would have been fine. Most likely my original donor was not a carrier; most people aren't. But if my donor *were* a carrier, my baby's chances of being born with the disease would be unacceptably high. If I chose to heed the warning of my test results, I could theoretically select a donor without the mutation and reduce this risk to zero.

Unfortunately, as I discovered when I started calling around, out of all the sperm for sale across the country, none had yet been tested for my mutation. Not a single sperm cell was certified safe. And now that I knew the danger in my genetic code, I couldn't move forward.

Over the course of the quest, my number of options had gone from two to infinity to seventeen to one to zero.

Or maybe not quite zero.

After days of desperate research, I discovered two remaining routes, neither of them certain.

Through another deep dive into Big Sperm websites, I found out that commercial sperm banks would allow me to buy some sperm and then subsequently request that the donor be tested. Since the test requires fresh saliva, this would require the bank to track down the donor (who might have donated many years earlier) and persuade him to get tested at my expense. There was no way for me to know in advance which donors might be available for testing. It would be a long, convoluted, and expensive process.

I discovered the other option through extensive emailing with the empathetic Yale sperm lab employee I always thought of as Joan the Sperm Lady. This choice was much simpler, but just as fraught. In six months, Yale would have one new donor coming out of quarantine, which meant that he would return to the clinic for final STI tests before his sperm was approved for service. The lab could administer the genetic test then, and he would either have the mutation or he wouldn't. Meanwhile I would simply sit tight and wait.

It was all-or-nothing. It was almost literally putting all my eggs in one basket.

The six months felt like forever.

≈

How do you end a story in the middle?

I could end this essay with the long-awaited email from Joan that informed me (after a suspenseful ellipsis followed by a line drop—the typed equivalent of a drumroll) that the donor sperm had tested negative, and was safe to inject into my womb.

Or I could end with my first insemination. The night before, Cathy and our friend Jill improvised a fertility ritual: Jill cast a witchy spell from the internet that involved burying a piece of ripe pear in a small cup of soil, and Cathy recited a litany of pregnant saints and placed a bag of strong-swimming Swedish Fish in front of my makeshift shrine, which consisted of an erect turkey baster surrounded by votive candles. Then, after I stabbed myself in the stomach with a "trigger shot" full of hormones that would cause my egg to drop, I came to the clinic for sperm infusions two days in a row.

The first day, the hapless male fertility fellow had a terrible time finding my cervix. He raised the examination table as high as it would go and knelt on the floor and looked up at my crotch with confusion. "I think everything's in the usual place," I told him. I thought: If dicks can do it, how hard can it be? But he had to remove and reinsert the speculum three separate times. After the second time I started giggling and messaging Mira, which definitely didn't help. The next day the female fellow found my cervix in a second. She said the sperm went in "like butter."

I could end with my first pregnancy. Eight days after I was first infused with sperm, I woke up to discover my breasts had doubled in size overnight. They spilled over the top of my bra like I was an Oktoberfest barmaid or a Jane Austen heroine. I took a pregnancy test the first day I could, and every day after that. Pregnant. Pregnant. Pregnant. Pregnant. I was so happy. For weeks I felt like I was swimming in a cloudy substance that slowed down my brain and made my body languid. I fell asleep each night at seven P.M. and I couldn't eat oysters and I didn't even care.

I could end with my first pregnancy loss. One morning I woke up and felt like myself again, clearheaded and disenchanted. At the doctor's office they told me my hormone levels weren't rising fast enough for the pregnancy to be viable. I felt like a time bomb, waiting for my body to expel what it had started to create. They said it could take a week or it could take a month. It took three days, and it started right before a high-stakes interview for a tenure-track job. I had full-body cramps that hammered the small of my back and scourged the back of my legs, and I was losing blood so fast I could feel darkness flickering around the edges of my eyes. All I could think during the interview was "I must try to seem normal. I can't afford to faint." When it was finally over I went home and bled until there was no blood left. I felt that if I could somehow hold on to the blood I could hold on to the baby, but I had to let it go. Afterward I sunk into grief and shame and couldn't find my way out for a long time.

I could end with deciding to try again. I am starting IVF now, which I can't afford, but I like that at least some of the nonviable embryos will expire peacefully in a petri dish so my body won't have to forcibly expel them. Cathy and her husband Marc are lending me IVF money until I get the next installment of my book advance. (Marc joked, "This is a Rumpelstiltskin deal, right?") Mary and Lisa are lending me money too. Someday I hope to have children whom I can tell about all the friends who brought them into being.

≈

Last summer, in between a pregnancy she lost and a pregnancy she expects to keep, Cathy reread *Moby-Dick*. She remembered how it ends. (Spoiler alert: It does not end well.) As she neared the final pages, Cathy realized she couldn't bear to read about the aftermath of Ahab's obsessive quest, the fate of the crew, the vortex of doom. She closed the book early so she could keep imagining all the shipmates safe on the *Pequod* forever, voyaging together on the rolling sea.

GIRLS OF A GOLDEN AGE

THE OFFICIAL SLOGAN at my grandma's retirement home is "Enjoy your age," and the last time I stayed with her there I loved it so much she bought me an "Enjoy your age" mug to take home and ritually fill with my morning coffee. In her nineties, she is enjoying her age: growing fewer plants, sewing bigger stitches, loving great-grandkids without having to lift them. And I am enjoying my age, too—this midlife era of striving and caring and caregiving, of prying some old hopes out of my hands while reaching for new ones, of using all the skills I spent my youth cultivating. The present is more than enough.

≈

One day last year I stepped out the front door of my New Haven apartment building into the afternoon sunshine. My landlord and landlady were repairing the porch, so I stopped to chat.

I was glad to see they'd decided to repaint the porch in the same perfect colors (peach, cream, turquoise, and pink).

I never thought I would get to live in an 1898 Italianate painted lady with a bubblegum-pink door, and I never take it for granted.

We chatted for a while, and then my landlord said, "You've lived here longer than anyone. At some point in the next few years we are probably going to be scaling back on the rental business a bit. Do you think you might be interested in buying the house?"

It felt surreal to be mistaken for a potential homeowner, but it also felt like heaven in a way that surprised me. "I do love it here," I said. "I have no plans to leave." I let myself lean against the cream-and-turquoise railing, and imagined what it might be like to settle in and stay.

This tall, narrow, sways-in-the-wind house has been my sturdiest home since childhood, and I feel like it has real restorative properties. Many essays and chapters and lectures and sermons have been written in it, many CSA tomatoes have ripened on its windowsills, many dinnertime candles have been lit at the table rescued from the side of the road, and many cans of seltzer have been drunk on the back patio, which is always called "the lanai," after the patio in *The Golden Girls*.

For most of my years here the apartment has nonetheless felt provisional, dependent on my finding friends to share it with and convincing Yale to renew my teaching contract. Staying for the long haul has been merely a dream. But once I'd let myself slip into it, it was a dream I couldn't quite let go of without some self-indulgent wistfulness. Later that day I went on Facebook and wrote, "I have serious landlady fantasies. I want to be Mrs. Madrigal from *Tales of the City*. Of *course* I want to buy a peach and pink Victorian house to fill with found family. But instead I will have to make do with wearing amazing kimonos and renting forever."

I thought I'd nipped my longing in the bud by performing melodramatic resignation in public, but I kept feeling flickers of utopian desire. I impetuously texted Lisa: "I couldn't do it on my own but I was thinking it might be fun to make a little commune." Her enthusiastic response included six exclamation marks and the words "yes," "magical," and "dream," plus "LOVE" three times, twice in all caps. Then, out of the blue like a confirming omen, I got an unsolicited text from an old friend from grad school: "I kind of feel like we should all go in on your apartment building." There were three of us; there were three apartments in the building. Suddenly a *Golden Girls* dream seemed possible.

I always knew that our dream might end in disillusionment. Homeownership is not necessarily a happy ending, and neither are communes. Roofs leak, basements flood, snow must be shoveled and taxes must be paid, neighborhood watch lists can be casually racist, and proximity and property can cause friendships to fray. The lust for real estate is as dubious as any capitalist craving, and a mortgage is just an arbitrarily dignified form of debt. Even the *Tales of the City* series itself eventually turned into a meditation on gentrification and the San Francisco housing bubble, with Mrs. Madrigal forced to leave her home behind. But even though I knew I might never get to live out this particular fantasy, I was glad to get to share it with my friends for a while. In our hopeful real estate texts, we were converging on a shared future.

~

In the end, it wasn't disillusionment or frayed friendship that caused me to give up on buying the house, but some unexpected and earthshaking good news. After surviving a forty-five-minute interview while in the throes of losing a pregnancy (the most badass thing I've ever done, and the worst interview of my life), I'd completely given up on getting the job I'd applied for. But miraculously, two months later, there it was in my inbox: an email from a professor at the City University of New York offering me a position as an assistant professor of creative nonfiction. The offer meant job security, a $25,000 raise, and the prospect of midlife New York City adventures.

Instead of buying my old home, I would need to start looking for a new one. Instead of settling in, I would need to let go.

~

I've never wanted to live alone, and for so many years I haven't had to. Now, as I stock up on boxes and bubble wrap and prepare to pack up my New Haven home, I'm grateful for everyone who has spent time with me here and enjoyed the light that streams and slants in every season and the slumped comfort of the falling-apart century-old love seat in the bay window. I'm grateful for everyone who has baked and cooked in the comically small alcove kitchen, and everyone who has slept soundly in the small quiet third bedroom in the bed that takes up the whole room. I'm grateful to my roommates past and present for putting up with me in all my harried Havisham-ness, and I'm grateful for the many times this has been a place of surviving and gathering strength and discovering a reprieve and making it through an extraordinary or tedious time.

At my happiest and best here, I've felt like the caretaker of a roadside shelter for pilgrims or like the lady who clangs the triangle in a boardinghouse. It makes me joyful to know that people in Houston and Paris and Pune and Norwalk and the Bronx all have keys to this place and consider it a home.

As soon as I find a New York apartment, I need to make them all new sets of keys.

∾

Maybe someday everyone I love will join me on a lanai to recline on rattan. But in the meantime, wherever we are, we will gather around the table and in the streets, in classrooms and bars and by hospital beds. We'll look for one another at the movie theater and on the TV screen and in the glow of our phones, in libraries and museums and at voting stations. What matters is that we will find one another.

ACKNOWLEDGMENTS

Really this entire book is just acknowledgments in essay form. But since I haven't managed to write individual essay-shaped love letters to everyone just yet, this litany will have to serve as a placeholder.

Heartfelt thanks:

To Rob McQuilkin, my angelic agent. Among many other miraculous things, *Hard to Love* got me a tenure-track job and paid for a bevy of frozen embryos. Rob, I owe my financial security and future offspring (if any) to you! Thanks for making my dreams come true. I am so excited to write more books and chat about them with you!

To Lea Beresford, my endlessly encouraging editor. Thanks for caring about and believing in this book from the beginning, and for your consistent kindness and thoughtful advice at every stage of the process! I'm so delighted with what we were able to accomplish together. Thanks also to Barbara Darko and everyone else at Bloomsbury for turning my messy Word documents into a real book.

To the original editors of the previously published pieces, who have taught me so much about writing over the years: Sarah Mesle ("How to Be Single," "On Spinsters," "Remembering How It Felt to Burn," "Young Adult Cancer Story" [whew!]), Merve Emre ("Coming Home to the Best Years of Our Lives"), Brook Wilensky-Lanford ("Dear Flannery"), Anna Shechtman ("On Sisters"), Rumsey Taylor ("The Stars"), and Dinah Lenney ("Waveforms and the Women's March").

To all the other editors, writers, and publishing people who have supported my writing, including Chloe Angyal, Nona Willis Aronowitz, Mary Curtis, Sara Eckel, Marie Griffith, Evan Kindley, Lyz Lenz, Clare Mao, Sara Marcus, Steve Prothero, Paul Raushenbush, Tiffany Stanley, Susan Stinson, Meera Subramanian, and Rebecca Traister.

To Stefan Tobler, my oldest literary friend, who believed in this book years (decades?) before it existed.

To Colleen Kinder, my beloved book doula. I'm saving your voice memos forever. I can't wait to read your books!

To Tom Cusano, one of the most brilliant editors of my acquaintance, and research assistant extraordinaire.

To Tara Menon, Cathy Nicholson, and Rebecca Rainof, who read every word.

To Leslie Jamison, for our continuing conversation and correspondence about writing and intimacy, and for your lavish and steadfast support of my work.

To Alana Massey, for your helpful, practical advice when I was trying to figure out how to write a book proposal. It worked!

To Aaron Ritzenberg, for shelter and pep talks during the week I was traipsing from skyscraper to skyscraper trying to find the right home for *Hard to Love*.

To the friends who turned their spare rooms into informal writing residencies when I needed peace and company: the Rainof-Mas family (Becca, Alex, Anya, Clara); the Nicholson-Levenson family (Cathy, Marc, Miriam, Ruthie, and Eli); and the Brooks-Jacobson family (Daphne, Matt, and Gibson).

Some essays require acknowledgment sections of their own. (Note: Some people should rightfully appear in almost every section, but I have tried to avoid too much repetition!)

"Lean On": To my beloved parents, Anne and Douglas Hopper, who first taught me about love and difficulty.

To my exes, for breaking my heart so I had stories to tell and sell.

To my friends, for mending my heart so well—especially the Bitch and Boast Club (J. K. Barret, Mary Noble-Tolla, Rebecca Rainof, Jacky Shin) and the other habitués of Thursday Gin and/or members of much-missed Princeton writing groups: Adrienne Brown and Andy Ferguson, Michelle Coghlan, Will Evans and Jacob Meister, Erin Forbes and Jason Baskin, Wendy Lee, Greg Londe, Anne Hirsch Moffitt, Sonya Posmentier and Jess Row, Lindsay Reckson and Ben Leavitt, Alyson Shaw and Jessie Bumpous, Ellen Smith, Dave Urban and Celina Fang, Keri Walsh and John Bugg, and Amelia Worsley.

I wrote "Lean On" at Jentel Artist Residency and I'm grateful to Neltje, the Jentel staff, and my fellow Jentellians for our Wyoming adventures! (Brittney Denham, Christine Carr, Eric Diehl, Raphael Dagold, and Barb Putnam: Look, I finally finished the damn essay!)

"On Spinsters": To all those who have discussed spinsters and single life with me or who have cameos here, including Sofia Betancourt, Jadzia Biskupska, Daphne Brooks, Claudia Calhoun, Genevieve Carpio, Barbara Cooper, Lydie Dews, Rachel Duncan, Merve Emre, Rachel Gross, Leslie Harkema, Leslie Jamison, Emily Johnson, Wendy Lee, Lisa Levy, Ashley Makar, Ivy Onyeador, Kristen Proehl, Dixa Ramírez, Lindsey Reckson, Val Smith, Keri Walsh (thanks for *SOLO*!), and Leslie Wingard.

"Pandora in Blue Jeans": To Keri Walsh, a fellow Hilton Als fanatic, for all our 1950s sex and gender conversations; and to New Hope and Lambertville—the territory of youthful love for Marijane Meaker and Patricia Highsmith, and for me as well.

"Dear Octopus": To my beloved brother Ian. Thank you for a lifetime of words, and for giving me your blessing to tell our story.

To Alex Verdolini, with sisterly thanks for reminding me about brotherly love, and for your editorial acumen.

"Remembering How It Felt to Burn": To Robin Wasserman, for writing such a searing book; to Emily Johnson, who read it with me in our temporary home in the Smoky Mountains; to Lizzie Neuhoff, who knew me when; and to all the former friends I never speak to, for leaving their mark.

"Coming Home to the Best Years of Our Lives": To everyone I've watched it with, especially Sarah Hammond, Katie Unterman, Keri, J. K., Rebecca, and my sisters.

This essay is in loving memory of Sarah Hammond.

"Acquainted with Grief": To Becca, with all my heart.

This essay is in loving memory of Mila Rainof.

"Hoarding": Dearest Cathy, 9,925 words are not nearly enough to convey the depth and breadth of my love for you! Thanks to you and yours, the best godfamily that ever was.

To my beloved aunts, Janis Zubalik, Susie Zubalik, and Katie Rhodes; my mama, Anne Hopper; and my grandma, Yvonne Zubalik, for showing me the way. Ariel Engle, I am so thankful for our cousinly connectedness despite distances of space and time, and for your music.

Adrienne, thanks for telling me to read *Housekeeping*. Maddie Duff, Chase Ebert, and Sophia Nguyen, thanks for visiting Marilynne Robinson in the Beinecke with me. Becca, thanks for your scholarly brilliance.

"Dear Flannery": With dearest love for my past, present, and future co-writer Ashley Makar.

This essay is in loving memory of my grandma Bette Hopper.

"Tending My Oven": To Rhiana Gunn-Wright, Angharad Davis, and Cathy Nicholson, and all the other friends, students, and roommates I've baked with and for over the years, including Abigail Braden, Emily Boring, Daphne Brooks, Michelle Coghlan, Larissa Galante, Micah Jones, Tara Menon and Alex Verdolini, Richard Morris, Eshe Sherley, Grace Shu, Elizabeth Spenst, Greg Suralik, Alex Thomas, and Baobao Zhang. Jordan Stein, your baking photos inspire me.

"Young Adult Cancer Story" and "Coasting": To the easy-to-love Care Team—Sarah Gollust, Lisa Levy, and Ritu Sen—and, with earthshaking care and delight, to Ash.

To Annette Georgia, founding member of the *TFIOS* Book Club, and to John Green, for giving my essay his stamp of approval.

Lisa, I am so glad we are forever family, and I'm so grateful for all the ways we've been able to lean on each other over the years. The best is yet to come!

Emily, I'm so grateful for our conversations about and during care and cancer, and for everything else.

"Everything You've Got": Dear Xiao Situ, this essay's for you! I wish I were in a basement bar right now with you and the rest of my *Cheers*-loving friends and colleagues—Nurfadzilah Yahaya, Brandon Menke, Katie McEwen, Heather Radke, Lisa Levy, Marc Levenson, Joe Stadolnik, and David Ellis Dickerson.

This essay is in loving memory of my grandpa Stanley Zubalik.

"On Sisters": To the Anchor Cistern—Kat Hopper, Ailsa Hopper Court, Liese Eo'ao Hopper, and Joey Hopper, always and forever. There's no one I'd rather eat oysters with, and no one I love and respect more.

To Gena Samqui Hopper, my wonderful sister-in-law and fellow big sister.

To Leslie Harkema, my movie buddy and neighbor and ally and dear friend.

This essay is in loving memory of Aunt Leona and Uncle Freddy, for inspiring the Hopper sisters' matching tattoos and loving us so well.

"The Stars": To Ivan Ortiz and James Campbell, for our many years of shared Bette-love. Nadia Ellis, finding your sparkling and searching essay on *Now, Voyager* felt like emotional time travel, and I'm glad to be one of its readers.

"The Foundling Museum": To my mother, with gratitude and awe; to Beth Boyle Machlan, for writing so heartrendingly about mothers and daughters; and to Rebecca and Tara, for saving this essay from solipsism at the eleventh hour.

Thanks to Nyasha Junior for the reading recommendations.

This essay is in loving memory of my brother Isaac.

"Waveforms and the Women's March": To Samira Mehta, Shirley Wong and Colin Blair, Kimberly Pendleton, Katherine Demby, Heather Reynolds, Steve Poland, Kimberly George, Jessica Spring, Chandler O'Leary, Greta LaFleur, Emily Mace, Rachel Kranson, Amelia, Sonya, Erin, Cathy, and Rebecca, and everyone else who marched, and everyone who marches on.

"Moby-Dick": Thanks to Courtney Baker for turning me on to DICK. And thanks to everyone else who has chortled, chatted, or wept with me about Melville, motherhood, and/or sperm, or supplied help and courage on this voyage, especially Sarah Blackwood, Kameron Austin Collins, Elise

Dunphe, Rae Gaubinger, Jared Gilbert and Alex De Looz, Brooke Jones, Katja Lindskog, Jenny Mellon, Margaret Middleton, Ginger Nash, Ivy Onyeador, Mimi Pillinger, Natalie and Kelly Prizel, Liz Reich and Laurie Marin and Jacob, Jill Richards, Sarah Robbins, Francisco Robles and Brandon Menke, Jim Steichen, Catherine Stephens, Arvind Thomas, Van Truong, Sara Utzschneider and Julie Robens and Jacob, Xiao and Will, Will and Jacob, Tara and Alex, Marc and Cathy, Mary, Becca, Leslie, Lindsay, and Lisa.

To Savion and all the other niblings who inspire me to try to create an extra cousin: Hannah, Joshua, Naomi, Tallulah, and Alden.

To pretty much everyone at Yale Fertility Center, especially Dr. Winifred Mak, Dr. Pinar Kodaman, Jill Stronk, all the staff, all the IVF nurses, and three out of the four fellows.

And last but not least, to that anonymous undergrad. I couldn't do this without you.

"Girls of a Golden Age": To my Tacoma grandma, Yvonne Zubalik, who was been teaching me how to live a creative life from the time I was old enough to borrow books from her teeming shelves, eat green beans from her garden trellises, and learn to sew a running stitch.

To my New Haven landlords, Nathalie Bonafé and Donald Harvey, who helped make my apartment feel like a home.

To my New Haven roommates, especially Alex Verdolini and Dixa Ramírez, who put up with me while I was finishing the book.

To Shirleen Robinson and Sunny Xiang, in honor of New Haven Writing Bees Past and New York Writing Bees Future.

To everyone who helped me apply for my new job, especially Richard Deming, Leslie Jamison, Tara Menon, Steve Pitti, and Jess Row. Abundant thanks to Gloria Fisk for playing matchmaker.

To my new colleagues and students at Queens College, CUNY. I am so looking forward to getting to know you!

To the Study at Yale, where this book was finally finished, and toasted with an impeccably cold and green Last Word.

To the Tacoma Public Library, where it began, and to Tacoma Community College and the University of Puget Sound, for educating me and so many others. To my Tacoma teachers, Bill Breitenbach, Jeannine DeLombard, Doug Sackman, and John Lear. Bill, I hope you have saved my retirement tribute to you, since reprinting it here would put me over my word count. Now is a good time to re-read it.

To the East Coast people I've loved the longest, Marilyn Nelson and Debbie Hopper. To Nancy Hauswald, honorary extended family.

To Minna Scholten and Drew Jameson, and to Sarah Boddy, with love.

To past and present Princetonians not named above, in the English department and Comp Lit (Bill Gleason, Jennifer Greeson, Tim Watson, Elaine Showalter, April Alliston, Angela Ards, Rachel Galvin, Kinohi Nishikawa, and Pat Guglielmi), on the Civil Rights Movement in Alabama pilgrimage (Val, Al Raboteau, Garrett Brown, and Carl

Owens), on the Religion in Tanzania trip (Alison Boden, Jeremy Borjon, and Sitraka St. Michael), in the Religion department and the Center for the Study of Religion (Rachel Gross, Elizabeth Jemison, Nicole Kirk, Rachel Lindsay, Leigh Schmidt, Judith Weisenfeld, Heather White, and Jenny Wiley-Legath), and everyone at Witherspoon Street Presbyterian Church (especially Barbara and Jerry Cooper, the Rev. Muriel Burrows, and the Witherspoon Quartet).

To my past and present New Haven friends and colleagues not named above, at the div school (Tisa Wenger, Sally Promey, Suzanna Krivulskaya, Kate André, Rachel Sommer), at the University Church in Yale (Ian Oliver, Candice Provey), in the English department (Felisa Baynes-Ross, Jane Bordiere, Anne Fadiman, Craig Fehrman, Jackie Goldsby, Lanny Hammer, Margaret Homans, Mary Kate Hurley, Brittany Levingston, Katya Lindskog, Pam Newton, Sue Penney, Sarah Robbins, John Rogers, Erica Sayers, Shifra Sharlin, Rasheed Tazudeen), and beyond (Sonja Anderson, Kati Curts, Anne Eller, Crystal Feimster, Irene Garza, Karin Gosselink, Jill Jarvis, Katie Lofton, Leah Mirakhor, Lynda Paul, Shari Rabin, Karin Roffman, Maytal Saltiel, and Alicia Schmidt Camacho). Thanks to the Yale Center for the Study of Race, Indigeneity, and Transnational Migration for their support of my research and teaching while I was completing this book.

And finally, to my students, past, present, and future, who brighten my days and fill my life with words. If I start to name you I will never end.

A NOTE ON THE AUTHOR

BRIALLEN HOPPER HAS written about books, pop culture, religion, politics, friends, family, and herself for the *Los Angeles Review of Books*, *New York Magazine/The Cut*, the *New Republic*, the *New Inquiry*, and *Avidly*, among other publications. Her essays have been recommended by the *New York Times*, the *Rumpus*, *Flavorwire*, *Longreads*, and *Slate*. She is the editor of the online literary magazine *Killing the Buddha* and an associate editor at And Other Stories, an independent publisher. Hopper grew up in Tacoma, got a PhD in American literature from Princeton, and attended divinity school and taught writing at Yale. She is now an assistant professor of creative nonfiction at Queens College, CUNY. She lives in New York City.